Sex, Sexuality and The

MW00529259

Sexuality is an important area of clients' lives yet it is often neglected, both in the consulting room and in training. This book examines issues of sexuality in a positive and affirming light and considers how sexuality-related issues can be introduced into therapy and training. Sex and sexuality are important to consider in psychotherapy, psychology, counselling and health provision across a variety of contexts and are relevant to clinicians and therapists working in health and mental health settings as well as in specialist services such as sexual and reproductive health and HIV.

Sex, Sexuality and Therapeutic Practice opens with a general discussion of sex and sexuality before considering how the therapists can think and talk about sexuality in practical and self-reflective ways across a variety of contexts. Each chapter in the book focuses on a specific topic with areas covered including:

- sexual diversity across the lifespan
- health and disability
- sexual and gender minority issues
- how culture and sexuality interact.

The manual provides up-to-date information, further reading, handouts for clients, self-reflective exercises and examples of training exercises for workshops and teaching. It is an essential resource for health professionals, therapists, clinicians, academics and trainers, and will support the practising therapist as well as those in training.

Catherine Butler is a Principal Clinical Psychologist, trainer and systemic psychotherapist in Adult Primary Care Psychology in City and Hackney Community Health Services.

Amanda O' Donovan is a Consultant Clinical Psychologist in sexual health and HIV at St Bartholomew's Hospital, London.

Elizabeth Shaw is a Consultant Clinical Psychologist in sexual health and HIV at St Ann's Hospital, London.

Sex, Sexuality and Therapeutic Practice

A Manual for Therapists and Trainers

Edited by Catherine Butler,
Amanda O'Donovan & Elizabeth Shaw

Routledge
Taylor & Francis Group

LONDON AND NEW YORK

First published 2010
by Routledge
27 Church Road, Hove, East Sussex BN3 2FA

Simultaneously published in the USA and Canada
by Routledge
270 Madison Avenue, New York, NY 10016

Routledge is an imprint of the Taylor & Francis Group, an Informa business

Typeset in Times by Garfield Morgan, Swansea, West Glamorgan
Printed and bound in Great Britain by TJ International Ltd, Padstow,
Cornwall
Paperback cover design by Andy Ward

British Library Cataloguing in Publication Data
A catalogue record for this book is available from the British Library

Library of Congress Cataloging-in-Publication Data
Sex, sexuality, and therapeutic practice : a manual for therapists and trainers
/ edited by Catherine Butler, Amanda O'Donovan & Elizabeth Shaw.
      p. ; cm.
   Includes bibliographical references and index.
   ISBN 978-0-415-44808-6 (hbk) – ISBN 978-0-415-44809-3 (pbk.) 1.
Mental illness–Sex factors–Handbooks, manuals, etc. 2. Psychotherapy–
Erotic aspects–Handbooks, manuals, etc. 3. Sex–Psychological aspects–
Handbooks, manuals, etc. I. Butler, Catherine, 1972- II. O'Donovan, Amanda,
1968- III. Shaw, Elizabeth, 1961-
   [DNLM: 1. Sex Counseling–methods. 2. Psychotherapy–methods. 3.
Sexual Behavior. WM 55 S5175 2009]
  RC455.4.S44S49 2009
   616.89'14–dc22

                                                          2009022992

ISBN: 978-0-415-44808-6 (hbk)
ISBN: 978-0-415-44809-3 (pbk)

Contents

Contributors

Catherine Butler, D Clin Psy, MSc in Systemic Therapy
Catherine is a principal clinical psychologist, trainer and systemic psycho-therapist in Hackney Primary Care Trust. Prior to her work in adult mental health, she worked in NHS sexual health services in central and south London for five and a half years. During this time she developed a couples' service, an HIV training programme for African Communities, and pro-vided national training on working with lesbian and gay clients and motivational interviewing. Alongside her clinical work, Catherine worked part time as a clinical tutor on the Doctoral Degree in Clinical Psychology at the University of East London. For three years she was the research officer on the British Psychological Society (BPS) HIV and Sexual Health Faculty committee, where her work included organising national confer-ences, writing BPS guidelines, conducting audits and publishing articles. Her research interests include sexual assault, the use of interpreters, and the personal and professional integration for lesbian and gay psychologists. Catherine has also worked in the private and voluntary sector, including as a couple/family therapist at PACE and as a therapist, trainer and clinical associate with Pink Therapy. She was previously on the BPS Lesbian and Gay Psychology Subsection committee and won their postgraduate research prize in 2003.

Angela Byrne, PhD, D Clin Psy
Angela Byrne is a clinical psychologist who has worked primarily in the field of HIV/sexual health. She is currently working in a service to improve access to psychological therapy among Black and minority ethnic communities in City and Hackney, East London. She also works with Positive East, an organisation for people living with HIV in East London, where she provides a service to refugee women living with HIV. In the past she worked as a clinical tutor at the University of East London and with international organisations such as the World Health Organization, UNAIDS, and UNICEF on HIV programmes in countries of the former Soviet Union and the Middle East. Her clinical and research interests include women's sexual

health, service provision for refugees, Black and minority ethnic communities and community psychology.

Amanda O'Donovan, BA, M Psych, C Clin Psy
Amanda O'Donovan is a consultant clinical psychologist at St Bartholomew's Hospital, London. She trained at the University of Western Australia and has worked in both mental and general health settings in the UK and Australia. She has specialised in Clinical Health Psychology since 1998 in areas such as HIV, sexual health, chronic fatigue syndrome, women's health and trauma. She has a long-standing interest in mindfulness and compassion-focused work both in clinical settings as well as applied to supervision and service development. She is an Honorary Lecturer at Queen Mary, University of London and the University of East London and teaches and provides training on psychological issues and HIV, sexuality and talking about sex. Her current research interests include body changes and illness, gender and health.

Elizabeth Shaw, Msc Clin Psy, AFBPsS
Elizabeth Shaw was the chair of the Faculty of HIV and Sexual Health of the Division of Clinical Psychology of the British Psychological Society (BPS) from 2005 to 2007. During this time she took an active interest in promoting training in sexuality within the profession by developing training standards, surveying clinical psychology courses' contents, encouraging sexuality awareness training, setting up an applied psychologists working party to develop guidance for working with clients from diverse sexualities, and guiding the development of this book. She works as a consultant clinical psychologist in Haringey North London in HIV and sexual health settings and has been committed to this field and professional issues in psychology for the last 14 years. This has included encouraging research in the area of HIV and sexual health by supporting and supervising clinical psychology doctorate research and organising relevant symposia in BPS conferences. Her research interests have included working with refugees and asylum seekers, aspects of living with HIV, researching and writing useful documents for psychologists working in sexual health settings, termination of pregnancy, attitudes to sexuality, and sexual trauma.

Clare Stevenson, D Clin Psy
Clare Stevenson is a Chartered Clinical Psychologist. She worked at St Bartholomew's Hospital and the London NHS Trust in the department of HIV, sexual health and chronic fatigue for five years, where she took a particular interest in women's psychosexual problems, providing individual and couple therapy. Clare also took a lead in the provision of a specialist clinical psychology service for commercial sex workers in close liaison with the Open Doors Women's Health Project in Hackney. From 2006 to 2008

Clare was newsletter editor on the committee for the Faculty of HIV and Sexual Health, Division of Clinical Psychology of the British Psychological Society. Her research interests have been in psychological service provision and evaluation, and chronic fatigue syndrome. In 2008 Clare started a new post as lead clinical psychologist in cancer and palliative care in City and Hackney. She has a particular interest in addressing issues of sexuality in cancer survivorship and palliative care.

Tables and figures

TABLES

FIGURES

Foreword

I'd thought sexuality was instinctive or natural, but it's profoundly linked to inner security and cultural context.

Tahar Ben Jelloun

Sex, sexual dynamics and how we define our sexuality, is one of the major deals in everyone's life.

Molly Parker

These two quotes, one from a poet and the other from an actress, demonstrate something that has been known and explored in the arts since the beginning of our cultural development. However, sexuality within the social sciences, while placed under the microscope at the beginning of our scientific awakenings, has largely been objectified and removed from the cultural, historical and political context of its time. It is only in later years that within our understandings of human relations have we only really been willing to recognise that sexuality is not just an instinctual, natural event, but is shaped and governed by our interpersonal and social context, and indeed for all its expression or repression is a 'major deal'.

This manual is an important addition to the field of understanding and working with human sexuality. It is highly relevant to the sexuality of today as it is expressed and communicated globally. With the rise of new forms of communication and the global networking of content, people have access to presentations of sexuality, diversity and difference not previously available. With this comes an ever-richer mosaic of human experience, raising options and potential choices never known about previously. However, accompanying such expressions come hand in hand other more repressive forces, positioning and relating sexuality to more restrictive and categorical world views. This leads me to a further quote by Michel Foucault, as one cannot talk about sexuality without talking about power, and in this text he eloquently ties our struggle to express sexuality into the context of our power structures.

If repression has indeed been the fundamental link between power, knowledge, and sexuality since the classical age, it stands to reason that we will not be able to free ourselves from it except at a considerable cost.

(Michel Foucault, 1978: 5 [French publication: 1976])

This manual will help both trainers and practitioners alike to start to address constructions of sexuality in a positive and affirming way. It uses the evidence that we have at our disposal to dispel myths, change attitudes and address sexuality in the wider clinical context, outside of the sexual health clinic. It will engage the intellect, address your experiences, thoughts and feelings in a way that will both challenge you, but also facilitate you to engage with your clients, or if a trainer with your participants, in stimulating and practical ways.

In 2002 the World Health Organization brought world experts together to define sexual health and distal, from global experience, guiding principles for services promoting sexual health. Among these principles the following stand out as particularly relevant to this manual:

- comprehensive understanding of sexuality;
- cultural diversity;
- equity;
- non-judgemental services and programmes;
- accessible programmes and services;
- accountability and responsibility.

This manual provides a comprehensive and up-to-date understanding of sexuality, using research to evidence practice. It acknowledges diversity and difference and considers the role of not just ethnicity, but also disability and age. A stance of equity and being non-judgemental is presented; an acceptance of difference between people is clearly modelled. That the authors are practising clinicians adds quality, as they are presenting resources and techniques that have been refined in practice and are known to be accessible to the audience and which demonstrate a professional accountability and responsibility that should be central to therapeutic practice. Given these ingredients I am confident that if you work either, or both, as a clinician or trainer within psychotherapeutic practice you will find this manual an illuminating and practical addition to your bookshelf.

Professor Jan Burns
Department of Applied Social and Psychological Development,
Canterbury Christ Church University

REFERENCES

Foucault, M. (1978 [French publication: 1976]). *The history of sexuality, vol. I: an introduction*, translated by Robert Hurley. New York: Vintage Books.

World Health Organization (2006). *Defining sexual health: Report of a technical consultation on sexual health 28–31 January 2002*. Geneva: WHO.

Acknowledgements

We would like to thank the following for their inspirational thinking and ideas that informed earlier drafts of this book: Sarah Zetler, Iseult Twamley, Philip Henshaw, Sarah Davidson and John Newland. Our thanks also go to the two graphics artists, Simon Thompson and Jim Broughton, who contributed their talent and time to produce the illustrations in Chapter 1. Finally, our gratitude and thanks also go to our family and friends for their support and patience throughout.

Introduction

Elizabeth Shaw

> By three methods we may learn wisdom: first, by reflection, which is the
> noblest; second, by imitation, which is easiest; and third by experience,
> which is the bitterest.
> Study without reflection is a waste of time; reflection without study is a
> waste of time.
>
> Confucius

This book is designed to help therapists and other health professionals
develop their understanding and practice around the complex area of
human sexuality in all its diversity. As well as being helpful for clinicians in
reflecting on issues of sexuality and how they are present and inform their
practice, it is also intended to be a resource for training in the area of sex
and sexuality. Current thinking around the concepts, activities and beliefs
around sex and sexuality can be regarded as historically, regionally and
culturally determined, and can be engaging and controversial. These ideas
are therefore part of a changing cultural discourse involving social and
moral judgements about what is acceptable or usual, and what might be
problematic (Foucault, 1978).

Therapists and clinicians are as influenced by the pressures of these social
discourses as any other person and our attitudes and beliefs can and do
affect how we practise and our ability to relate to clients in a therapeutic
way. These attitudes could become unhelpful to a client unless we are able
to remain grounded and maintain our non-judgemental curiosity and
openness within therapeutic conversations. There is increasing awareness
that this can be enhanced when a therapist reflects on their own values and
beliefs about sexuality, and have been able to develop and review their own
constructs about sex and sexuality through exploration in supervision and
training. Therapists need to develop theoretical understandings as well as
simply being open to the possibility of relating to the unknown in sexual
diversity (Davies & Neal, 2000; Garnets *et al.*, 1991; Godfrey, 2006;
Murphy *et al.*, 2002; King *et al.*, 2007). In this spirit the book is based on
the reflective-practitioner model of learning (Dewey, 1933; Schon, 1983,

1987) where the learner is invited to look at their experiences, feelings and beliefs in relation to therapeutic practice in order to build deeper, new understandings to inform their actions in therapy around issues of sex and sexuality (Doris *et al.*, 2003; Nelson, 1998).

The last 50 years in the UK have seen considerable change in how sex and sexuality have been experienced and discussed. It can be argued that there has been a socio-political shift towards greater affirmation and acceptance of the diversity of sexuality since the advent of the pill, feminism, 1960s sexual freedom and the declassification of homosexuality as a mental illness. This has served to contribute to greater sexual freedom and expression, despite the increased medicalisation of male and female sexual problems (Kaschak & Tiefer, 2002). These changes have been underpinned by changes in legislation, such as the legalisation of abortion, the decriminalisation of consenting sadomasochistic sexual relationships, and civil partnerships for lesbian and gay couples. These changes have been mirrored in developments in psychotherapy, such as social constructionist understandings of relationship problems and sexuality affirmative psychotherapy, (e.g. Davies & Neal, 2000; Ritter & Terndrup, 2002). This has been accompanied by increased openness in social and media discussions about sexuality, moving away from arguments based on suppression, silence and beliefs that there are only either standard male and female, sexes and genders, that are fixed over a lifetime, which have dominated until recently. This is also reflected in the expanding range of self-help books on sex and sexuality and more positive sexual media portrayals in television and in films such as *Brokeback Mountain* and *Juno*. Similarly in health settings there is increasing recognition that issues of sex and sexuality are relevant to all therapeutic settings and presentations.

With this approach and these ideas in mind, readers of this book can gain:

- a working knowledge of current thinking and models of sex and sexuality;
- an increased awareness of personal values around sex and sexuality;
- further knowledge about sexuality and sexual practices that may be different from our own;
- an increased confidence and the skills to raise issues of sex and sexuality with clients;
- structured exercises and ideas to run training programmes about sex and sexuality with other professionals or students;
- access to resources and handouts to share with clients or for training purposes.

THE BACKGROUND TO THIS MANUAL

The authors of this book are members of the Faculty of HIV and Sexual Health of the British Psychological Society (BPS) and are experienced clinical psychologists working, teaching and researching in the field of sexual health and human sexuality. This book was conceived out of a need for more guidance in this area expressed by clinical psychologists at different stages of training and practice that we have come across in our professional practice, as we serve very diverse clinical areas with sex and sexuality issues being encountered at different levels of prevalence and complexity. In order to encapsulate this we undertook a focus group with clinical psychology trainees and asked them what would help them learn about working with issues around sexuality. The contents of this book are the product of this research. We also surveyed training courses to think about how sex and sexuality was taught and how this could be improved (Shaw *et al.*, 2008). In addition the book reflects standards for training in clinical psychology in the area of sexuality (Division of Clinical Psychology, 2007), and the British Psychological Society guidelines for psychologists working with sexual and gender minority clients.

THE CONTENT OF THIS MANUAL

This book is not a sex therapy manual, nor is it about disease and illness; rather we hope it celebrates our bodies, desire, arousal and the pleasure that sexuality can engender while also being mindful of its more problematic side, such as when a person's sexuality does not fit into what we are familiar with. We also hope to make current thinking accessible and enabling, rather than academic and dry, allowing for self-directed learning with the explicit understanding that contexts and beliefs around the issues are constantly evolving. The book starts with an overview of how sex and sexuality are conceptualised and then moves into helping therapists and clinicians talk, think and theorise about sexuality in a practical and self-reflective way. It then discusses the specific areas of sexuality as related to health and disability, sexual and gender minorities, sex across the lifespan and the interaction of sex and sexuality with culture.

The book has been designed as a foundation training manual and each chapter has exercises and resources to help with the readers' assimilation of what has been discussed, which can also be adapted to client work and training. Mainly social constructionist, systemic and cognitive behavioural approaches are drawn upon, but the text will be of interest to therapists and trainees of all therapeutic orientations at every level of training. The chapters can be used to dip into particular areas or read in sequence. As a basic text it covers much ground and signposts the reader to more in-depth reading and useful resources for clinicians and trainers where possible.

The interspersed reflective exercises are the cornerstone of the method of learning we advocate. We ask you to consider questions and clinical vig-nettes that may challenge you, make you think, and lead you to explore them in more depth, although not always giving you definitive answers 'for action, in action or on action' (Dewey, 1933). This will enable you to open up to possibilities at your own pace with your own self-evaluations in line with the constructivist approach (Sexton & Griffiths, 1997).

We hope you find the exploration of issues in this book stimulating, helpful and inspiring for your work with your clients, and teaching and training in this area. Perhaps you may know if the book has helped you if through using it you feel more able to talk about sex, and feel more open and confident in working clinically with sex and sexuality.

REFERENCES

Davies, D. & Neal, C. (eds) (2000). *Pink therapy 2: Therapeutic perspectives on working with lesbian, gay and bisexual clients*. Buckingham: Open University Press.

Dewey, J. (1933). *How we think: A restatement of the relation of reflective thinking to the education process*. Boston: DC Heath.

Division of Clinical Psychology (2007). *Best practice guidelines for the training and consolidation of clinical psychology practice in HIV and sexual health settings*. London: BPS.

Doris, Y.P., Kember, L. & Kember, D. (2003). The relationship between approaches to learning and reflection upon practice. *Educational Psychology*, 23 (1), 61–71.

Foucault, M. (1978). *The history of sexuality, vol. 1: An introduction*. Harmondsworth: Penguin.

Garnets, L., Hancock, K.A., Cochran, S.D., Goodchilds, J. & Peplau, L.A. (1991). Issues in psychotherapy with lesbians and gay men: a survey of psychologists. *American Psychologist*, 46 (9), 964–972.

Godfrey, K., Haddock, S.A., Fisher, A. & Lund, L. (2006). Essential components of curricula for preparing therapists to work effectively with lesbian, gay and bisexual clients: A Delphi study. *Journal of Marital and Family Therapy*, 32 (4), 491–504.

Kaschak, E. & Teifer, L. (eds) (2002). A new view of women's sexual problems. New York: Haworth Press.

King, M., Semlyen, J., Killaspy, H., Nazareth, I. & Osborn, D. (2007). *A systematic review of research on counselling and psychotherapy for lesbian, gay, bisexual and transgender people*. Lutterworth: BABCP.

Murphy, J.A., Rawlings, E.I. & Howe, S.R. (2002). A survey of clinical psychologists on treating lesbian, gay, and bisexual clients. *Professional Psychology: Research and Practice*, 33 (2), 183–189.

Nelson, M.L. (1998). The pedagogy of counselling: A critical examination. *Counsellor Education and Supervision*, 38 (2), 70–88.

Ritter, K.Y. & Terndrup, A.I. (2002). *Handbook of affirmative psychotherapy with lesbian and gay men*. London: Guilford Press.

Schon, D.A. (1983). *The reflective practitioner: how professionals think in action*. London: Temple Smith.

Schon, D.A. (1990). *Educating the reflective practitioner: towards a new design for teaching and learning.* San Francisco, CA: Jossey-Bass.

Sexton, T. & Griffin, B. (1997). Constructivist thinking in counselling practice, research, and training. New York: Teachers College Press.

Shaw, E., Butler, C. & Marriott, C. (2008). Sex and sexuality teaching in clinical psychology. *Clinical Psychology Forum*, 187, 7–11.

Chapter 1

Sex: body, behaviour and identity

Amanda O'Donovan and Catherine Butler

Sex is emotion in motion.

Mae West

INTRODUCTION

The question 'What is sex?' may seem fairly straightforward, but depending on the frame of reference used there will be a variety of different answers. The word 'sex', as well as being both evocative and provocative, holds an array of diverse meanings and concepts and usually refers to the physical distinction between men and women or penile penetration of the vagina. However, it can also refer to sexuality, attraction, body parts and a wider range of sexual behaviours. This chapter seeks to explore the differences between these concepts, to challenge some of the myths that are prevalent in the area and to develop an understanding of the complex interactions between them.

As sex has been a somewhat silenced conversation in many arenas, therapists may be less familiar with ideas and knowledge in this area. Sexual health, sexual behaviour, sexuality and gender are often neglected in training for health professionals and therapists. This chapter seeks to provide a useful exploration of these areas and to assist the therapist to reflect on his/her own areas of knowledge as well as beliefs he/she may hold about a wide variety of sexual practices, roles and identities. It is hoped that with an increased understanding of this range of concepts and behaviours, therapists will feel more skilled and confident in addressing these issues, opening conversations and exploring areas of difficulty with clients. Ideas about 'normality' in the field of sex and sexuality are problematic and the lack of open, clear communication in this area means that unhelpful or outdated myths about sex often persist. This chapter aims to reflect useful ideas and conversations that may be helpful for therapists in thinking about these different concepts and considers the psychological and biological components of sexual identity, gender and sexual acts.

Many of the exercises in this chapter can be used to conduct training with others. When doing training in sex, sexuality and related areas however, careful consideration is required about which exercises are appropriate in different contexts (e.g. level of training, length of course, closeness of group etc.). Consider what information or disclosures participants may feed back to the group and what will happen with this information. Aside from contracting for confidentiality, some groups may not wish to share intimate details or, there may be people in the group who have been sexually abused or assaulted. Because of this some exercises might be difficult or inappropriate for use in a group setting and so should not be used.

WHAT IS SEXUALITY?

Sexuality has a highly varied set of meanings and mainly refers to erotic desires, practices and identities (Jackson & Scott, 1996). The main tensions about the meaning of sexuality centre around accepting essentialist biological origins of sexuality, as opposed to post-structural and post-modern positions which affirm that sexuality is open to reconstruction and reinventions, enabling the embracing of sexual diversity and a greater classification of sexuality than hetero- and homosexual. Sexuality is related to emotions, roles and ideas and shaped by diverse experiences throughout the lifespan and encompasses far more than the gender of sexual partners chosen or the type of sexual acts engaged in. Our sexual selves are shaped by many of the same contexts and events that shape the kind of individuals we become.

Our relationship to sex, sensuality and our body develops well before we become sexually active. Arousal and sexual functioning are influenced by past and present relationships, life stresses, early experiences and knowledge of sex. There are multiple complex links between social context, relationship, mood, thoughts, feelings, assumptions, physical health, bodily sensations and stimulation that determine the quality of each sexual experience. How sex and sexuality plays out in relationships is a longer, more complex dance that reflects the factors above but is also determined by relationship quality, trust, communication, attraction and respect.

Exercises 1.1 Our sexual selves
This exercise facilitates self-reflection on your early messages about sex. It can be done on your own or used as a training exercise, perhaps encouraging participants to discuss their thoughts in pairs given the potentially sensitive nature of their answers (because of this participants should also be given the option of doing the exercise alone).

- How was affection or demonstrations of love shown in your family?
- What is your parents' relationship to their masculinity/femininity and sexuality?
- How attractive and loved did you feel as a small child? Teenager? Young adult?
- What messages have you received about your physical body and nudity?
- How did you learn about sex?
- How do you feel about your early sexual experiences?

Completing this exercise should start to break up the idea that there is one way of 'doing' gender and sex; that these ideas are socially constructed and may change for us over time as we encounter new experiences and influences.

Sexuality could be considered as fairly central in our society and as therapists we will also be influenced by this context. In the last quarter of a century feminism and other social and political changes have challenged ideas about sexuality and gender. The 'right' of men to women's bodies, the privilege given to heterosexuality, ideas about masculinity and femininity have changed and changed again (Cartledge & Ryan, 1983). How sexuality expresses itself through behaviour is discussed later in this chapter and Chapter 4 covers sexual and gender minorities.

WHAT IS SEXUAL ORIENTATION?

Sexual orientation, sometimes referred to as sexual identity or sexuality, describes an enduring sexual, emotional, romantic, affectionate or erotic attraction for individuals of the same and/or different sex. The concept of sexual identity is important in how a person understands themselves and how they communicate their sexuality. It can bring a person security and belonging, however if an identity is not well established within society, such as transsexuality or bisexuality, this can create difficulties as a result of a lack of understanding and prejudice. Most people identify with the ends of the sexual orientation continuum (homosexual/heterosexual) but may occupy some position in between. There are an increasing number of people who challenge the notion of fixed sexual identities and prefer to see sexuality as what they do rather than what they are and this sexual identity may shift over time or context. Terms such as 'queer', or 'heteroflexible' might be used as an identity label by someone who chooses not to conform to mainstream sexual orientation labels or sexual practices. Many other terms have emerged in social discourse since the sexual revolution in the 1960s, including asexual (individuals who choose not to be sexual) and pansexual (attraction to others irrespective of gender, including attraction to those identifying as transgender, bigender or intersex), and may be rejecting of the gender binary as discussed later in this chapter. More contemporary theories about sexuality such as queer theory and the assumptions of heteronormativity are explored in Chapter 4.

The sexual orientation continuum can be represented thus:

attraction/erotic/romantic response

attracted to males ——— bisexual/asexual ——— attracted to females

People may also have sex with others of the same sex but not identify their sexuality as lesbian or gay due to situational or cultural facets. A continuum can therefore be conceptualised which is based on sexual partners rather than defined sexual identities such as hetero/homosexual:

sexual partners/attraction

sex with men — sex with men & women/no sex/self-sex — sex with women

These ideas were developed by Kinsey (1948, 1953) with a scale of a continuum of sexuality (for more information visit http://www.kinseyinstitute. org) and furthered by Klein *et al.* (1986) to include past, present and ideal reflections of sexuality and fantasy, attraction and sexual identity in the Klein Sexual Orientation Grid. Klein also emphasised that self-awareness about sexuality can be an evolving process that is highly context dependent. These more complex understandings of the interplay between sexuality and sexual acts highlight the need to work with clients' self-descriptions of identity and behaviour and validate these rather than make assumptions or impose your own values or understandings.

WHAT IS GENDER?

The term 'sex' often refers to an individual's gender of biological sex, most often thought of as 'male/female', and includes physical attributes such as external genitalia, internal reproductive structures, sex chromosomes and hormones. The hard and fast dualism of male/female gender is being questioned more recently with recognition that biological gender, like other physical attributes, can also be conceived as being on a continuum. This move from seeing gender as two opposites to understanding it as a range (where most people will lie towards the ends of the continuum) can be difficult to conceptualise. The 'fact' of two sexes is almost hard wired and can feel like a 'truth' of nature in Western cultures. However, increased understanding of the variation in the factors that determine gender, such as hormonal and chromosomal make-up, secondary sexual characteristics, external genitalia and internal reproductive structures, has challenged the concept of two separate and completely distinct sexes. The diagnostic category of disorder of sex development (DSD) has recently been used as an umbrella term to include diagnoses where genital, chromosomal or anatomical sex development is atypical. DSD was previously referred to as 'intersex' and 'hermaphroditism'. There has been some criticism of the term DSD because it classifies anything outside of the dichotomy of male/female as a 'disorder'.

A biological continuum of gender could thus be represented:

anatomy/chromosomes/hormones
male ——————————— DSD ——————————— female

The male/female paradigm is also unhelpful as it does not encompass individuals, such as those with DSD conditions, who do not fit the dualism of male or female. DSD individuals share some or many features of both male and female genitalia and reproductive anatomy. There are many biological reasons why this occurs including natural variation, hormonal factors during pregnancy and chromosomal make-up. For more information visit the UK Intersex Association website at http://www.ukia.co.uk.

The shared biology of males and females can be seen during foetal development in the similarity of genital structures at 10–12 weeks gestation. Sexual organs develop from the same embryonic bud tissue while the glans tissue becomes either a glans clitoris or penis determined if androgens are released through the Y chromosome. The vestiges of this shared biology can be seen in adult anatomy where the head of the clitoris has as many nerve endings as the head of a penis. Similarly, the G-spot in females is located roughly in the same area where the male prostate gland is situated as they share a common embryonic origin. The scrotum in men finds its counterpart in the female labia.

Ideas of gender are strongly culturally determined and constructed. Although Western societies often view gender as a dichotomy, many other cultures conceptualise gender in broader ways than this. For example 'lady boys' in Thailand, the hijra of India who are considered to be 'third sex', and 'two-spirit' individuals in North American indigenous groups who fulfil mixed gender roles, dress and work as both male and female genders and are thought to have a masculine and feminine spirit living in the same body.

GENDER IDENTITY

Gender identity is the term used to describe how we understand and identify with our biological sex. It is a psychological quality although biological factors play a role in its development. Sex and gender categories are probably the most dominant and fundamental in human roles and functioning

(Bem, 1989) and are well established in preschoolers. From the moment a child is born and his or her sex is 'determined', he or she is then treated differently dependent on whether they are a 'boy' or a 'girl'. In many Western cultures, female babies are picked up sooner than boys when they cry and given more verbal interaction whereas male babies are given stronger physical handling, stimulation and cues (Maccoby & Jacklin, 1974). At age three, a level of awareness of being a 'boy' or 'girl' is present and this is reflected in children showing preferences for behaviours ascribed to their gender (e.g. trucks v. dolls) and to having playmates of the same gender. In parallel with other areas of cognitive development, the concept of gender categories as being stable comes later in development. Gender identity is fixed and stable and resistant to change and has significant effects on personality and coping styles (Renk & Creasey, 2003). When looking at individuals, attributions about their gender are made instantly and unconsciously and any ambiguity around the presumed male/female dichotomy is usually experienced as troubling.

Gender identity can also be more diverse than categorical-based concepts of male–female. Transgender is a term for people who do not fit with the dichotomous categories of male/female gender identity and may include transsexuals or gender queer individuals, transvestites and drag queens. Transgender or gender queer individuals may not identify with either end of the male/female continuum but at several places along it or even outside of traditional gender categories. This fits with the idea of 'not passing completely' as one sex or the other. Transgender identities do not equate to particular sexual orientations or sexual identities.

Transsexuals are individuals who wish to live and be recognised as a different sex to that which they were born into. They may seek medical interventions such as hormone treatment or surgery to make their bodies as congruent as possible with their preferred gender identity. Cross-dressers or transvestites choose to wear clothing that is different to stereotypical gendered clothing, e.g. a man who wears a dress. This may be for emotional comfort or sexual arousal, or as a way to express a broad range of feelings. The majority of people who identify as cross-dressers are biological males. Other categories or terms used in the UK include: drag kings or queens who often identify as gay and lesbian who dress up in the stereotypical clothes of the sex different to their own, often for performance or entertainment and gender queer people. Further discussion of trans issues, and exercises to use in training, are given in Chapter 4.

GENDER ROLES

Gender roles and expression reflect how we communicate or signal our gender. These communications are socially constructed and vary across culture, society and peer groups. Early twentieth century Western gender roles were based around the idea of heteronormativity and are now widely seen as outdated stereotypes. Similarly, gender roles were viewed as comparatively fixed and transgression of these roles was met with disapproval or discrimination. However, more recently, gender roles are considered as more fluid than originally thought, e.g. a man might be able to now wear make-up in a night club without attracting comment. Gender could also be though of as fluid across context, culture and time, viewed as a spectrum.

communication of sex/gender
masculine ——————— androgynous ——————— feminine

Denman (2004) outlines how stereotypical gender roles are reinforced and accounted for by various social and psychological explanations including behavioural, psychoanalytic and social constructionist theories.

Exercise 1.2 Gender self-awareness

This exercise challenges the assumptions of fixed gendered identities by using self-reflection to highlight a person's journey of gender awareness. It can be used individually or in small groups if running training.

- Discuss when you first became aware of your identified gender?
- What were the differences you noticed between being 'a boy' or 'a girl'?
- What were the ways in which boys and girls were treated differently in your home, family, school or culture?
- Were there differences in how boys and girls behaved?
- Were there different expectations placed on boys and girls? How were these communicated?
- Were there any contradictory messages given about gender roles and expectations (e.g. the idea of a 'new man' who was sensitive to feelings)?

There are no right or wrong answers to these questions but hopefully completing them, and perhaps having the opportunity to share your answers with a group, will highlight the socially constructed nature of gender.

WHAT IS SEX?

Behaviours that are defined as sexual vary widely across different groups of people, over time and across cultures. Ideas about what sex is, and what it is not, depend on ideas about the 'normality' in sex, men's and women's roles, culture and social context. These frames of reference are complex and interacting and shape understandings about what qualifies as sexual behaviour. For instance, within a legislative and moral framework in the 1800s, Queen Victoria could not conceptualise the idea of two women 'having sex'. Ideas of 'normality' in sex are also dependent on the frame of reference applied.

Exercise 1.3 First learning about sex

Taking the time to reflect on our sexual selves is often something that people may not have spent much time doing, so conducting this exercise on your own or with workshop participants may result in new things about oneself, as well as about sex, being learnt!

Consider the sets of questions below; each can be considered in turn or they can be read through quickly and the few that are of most interest focused on:

- What are the stories/images/messages about sex you received from your culture? How do these relate to gender? To relationships? To sexual knowledge and contraceptive use? To responsibility? How have these stories changed over time?
- What are the stories/images/messages about sex you received from your family? Did you hear different messages from different family members? Which ones would you want to pass on or hold back from your own children?
- What are the stories/images/messages about sex you received from your relationships with friends and sexual/romantic relationships? Have you noticed yourself shocked, surprised or embarrassed by sexual differences you have had with lovers? What do you think you can teach lovers or would like to be taught?
- What you would consider your values/morals about sex? Can you think of defining moments you have had on your own sexual journey? Are there things you have regretted doing or not doing up to this point? Is there anything you can do about this? How would you describe your sexual self?

Some of the contextual frameworks dominant in Britain today that may inform our understating of sex are outlined below.

Sex as human behaviour

Sex as a legitimate area of human behaviour to study and research first emerged through the ground-breaking work of Alfred Kinsey. Kinsey, who originally trained in taxonomy, described in detail the sexual behaviour of males in 1948 and females some five years later. These studies were based on thousands of interviews within the (majority White American) general population and reported on the frequency of a wide range of sexual practices such as same-sex sexual experiences and masturbation. At the time his findings caused outrage by challenging traditional ideas about sex, particularly the ideas about which sexual behaviours were and were not 'normal' in women. Masters and Johnson developed these understandings of sexual behaviour in 1966 with the publication of *Human Sexual Response*. Their findings informed the biological understanding of the sexual response cycle that is dominant today and outlined later in this chapter.

Sex as defined by psychiatrists

Psychiatry and medical contexts have a powerful influence in sanctioning sexual behaviours in Western contexts. In contemporary psychiatry, sex is currently conceptualised as including most means of sexual gratification between consenting adults, regardless of the gender of partners (American Psychiatric Association (APA), 1994). This has not always been the case: homosexuality was viewed as a psychiatric condition until relatively recently and Freud considered masturbation and oral sex to be immature forms of sexual expression.

There are a range of sexual fantasies, urges or behaviours, e.g. sado-masochism, fetishes, voyeurism and exhibitionism, that are still considered to be mental disorders and are classed as paraphilias (APA, 2000). Para-philias are diagnosed if they have been present for over six months and cause the individual marked distress or impair social or occupational functioning. Critics of sadomasochism being pathologised (e.g. Baggaley, 2005; Kleinplatz & Moser, 2005; Langdridge & Barker, 2007) emphasise that as the code of practice within sadomasochism insists that activities should be safe and consensual, this type of sex should not be positioned as a disorder. However, distress may be more likely in the partner who is not interested in this form of sex, and this may impact on relationships. The narrow criteria for diagnosis of a transvestite fetish have also been the subject of criticism as they only apply to heterosexual men who dress in female clothes. This definition does not apply to bisexual or gay men or heterosexual men who may cross-dress for other reasons than for sexual gratification (such as for relaxation, Denman, 2004). Butler (1999) reflected that women also dress to perform gendered expectations, but because this is normalised in our culture it is not considered a fetish. Although homosexuality was removed from the APA *Diagnostic and Statistical Manual of Mental Disorders* (*DSM*) in 1973 and the World Health Organization (WHO) *International Classification of Diseases* (*ICD*) in 1992, transgender identities remain pathologised in both manuals as gender identity disorder (*DSM–IV–R*, APA, 2000) and transsexualism (*ICD-10*).

Sex as defined by the law

The legal framework is also a dominant discourse in ideas about 'normal' sex and a number of sexual behaviours fall into the realm of criminal acts. These include paraphilias, paedophilia, rape and sexual assault.

Paraphilias are illegal when involving non-consenting people, including observing an unknown/non-consenting person while unclothed and/or engaged in sexual activity to produce sexual excitement (voyeurism); exposing one's genitals to a stranger (exhibitionism); and touching or rubbing one's genitals against the body of a non-consenting person (frotteurism). Sexual activity with children (paedophilia) is also covered robustly by the legal framework and also carries strong moral and psychiatric censure. Paedophilia is defined as sex with a child of age 13 or younger, or in the case of an adolescent if the individual is five or more years younger than the perpetrator. Illegal non-consensual sexual activity includes rape and sexual assault. Rape has only been legally recognised to occur within marriage in the UK since 1991. Before this, a woman was considered to have consented to all future sex with her husband when she took her marriage vows. Male rape has only been recognised since 1994 and prior to this rape was only conceived as being committed by a man against a woman (Sexual Offences Act 2003).

Consent is a key concept within the legal framework and covers whether a person agrees or chooses to engage in the activity. Consent also considers whether an individual has the freedom and capacity to make that choice and it is informed by broader understandings around issues of power (a more in-depth consideration of issues of consent is given in Chapter 3).

More recently, the transmission of some sexually transmitted infections has also come under the domain of the legal system, most notably the criminalisation of HIV transmission. Convictions have been sought where sexual behaviour was viewed as reckless and information about HIV status was withheld from partners, or partners were misled about the individual's status, which highlights the legal importance of disclosure and consent. Guidance for therapists around criminalisation and relevant clinical management issues such as confidentiality, risk and disclosure can be found in the British Psychological Society Faculty of HIV and Sexual Health publication *Criminalisation of HIV Transmission* (Gibson & O'Donovan, 2009).

Sex as defined by public health

The Department of Health, National Institute for Health and Clinical Excellence (NICE) guidelines and health promotion agencies emphasise the importance of 'safe' sex and are concerned primarily with issues of transmission of sexually transmitted infections (STIs) across the population. In this context, 'sex' should only occur with a condom. Sigma (2007) point out that in public health campaigns the responsibility for enforcing condom use is often placed on the individual who knows they have a STI, disregarding the view that sex and health consequences are a shared responsibility. The same positioning of responsibility is used in campaigns that target women to protect themselves against being raped (e.g. by watching their drink to prevent drug rape, or not getting a taxi alone), rather than targeting the men who offend (O'Byrne *et al.*, 2006). This is an interesting paradox, as vulnerable groups are being identified in the campaign and these same groups are then given the responsibility for their own safety and protection. O'Byrne *et al.* (2006) also critique campaigns aimed at men that suggest that rape is a result of men 'not knowing' that consent is important in sex or men being unable to understand such communications.

Sex as defined morally

As social and historical values shift and change, so do attitudes to sex and sexuality. Psychiatry pathologised homosexuality for many years and many of the world religions have difficulty with viewing same-sex relationships and behaviours as valid and healthy forms of sexual expression. Sex has often been viewed as being permissible only within marriage and often with the emphasis on procreation rather than pleasure, including prohibitions on contraception. Masturbation is disapproved of in some cultures and religions, as are various other sexual behaviours such as oral sex and anal sex. Some cultures and religions also prize celibacy or forgoing sexual acts entirely or at various times of a woman's cycle such as menstruation. Sex is also positively connoted in some moral and religious contexts as a fulfilment of human roles, a pleasure or blessing and viewed as natural, 'God-given' and therefore good. Further consideration of the interaction between sex and culture is discussed in Chapter 6.

Sex and spirituality

Sexuality has been linked to spirituality over the centuries within many of the great spiritual traditions. Perhaps the most well known of these is in the Tantric tradition from India and Tibet where sex may be practised as a purification ritual and a celebration of the unity of beings. This tradition suggests that there is inherent in our bodies a life force that expresses itself as energy that can be channelled and embodied in order to bring greater intimacy with another person and the divine. Here the emphasis is on using the breath and sexual energy generated in the pelvic area to raise the energy in a conscious and embodied way.

Within other traditions, such as some interpretations of the biblical stories, less positive and more prescriptive interpretations have been made about the functions of sex. For example the Garden of Eden story has been interpreted as man's fall from innocence when woman tempted man to eat of forbidden fruits as an account of sexual sin. This is despite other accounts that tell us that humans were created in the image of a passionate God with a deep longing for connection. Similarly the Song of Solomon verses that tell of love between man and woman can be seen in a multilayered way to also allude to love towards God. Either way they have influenced how sexual morality has been constructed. It can be helpful clinically to understand a client's views and dilemmas resulting from their belief systems. Conflicting ideas about sex and religion or morality can be complex and may be encountered in personal or clinical contexts. For example, a divorcee who ends an unhappy marriage and is in conflict over feelings of living in sin with a new partner as well as experiencing satisfaction and fulfilment in a new and more rewarding relationship (Carr, 2003).

Freud, Reich and Jung, founders of modern psychology and psychotherapy, drew richly from these traditions and to differing degrees linked their theories of sexuality around them. At the beginning of the twentieth century, Jung departed from Freud's theory of sex as a basic instinct (Freud, 1905) and suggested that sex was more part of a creative, spiritual instinct or drive towards wholeness within the psyche. In his archetypal psychology he describes sexuality and gender in spiritual terms when discussing the 'anima' and 'animus', the anima being the unconscious feminine part of a man and animus the unconscious masculine part of a woman. Jung proposed these develop from a collective unconscious of primordial origin that everyone is born possessing. However, he also suggested that the anima/animus development can be shaped by our parents and so create positive or negative images, which will in turn affect how we relate to different sexes or with different parts of oneself. Jung also suggested that 'psychic energy' can be channelled via sexuality, building on Freud's idea of the libido as 'sexual energy' (Samuels, 1986; Hopke et al., 1993; Stein, 1984).

The psychoanalyst Wilhelm Reich departed from Freud to reconcile the mind and body by developing body-centred psychoanalytic techniques and 'Orgonomy' (Staunton, 2002). He wrote about neurosis being caused by psychic conflict and resulting blocked 'orgone energy' or 'sexual/life force energy' in our bodies. To live healthily, Reich proposed the accumulated orgone energy should periodically be released through sex. Reich built an 'orgone accumulator' to assist the flow of orgone energy (Reich, 1989) and one of Jack Kerouac's characters (Old Bull Lee) uses such a device to boost his sex drive in the novel *On the Road* (Kerouac, 1957).

Sex as an erotic or romantic act

Eros was the Greek god of lust but also of love, intercourse and fertility. The term 'erotic' has since come to reflect lust and sex independent of these other contexts. Sex can be experienced as an erotic act, a feast of sensuality, a way of expressing 'carnal desires' and individual sexuality. These eroticised narratives about sex may be less present in settings in which therapists work but may form the major part of a client's own understanding or experience of sex. Losing oneself, being transported by desire – these phrases evoke the sensual, pleasure-driven narratives of sex and emphasise the power of the erotic experience. Often these stories can be positioned as sordid, decadent or deviant, particularly in a health or moral context and reflect societal anxieties about pleasure-driven narratives.

Romantic ideas about sex stem from eighteenth century courtly traditions. Knights and quests, heroes and princesses populate these narratives that often echo traditional gender-based power imbalances where the man is the active agent and the woman as a passive recipient who is wooed by her suitor. Romantic sex is often depicted through its relational role in developing emotional feelings and bonding between partners. The sexual act is seen as an expression of love and other 'finer feelings' rather than as an expression of arousal or desire. The physical element of sex and the potential for problematic or difficult experiences is marginalised within these discourses where boy meets girl, boy woos girl and sex is seen through the soft-focus lens of mutual pleasure.

Erotic and romantic narratives about sex are found in abundance in fiction and in inner-fantasy life. They may shape expectations about what a sexual experience should feel like or be like and are also often mirrored in the contemporary media depictions of sex, discussed next.

Sex as defined by the media

Information, ideas and images of sex are widely available in our culture. Sex is present in films, on television, featured in magazines, commented on in newspapers and written about in books. Frequently represented in advertising images, sex is not only seen as a commodity but also as a way to facilitate purchases of other commodities. Sex sells. Often these depictions or discussions reflect one of the narrow frameworks above e.g. sex as purely erotic, sex as a heterosexual activity, sex as deviant or criminal. Some of the material in these frameworks is reiterated so frequently that it has come to be believed as fact.

The following exercises challenge some of the 'facts' learnt about sex.

Exercise 1.4 Sex myths

This exercise highlights the myths that abound in popular culture, as well as inviting the reader/participant to draw on alternative discourses.

Which of these statements reflect ideas that you, your colleagues or clients may hold? What are alternative positions to those stated below?

- Men always want sex.
- In heterosexual sex, satisfaction of both partners is the responsibility of the man.
- Only young attractive women are sexually desirable.
- If you really love each other, the sex will be great.
- Real sex involves penetration.
- Good sex ends in orgasm.
- Simultaneous orgasm is a sign of good sex.
- It's physically harmful for a man to have an erection and not have sex.
- Gay men are attracted to young boys.
- All gay men like anal sex.
- In a same sex relationship, one partner is more sexually dominant than the other (e.g. butch–femme, active–passive, top–bottom).

Exercise 1.5 Sexual contexts quiz

This exercise considers how sex can be viewed differently in different contexts, and so again challenges the idea of sex as a fixed and stable concept.

Think about an example or situation in which these contexts may be relevant:

1   Sex as a public health issue.
2   Sex as a sign of group membership.
3   Sex as a way to demonstrate social power.
4   Sex as a cure.

Answers: 1 Sexually transmitted infections. 2 Teenage. 3 Rape/sexual abuse. 4 Myths re HIV cures.

Exercise 1.6 Your definition of sex

At this point it may be useful to consider what is your definition of sex with another person:

- How would you answer the question 'how many people have you slept with?' – just counting the incidences of penile/vaginal penetration, or other non-penetrative sex acts? Counting acts that just you performed or were performed on you?
- Do you view sex as good or bad dependent on the context? e.g. sex in casual relationships versus sex with long-term partners; sex on drugs or alcohol versus sex when sober; use of sexual fantasy and sex toys?
- Are intimacy, safety and closeness things you always consider important for sex?
- Are there times when sex feels more erotic than others? Under what circumstances?

Talking about sex in the therapy room

As therapists it can be helpful to take a curious and interested perspective of what might constitute sex. A person can be sexual when not having penetrative penile/vaginal or anal sex. This can be both with a partner (e.g. oral sex, mutual masturbation, sensuous massage etc.) or alone (e.g. masturbation, enjoying erotic underwear etc.). If a client presents saying that they are not having sex for whatever reason, it is important to explore other ways in which they might still be sexual. Do they ever fantasise? Do they find people attractive in real life or in magazines? Are they sexual with themselves in any way? Do they have any intimate contact with their partner? Helping clients realise the enormous numbers of ways that one can be sexual takes the pressure off the act of vaginal/anal sex and allows for new definitions of sexual identity and relationships that include being intimate and sexual.

Exercise 1.7 Ways to be sexual

This exercise explores ideas about sex that you might be taking into the therapy room (and bedroom). These ideas might influence how you view clients' descriptions of their sex lives or even be a resource to draw on when exploring the multiple ways that a client may express their sexuality. If used in training this exercise should be used for individual consideration due to the sensitive and intimate details of the answers.

Ask yourself the following questions:

- What is the most sexual thing you have done with all your clothes on?
- What is the most intimate thing you have done with a partner in public?
- If you did not have sex for a month, how else might you express your sexual feelings towards your partner or yourself?
- When you are attracted to someone, how do you let the other person know you want to become sexual with them?
- How are you sexual or intimate with a partner if one or both of you are tired?
- If one of you does not want sex, is there a way the other can still feel sexually satisfied?

THE SEXUAL BODY – AROUSAL AND PHYSIOLOGICAL RESPONSES

Historically, biological understandings of sexuality have been privileged over social, psychological and contextual theories and explanations. It is important to be mindful that the physiological processes of desire and arousal occur in a multiplicity of contexts that powerfully shapes the meanings ascribed to them.

Sexual anatomy – 'female' sexual organs and responses

Female appearance, body shape and size are the subject of immense scrutiny in contemporary Western society. Despite this focus on physical appearance, many women are unfamiliar with their genitalia and reproductive organs and may lack a vocabulary to describe them. Whereas male genitalia are prominent and visible, the more hidden structures of female anatomy often remain a mystery, even to the women to whom they belong.

Anatomy

Women's genital anatomy is often classed through a visible/not visible dichotomy. External genitalia, collectively called the vulva, comprise the mons, labia majora, labia minora, clitoral hood and clitoris (Figure 1.1). The outer lips, or labia majora, vary in size from woman to woman and may or not enclose the labia minora, or inner lips which are made from a continuous and often uneven fold of flesh. The inner lips join at the top to form a soft fold of skin or clitoral hood.

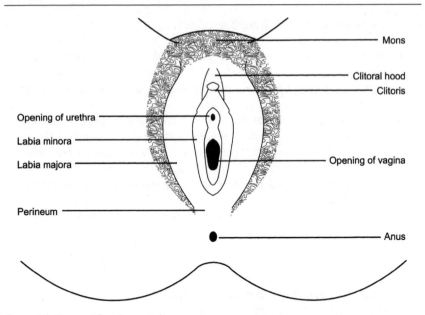

Figure 1.1 External female genitalia.

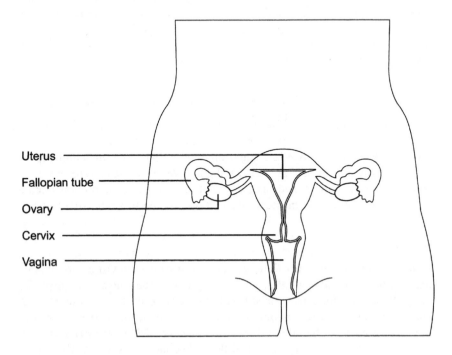

Figure 1.2 Internal female genitalia.

The clitoris sits inside the top part of the labia minora and contains many nerve endings especially at its tip, or glans, which is covered by the clitoral hood. Due to the sensitivity of the clitoris, some women prefer for stimulation to be focused on the base or along the side of the clitoris rather than the tip. Below the clitoris is the urethral opening for passing urine and below that is the entrance to the vagina which is separated from the anus by the perineum.

The internal genital organs include the vagina, uterus, fallopian tubes and ovaries. The clitoral shaft extends inside the pelvis to the pubis and then forks around the urethra before ending at the top end of the vagina (Figure 1.2). The G-spot is a region of spongy tissue 2.5 to 10 cm (1 to 4 inches) inside the front wall of the vagina and is another area that, for some women, is particularly pleasurable when stimulated.

The vagina produces a discharge or lubrication, which is generated by glands in the cervical passage. Vaginal discharge varies considerably in volume, odour and taste between women and also across the menstrual cycle. At ovulation, discharge is stickier, elastic and spinnbarkheit with the consistency of egg white.

Female sexual response

The most widely known model of female arousal comes from Masters and Johnson (1966) where it is conceptualised as having four phases.

Excitement

This phase can happen almost instantaneously in response to a range of visual stimuli, thoughts, images or physical sensations. Blood flow is directed to the pelvic region causing engorgement of the clitoris and labia with a resulting darkening of their colour and related sensation of fullness or pressure. The vaginal walls that usually lie close together begin to open or move apart and become smooth and lubricated. Lubrication may come from the vagina and cover the labia minora or majora. The amount of lubrication produced varies widely from woman to woman and may not be indicative of the degree or intensity of arousal. The uterus then starts to tip forward slightly in response to the cervix pulling at the top of the vagina, which causes the vagina to lengthen and balloon out near the cervix (Figures 1.3 and 1.4 illustrates these changes). Nipples may also become erect and, as arousal continues, this may generalise to the iris area around the nipple. This phase can be maintained throughout sexual activity.

Plateau

If excitement and arousal continue, further physical changes occur. The labia majora and minora continue to become full and engorged and open

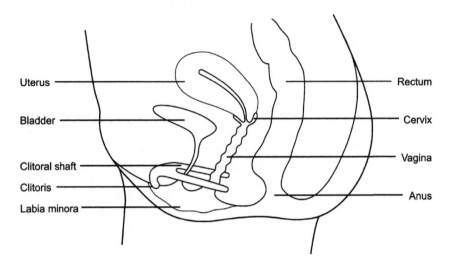

Figure 1.3 Female genitals during non-arousal.

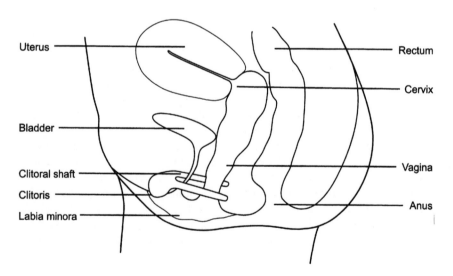

Figure 1.4 Female genitals during arousal.

out slightly. The vagina becomes fully expanded and ballooned at the top. This is thought to have an adaptive reproductive function as sperm will pool in this area near the cervix, facilitating fertilisation. Nipples may become more erect and other muscles in the body may tense as heart rate and respiration often increase.

Orgasm

This is the point of climax. During orgasm, the uterus, outer third of the vagina and anal sphincter contract rhythmically and the sensation is enjoyable or intensely pleasurable. The quality and sensations of the orgasm can vary in response to the type and frequency and location of physical stimulation. Further orgasms may be possible within seconds or minutes of orgasm with continued arousal or stimulation.

Resolution

After orgasm, if there is no further stimulation, the genitals return to their un-aroused state. This resolution phase is expedited by orgasm and is slower after the plateau phase alone and may be accompanied by feelings of congestion or heaviness in the genital region.

This model of sexual response, although facilitating descriptions of the physiological processes involved, is problematic in other ways as it is overly focused on genital activity and is stage-based, with orgasm seen as the end-point to sexual activity and penile penetration being synonymous with sexual intercourse. Non-genital sensual sites and erogenous zones are not included in this physiological account although mouth, lips, skin, and thoughts, fantasy and imagery play an integral part in sexual response and arousal.

More recent models of arousal have included contextual factors, emotional aspects of sex and the connection between thought processes and physiological responses. Kaplan (1995) describes a model of arousal where desire is the first and most important phase, that is then followed by arousal and orgasm. Basson (2000) describes how sexual contact may be sought for reasons other than sexual satisfaction such as reassurance-seeking, demonstrating affection or increasing emotional intimacy. This circular model of sexual response is illustrated in Figure 1.5.

Basson views the four-phase response described earlier as one possible pattern of arousal. For some women sexual response is not experienced as a single peak at orgasm, but rather a series of rolling hills or a mountain range with multiple peaks.

There is enormous variation in female arousal responses and orgasm with some women reporting always achieving an orgasm during sex or masturbation and others reporting that they never reach orgasm or are unsure

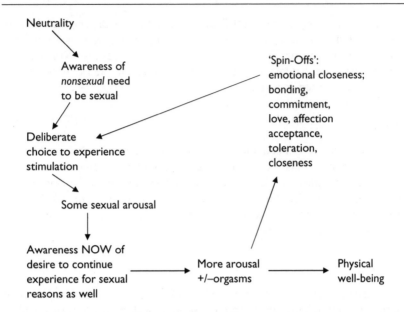

Figure 1.5 Basson female sexual response cycle. From Basson (2000) The femal sexual response. *Journal of Sex and Marital Therapy*, 26 (1), 51–65. Reprinted by permission of Taylor & Francis Ltd, http://www.tandf.co.uk/journals

about whether they do or not. It is difficult to clearly understand causal factors in these responses as it is almost impossible to account for all variables, such as the techniques of the women's partners, relationship, physical health, genetics and other factors that affect arousal. Problems and difficulties around sex and sexual functioning are well documented and discussed in other texts (e.g. Kaschak & Teifer, 2002; Hawton *et al.*, 1985). *A New View of Women's Sexual Problems* (Kaschak & Teifer, 2002) reflects broader contexts of sex and sexuality and may provide a useful departure point for conversations about when sex goes wrong (for more information visit http://www.fsd-alert.org), including considering the impact of sex in the contexts of problematic relationships, economic dependency, domestic violence etc.

Sexual anatomy – male sexual physiology and arousal

Male genitalia consist of the penis, scrotum and testicles or testes (Figure 1.6). The head of the penis, or glans, is the most sensitive part of these organs. The glans of the penis is covered by the foreskin, this is removed by circumcision in some cultures. The scrotum contains two testicles that hang outside the body to regulate temperature conducive to sperm production. The internal genital structures include the vas deferens, seminal vesicles,

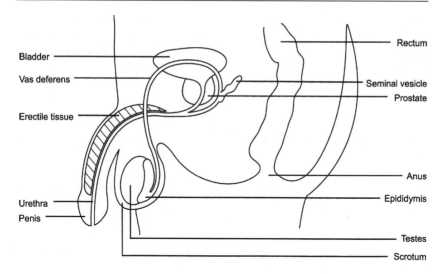

Figure 1.6 Male sexual anatomy.

epididymis and prostate. Sperm are stored in the epididymis in the testes and then travel up the vas deferens into the seminal vesicle where most of the fluid ejaculate is made. The prostate gland also contributes to the seminal fluid. Pre-ejaculate, the droplet of fluid that is produced in an erect penis, is a clear, sticky fluid produced in the Cowper's glands that lubricates the urethra in preparation for ejaculation.

Male sexual response

Male arousal is conceptualised as consisting of four stages: excitement, plateau, orgasm and resolution as outlined by Masters and Johnson (1966).

Excitement

This stage can happen almost instantly in response to a sexual thought, arousing image or physical sensation. The spongy tissue of the penis fills up with blood and becomes larger, firmer and more erect. The testicles are drawn up closer to the body and the skin of the scrotum thickens to facilitate this. If arousal is not continued the increased blood flow to the pelvic area is reversed and the genitals return to their previous state.

Plateau

If excitement and arousal continue, further physiological changes occur. The testicles are elevated and tightened, the foreskin, if present, rolls back and the glans is exposed and the coronal ridge becomes engorged and darkens in colour. The urethra will dilate marginally to facilitate the movement of ejaculate along the penile shaft. Arousal is also reversible at this stage and can shift to the unaroused state or the excited phase and then go back to the plateau as arousal returns or increases.

Orgasm

Male orgasm has two stages. In the first stage the vas deferens contract and the sperm is surrounded by seminal fluid in the seminal vesicles. If stimulation stops at this stage, ejaculation can be delayed. Any further arousal or excitement will lead to a point known as 'ejaculatory inevitability'. The sperm travel up the urethra and the entire penis contracts causing the seminal fluid to be ejected. Contractions occur at a rate of 0.8 seconds in both male and female orgasm. Ejaculation of sperm is usually, but not always, accompanied by the intense pleasurable feelings of orgasm. Similarly male orgasm is physiologically possible without ejaculation.

Resolution

All of the above changes are reversed after ejaculation. In the resolution phase the penis and scrotum softens and the testicles descend. During the refractory period there is no possibility of physiologically becoming aroused. This refractory period lengthens significantly with age from a few seconds in adolescents to a few hours in old age.

Developmental changes that occur are discussed further in Chapter 5. Problems in male sexual response or functioning are covered in detail in other texts (e.g. Hawton *et al.*, 1985; Zilbergeld, 1993).

In the chapters that follow many of the concepts and ideas outlined above are explored further and additional training exercises are suggested that could also be used in training and working therapeutically around these topics.

OTHER RESOURCES

Websites

Teen-friendly cartoon illustrations of different shapes of male and female genitalia: http://www.teenwire.com/interactive/movies/do-051019-figleaf. php

Sh! – friendly and low-key women only sexual emporium: http://www.sh-womenstore.com

Betty Dodson Workshops – DVDs, books and exercises on self-loving: http://www.bettydodson.com

Related organisations and professional groups

BPS Faculty of HIV and Sexual Health: http://www.bps.org.uk/dcp-sexhealth/dcp-sexhealth_home.cfm
British Association for Sexual and Relationship Therapy: http://www.basrt.org.uk
British Association for Sexual Health and HIV: http://www.bashh.org/
Gender Identity Research and Education Society: http://www.gires.org.uk
New View Campaign of sexual well-being: http://www.fsd-alert.org
Relate – sex therapy, relationship therapy and counselling: http://www.relate.org.uk

FURTHER READING

Anders, C. (2002). *The lazy cross dresser*. Eugene: Greenery Press.
Daniluk, J.C. (2003). *Women's sexuality across the lifespan. Challenging myths, creating meanings*. New York: Guilford Press.
Dodson, B. (1996). *Sex for one: The joy of self loving*. New York: Crown.
Heath, H. & White, I. (2002). *The challenge of sexuality in health care*. Blackwell: London.
Hopke, R.H., Carrington, K.L. & Writh, S. (eds) (1993). *Same-sex love and the path to wholeness*. London & Boston: Shambala.
Litvinoff, S. (2001). *Relate: sex in loving relationships*. London: Vermillion.
Rose, L. (2006). *How to change your sex: A light-hearted look at the hardest thing you'll ever do*. Lulu.com (http://www.lulu.com).

REFERENCES

American Psychiatric Association (1994). *Diagnostic and Statistical Manual of Mental Disorders* (4th edn). New York: APA.
American Psychiatric Association (2000). *Diagnostic and Statistical Manual of Mental Disorders* (4th edition – Revised). New York: APA.
Baggaley, M. (2005). Is an interest in BDSM a pathological disorder or a normal variant of human sexual behaviour? *Lesbian & Gay Psychology Review*, 6 (3), 253–254.
Basson, R. (2000). The female sexual response: A different model. *Journal of Sex & Marital Therapy*, 26 (1), 51–65.
Basson, R. (2005). Women's sexual dysfunction: Revised and expanded definitions. *Canadian Medical Association Journal*, 172, 1327.
Bem, S.L. (1989). Genital knowledge and gender constancy in preschool children. *Child Development*, 60, 649–662.
Butler, J. (1999). *Gender trouble – Feminism and the subversion of identity*. London: Routledge.
Carr, D.M. (2003). *The erotic word: Sexuality, spirituality and the bible*. Oxford: Oxford University Press.
Cartledge, S. & Ryan, J. (1983). *Sex & love*. London: The Women's Press.

Denman, C. (2004). *Sexuality: A biopsychosocial approach.* New York: Palgrave Macmillan.

Freud, S. (1905). Three essays on sexuality. In *Penguin Freud Library*, vol. 7. Harmondsworth: Penguin.

Gibson, S. & O'Donovan, A. (2009). *Criminalisation of HIV transmission: Guidelines regarding confidentiality and disclosure.* Leicester: British Psychological Society.

Hawton, K. (1985). *Sex Therapy: A practical guide.* Oxford: Oxford University Press.

Hopke, R.H., Carrington, K.L. & Writh, S. (eds) (1993). Same-sex love and the path of wholeness. London & Boston: Shambala.

Jackson, S. & Scott, S. (eds) (1996). *Feminism and sexuality: A reader.* New York: Columbia University Press.

Kaplan, H.S. (1995). *The sexual desire disorders.* Levittown, NY: Brunner-Mazel.

Kaschak, E. & Tiefer, L. (2002). *A new view of women's sexual problems.* New York: The Haworth Press.

Kerouac, J. (1957). *On the road.* New York: Viking Press.

Kinsey, A., Pomeroy, W.B. & Martin, C.E. (1948). *Sexual behaviour in the human male.* Philadelphia: WB Saunders.

Kinsey, A., Pomeroy, W.B. & Martin, C.E. (1953). *Sexual behaviour in the human female.* Philadelphia: WB Saunders.

Klein, F., Sepekoff, B. & Wolf, T. (1986). Sexual orientation: A multi-variable dynamic process. *Journal of Homosexuality*, 11, 35–49.

Kleinplatz, P.J. & Moser, C. (2005). Is S/M pathological? *Lesbian & Gay Psychology Review*, 6 (3), 255–260.

Langdridge, D. & Barker, M. (2007). *Safe, sane and consensual.* Basingstoke: Palgrave.

Maccoby, E.E. & Jacklin, C.N. (1974). *The psychology of sex differences.* Stanford, California: Stanford University Press.

Masters, W.H. & Johnson, V.E. (1966). *Human sexual response.* Toronto; New York: Bantam Books.

O'Byrne, R., Rapley, M. & Hansen, S. (2006). "You couldn't say 'no', could you?": Young men's understandings of sexual refusal. *Feminism and Psychology*, 16 (2), 133–154.

Reich, W. (1989). *The function of orgasm.* London: Souvenir Press.

Renk, K. & Creasey, G.L. (2003). The relationship of gender, gender identity, and coping strategies in late adolescents. *Journal of Adolescence*, 26 (2), 159–168.

Samuels, A. (1986). *Jung and the post-Jungians.* London: Routledge.

Sigma (2007). *Form and focus: Evaluation of CHAPS national interventions, 2003 to 2006.* London: Sigma.

Staunton, T. (ed.) (2002). *Body Psychotherapy.* London: Routledge.

Stein, R. (1984).*The betrayal of the soul in psychotherapy.* Dallas: Spring Publications.

World Health Organization (1992). *The ICD-10 Classification of Mental and Behavioural Disorders: Clinical Descriptions and Diagnostic Guidelines.* Geneva: WHO.

Zilbergeld, B. (1993). *The new male sexuality: The truth about men, sex and pleasure.* New York: Bantam.

Chapter 2

Talking about sex

Clare Stevenson

A chicken and an egg are lying in bed. The chicken is smoking a cigarette with a satisfied smile on its face and the egg is frowning and looking put out. The egg mutters to no one in particular, 'I guess we answered that question'.

Author Unknown

'WHEN WAS THE FIRST TIME YOU HAD SEX? HOW WAS IT?'

How would you feel about being asked those questions? Embarrassed? Puzzled? Liberated? Excited? Relieved? Horrified? How would you feel asking them? It is likely that your response will depend on the context in which the question is asked and why, your relationship with the person you are talking to, your social roles and how you think they will respond to you. Your answer may be influenced by your prior experience of talking about sex, whether there are problems with your sex life and your assumptions, expectation, values and beliefs about sex.

Talking about sex and sexuality within a therapeutic setting can be one of the most challenging areas we face as therapists. Fears, assumptions and sheer embarrassment can make us hesitate in addressing sex. For many of our clients, talking about sex may feel like a big step, even for those who wish to discuss it or who may already have addressed a range of other intimate and difficult issues with therapists (Daines & Perrett, 2000).

This chapter aims to be a guide to putting sex on the agenda in therapy conversations. It explores ideas about how therapists can have sensitive and useful conversations, with consideration of issues such as power, culture and gender, and the need for boundaries and ethical practice. The chapter will present literature from a variety of theoretical perspectives, exploring ideas, questions and exercises to guide self-reflection and curiosity in order to develop personal reflective practice.

WHY TALK ABOUT SEX AND SEXUALITY?

Usually a client is referred to or finds a therapist when seeking help for a specific problem. If that problem is directly related to sex or sexuality then it seems clear and obvious that as a therapist we will need to address such issues. However, if the client does not raise sex as an issue, then one might ask, is it relevant or necessary to ask about it? This section explores what might be missed in our understanding and formulation of the difficulties our clients present to us, if we leave sex off the agenda in our assessments and interventions.

Exercise 2.1 Why talk about sex?

This exercise involves questions to help guide individual reflection or a group exercise.

1   Reflect on the role sex and sexuality plays/has played in your own life; how important, or not, it has been in determining your general feelings of well-being?
2   If you have ever felt low, anxious or depressed at any time in your life, was there any relationship, either in terms of cause or effect, between your mood and how you felt about sex or how you had sex? For example, the lack of opportunity to have sex might have led to lowered self-confidence; or low mood made you 'go off' sex.
3   Would you have valued the opportunity to talk about any sexual issues you may have had? If so, what would have made that conversation possible for you? If you did talk to someone about it, what made it a helpful/unhelpful conversation?

Box 2.1 Tips for group work

When doing the exercises in this chapter with a group, ask group members to reflect privately, at least initially. Either keep answers private, or allow participants to discuss in a pair those aspects that they feel comfortable to share. It is also helpful to discuss boundaries and respecting confidentiality. For example discuss what you will share with the larger group and only share comments if agreed in your pair. Remind participants to take care of themselves while doing an exercise such as this and only disclose as much as they feel comfortable. Nevertheless encourage them to do as much as they feel able, as it could be a useful self-reflective exercise to help them to consider what might be missing if we do not provide the opportunity for clients to talk about the role of sex in their lives. If participants choose not to do it, it might be useful to reflect on why they do not feel comfortable doing so? Would they feel comfortable in different circumstances and if so what would these be? Although these guidelines are fundamental to any training group exercise, consider the potential unique issues related to sexuality that may arise. For example, there may be personal experiences of difficult or abusive sexual experiences within the group. Therefore it is even more important with such exercises to name the potential sensitivity of the topic and discuss boundaries where necessary.

IS TALKING ABOUT SEX RELEVANT TO ALL SERVICE SETTINGS?

Therapists may assume that sexual issues are only relevant to psychosexual presentations or within sexual health services, genitourinary medicine (GUM) or specific psychosexual or sexual assault services, and therefore may refer any issues related to sexuality to specialist services, or not address them at all. However, sex and sexuality are relevant to most, if not all, areas of clinical practice and may form part of a psychological formulation in relation to many presenting concerns.

Sex can be a source of pleasure, celebration and joy, or it can be the cause and effect of psychological difficulties and associated with a range of medical conditions. Therefore exploration of sex and sexuality can be a key part of understanding identity, relationships and emotional as well as physical health (Orbach, 1999; Wells, 2000; Yalom, 1989).

Exercise 2.2 Relevance of sex and sexuality

This exercise can be done either as individual self-reflection, or within small groups or pairs, feeding back to a larger group for discussion.

In order to explore the relevance of sex and sexuality in a wide variety of clinical presentations, think about how issues of sex and sexuality may be of relevance to the following vignettes:

1   A 29-year-old woman with recurrent depression recently separated from her male partner of four months. She has never had a relationship longer than six months.
2   A 14-year-old girl with an eating disorder.

3   A 66-year-old man recently retired and married for 40 years, who presents with insomnia.
4   A 45-year-old woman with chronic back pain, in a long-term relationship.

Note: there are many potential ways to approach these vignettes, and no 'right answers'. For the purpose of this exercise, try to generate ideas related to sex, sexuality and sexual orientation. Of course sexual issues may be only one of a range of relevant factors to explore in order to formulate and decide on an intervention with the above cases. If you have time, think about how the sexual issues may interact with other hypotheses or ideas you may have about the clients. If you work in other settings you can generate your own case examples.

When discussing the vignettes, a starting place may be to situate sexuality within the individual's current context, including age, culture and relationship status. We know that an individual's relationship to their sexuality will change over the lifespan, for example the burgeoning sexuality of adolescence and dominant Western cultural notions of sexual freedom in late teens and early twenties. Other developmental issues may include fertility issues, links between sexual functioning and physical health at any age, and especially during the later years of life (see Chapter 5). It is also important to consider direct links between sexual functioning and mental health e.g. depression and anxiety (Denman, 2004; Miller & Green, 2002; Orbach, 1999). Fear or anxiety about sexual issues can impact on both mood and relationships. Lowered mood or anxiety can reduce libido or desire for sex. Body image or self-esteem can impact on making and sustaining relationships and on a sense of sexual desirability.

Some other issues that may be elicited from the vignettes include:

- current problems with having sex, such as sexual pain or discomfort;
- possible issues of sexual orientation, cultural norms and identity;
- effects of previous sexual and relationship history e.g. sexual assault or child sexual abuse that can be linked with eating disorders, intimacy issues or psychogenic pain;
- chronic pain, physical health problems and common drugs used to manage conditions, including diabetes or heart disease, may affect a person's sexual desire and sexual functioning in ways they may or may not understand or anticipate.

The role of sex and sexuality in mental and physical well-being has been explored and debated extensively within philosophy, psychology, psychotherapy and nursing literature. The role of sexual problems in regulating intimacy and containing emotional problems is explored by a number of authors including Daines and Perrett (2000), Orbach (1991), Spence (1991) and Hawton (1985). For an excellent training manual on nursing care for sexuality in health and illness in particular see Wells (2000).

In summary, developing a curious, positive, affirmative, comfortable, non-judgemental and integrated approach can enhance practice in a range of areas not just those directly focused on sex or sexual problems. By placing sex on the agenda as an integral part of the client's well-being from the outset we are modelling its importance.

WHAT MAKES IT DIFFICULT TO DISCUSS SEX AND SEXUALITY FROM THE CLIENT'S PERSPECTIVE?

Some clients may be concerned about issues related to sex or sexuality and be keen to discuss them, but find it difficult to find the ways and means to do so. They may present with other concerns, or may wait to assess how comfortable they feel before disclosing further. Our questions and approach can close down or open up potential conversations. Daines and Perrett (2000) describe how clients may wonder: 'What words shall I use?, Will they offend?, Will the counsellor help me out or leave me to stumble?'. For some clients concerns related to sexual issues may have been kept secret and not talked about for years and they may need to be 'gently led' in order to talk about their sexual secrets or concerns.

This section will consider the reasons why clients may find it hard to have such conversations with a health professional and what might stop them or hold them back from doing so.

Exercise 2.3 Why might clients feel uncomfortable or not want to talk to their therapists about sex?

Generate some answers to the question of why clients might find it difficult to talk about sex and sexuality, and what issues they may bring to therapy about this. If you are doing this exercise with a group you may want to do this in pairs or threes. If you have trouble generating answers then try to think of yourself as a client and what might inhibit you talking to your therapist about sex or sexual problems.

Some of the issues that may be elicited include:

- client's feelings of embarrassment about sexual issues or feelings of shame about their own difficulties or desires;

- a belief that sex should be private or secret;
- anxiety about confidentiality and whether particular people might find out that they have spoken about sexual issues;
- religious or other cultural beliefs about discussing sex that might prohibit them from talking openly about it;
- power imbalances and difference, both visible and perceived, between the therapist and client, e.g. gender, cultural background and sexual orientation (McGoldrick, 1994; Lynne Ellis, 1997);
- concern that the therapist will not think that sexual issues are relevant or not being aware that sexual issues are something they could ask for help with (Reder & Fredman, 1996);
- a fear of being judged or thought to be strange/perverted/bad etc;
- worry that the therapist will not be able to understand or help them with sexual problems;
- worry about embarrassing the therapist and this affecting the therapeutic relationship;
- not knowing what words to use.

There is considerable evidence that clients find talking about issues of sex and sexuality particularly difficult (Dardick & Grady, 1980; Milton *et al.*, 2005; Hitchcock & Wilson, 1992; Daines & Perrett, 2000). Hook and Andrews (2005) explored shame and depression in non-disclosure in therapy and found that sexual problems were among the most common difficulties not disclosed to therapists when in therapy for depression. 'Feeling ashamed' was the most common reason given, followed by lack of trust in the therapist and lack of empathy from the therapist. Other concerns included fear of negative judgement; that the issue was too painful to talk about; fear of rejection from the therapist; feeling too guilty; thinking the information not important for treatment and that it was too private. Within nursing literature there is evidence that many patients wish health professionals would raise issues of sexuality with them (Waterhouse & Metcalf, 1991).

WHAT MAKES IT DIFFICULT TO DISCUSS SEX AND SEXUALITY FROM THE THERAPIST'S PERSPECTIVE?

There can be a number of reasons why therapists find talking about sex or sexuality with their clients challenging. Many of the reasons that clients find it difficult will hold true for therapists too. The therapist's beliefs about sexuality and talking about sex may make these conversations feel difficult or problematic. Self-reflection and developing awareness of our own feelings as therapists is an area recognised as important in psychotherapy, psychology and nursing practice (Wells, 2000; Boyd Franklin, 1989; Milton *et al.*,

2005). It is seen as essential particularly in this area, as it has been found to be one where therapists can hold unhelpful beliefs and prejudices (Annesley & Coyle, 1995; Bartlett *et al.*, 2001). Developing the skills to recognise such feelings and respond appropriately in order to address clients' psychosexual concerns is important for both responsive care and professional confidence (Wells, 2000). The assumptions we hold are likely to influence the questions that we ask and do not ask and the direction that the therapeutic work takes. In addition, attitudes towards sex and sexuality will be communicated to others through our use of language and questioning style, hence the exercises in this chapter strongly encourage self-reflective practice.

Exercise 2.4 Why might therapists feel uncomfortable talking about sex?

These questions can be used to guide personal self-reflection, or could be used in a training setting as a pairs exercise.

1 What are your personal fears/anxieties about talking about sex with clients?
2 What do you fear may happen if you do raise the issue?
3 What have been your experiences to date when the issue of sex has been raised in therapy?
4 What therapeutic models do you work with and what place does sexuality hold within them?
5 How able do you feel to address strong feelings such as shame and embarrassment that may be raised in the therapeutic encounter, either within yourself or within your client?
6 Do you have strong views, assumptions or notions about sex, sexual practices or sexual orientations that might limit your work with clients?
7 Do you feel inexperienced or unsure about addressing sex and sexuality issues and concerned this may come across or limit your work?
8 Are there other factors that might determine whether or not you put these conversations on your therapy agenda, for example your services approach or attitude to addressing sex in therapy?

Exercise 2.5 Reflection on clinical practice

This exercise can be used as an adjunct to the above questions. If using it with a group, arrange groups so that at least one person has a case they are comfortable to share.

Think of a client where either:

1 You think it may have been useful to raise the issue of sex or
   sexuality but did not. Discuss and reflect on what might have
   inhibited you from having the conversation.
   or
2 You did talk about sex, but it was difficult. What was difficult
   and why? What went well in the conversation?

As discussed, this is an area of practice that many professionals find difficult to address, therefore do not be surprised if you find the above questions challenging. Markovic (2007) investigated the ways in which systemic
psychotherapists addressed sexual issues in a qualitative study. She found
that for many participants talking about sex was at times experienced as
'provocative' due to personal vulnerabilities triggered by the topic. Also
that judgements and prejudices can be 'sparked off', and that there are
often pervasive, deeply embedded inhibitions and anxieties with regard to
topics of sex. This research highlights again the need for a self-reflective
approach to developing therapeutic conversational skills in this area.

You may want to return to these exercises at the end of this chapter and
consider whether any of your ideas have changed or if you feel better
informed or more confident in working with these issues. If you identify,
through the above exercises, that this is an area where you particularly
struggle, then it may be useful to highlight your own training needs in this
area. Who might you talk to about your concerns, for example, a supervisor, a tutor or a trusted colleague?

HOW TO START A CONVERSATION ABOUT SEX: SETTING THE SCENE

The context in which you are working will influence conversations you may
have about sex. In a sexual health or genitourinary medicine (GUM)
context, clients are likely to be expecting to be asked about sex, and indeed
be rather surprised if they are *not* asked. Therefore as a therapist, opening
such conversations may well feel more comfortable in this context. Of
course, issues of embarrassment and shame may still be present. In other
service contexts, where conversations about sex and sexuality may be less
expected by the client, and more easily sidestepped by both sides, opportunities to 'put sex on the agenda' might need to be created.

Drawing together suggestions from the literature, the following principles
or guidelines are suggested as a starting point for developing a personal
style in asking about sex.

1   **Start positive** – you do not have to start by making your opening question about *problems*, instead explore how your client feels about their current sexual life and experiences. Start with as few assumptions as possible, holding in mind the notion that 'normal' in sex is hugely varied and that 'problems' may be a matter of definition or expectation.

2   **Be transparent and 'locate' your questions** – tell your client about the reason you are asking a particular question at that time. Let your client know why you are curious about that aspect of their life or functioning, for example, in order to better understand their relationship, or the effect of an illness, etc.

3   **Be 'matter of fact'** – if you can be comfortable with the topic, then it is more likely that you will enable your clients to be comfortable too.

4   **Stay curious and open minded** about your client's lifestyle and choices, sexual orientation, the gender of any partner mentioned, the types of sex they may be having.

5   **Stay aware and reflective** about any cultural factors that are likely to be impacting on the sort of conversation you are able to have with your client (Chapter 6 explores this in more detail).

6   **Think about timing** – is rapport well established? Try to consider the timing of asking questions about sex, and consider the impact a question may have at a particular time.

7   **Be on the look out for openings and 'invitations'** – listen out for these. Daines and Perrett (2000) suggest that some clients, who may be less confident to talk about these issues directly, may approach the subject indirectly, or may drop 'hints' to see whether the counsellor/therapist follows up what they say. They suggest that statements such as 'My partner and I are really arguing recently'; 'She does not seem to be interested in me at the moment'; 'I wish he would not keep bothering me whilst I feel so ill' are vague and could mean anything, but one possibility is that there is some kind of sexual problem that the person would like to talk about. They could be an opener or an invitation for you to ask further.

8   **Use questionnaires and other assessment tools** – e.g. the Beck Depression Inventory (BDI-II, Beck *et al.*, 1996) has items on sex; you could use their answers as a starting point for a conversation.

9   **Normalise sex as a topic** – By letting your client know that sexual concerns are more common than they may think in their particular presenting context, this may enable them to feel less embarrassed in discussing the topic with you. For example, often sex becomes more complicated with chronic health problems or difficulties with mobility or pain. By normalising the concerns and the usefulness of talking about them you are more likely to provide a comfortable space for your client to disclose to you.

10 **Choose language that is comfortable for you and your client** – the following sections further explore how to find an agreed language in more detail.

Exercise 2.6 Starting conversations about sex and sexuality

For each of the vignettes in Exercise 2.2, generate some possible opening questions about sex. If you are doing this exercise with a group you could encourage role play in pairs to practise introducing the topic of sex and sexuality. Try using the guiding principles above to generate and develop open and curious questions that fit your work setting, therapeutic model or personal style.

SETTING AN AGENDA

Agenda setting is a cornerstone of many therapeutic approaches, including the range of cognitive therapies, systemic and family therapies, and some short-term analytic therapies. Within cognitive behaviour therapy (CBT), planning at the beginning of each therapy session is considered the opportunity to structure and clarify goals of the session to ensure the most effective use of the time available (Padesky, 1995; Beck, 1995). During the assessment phase, agenda setting may provide opportunities to invite conversations about a range of issues. It should be a collaborative process; therefore clients should be invited to reflect on what they consider to be the most relevant topics to cover in the time. However, due to the power imbalance inherent in the therapy relationship, it is important for the therapist to create the opportunities, set the scene and in some cases give 'permission' for the client to be able to raise issues that may be difficult to discuss or may not be considered relevant or important enough to put on the agenda.

Spence (1991) suggests that when assessing a client it is important to ensure flexibility, confidentiality and to be relaxed and comfortable talking about topics generally. Remember, particularly in the early stages of the therapeutic relationship that you and your client are still strangers to each other. She suggests that a mix of highly personal and less 'threatening' questions can help to facilitate conversation. Phrasing questions so as to create the assumption that a given behaviour is normal e.g. not 'have you' but 'how often . . .'. Be aware that language used will communicate assumptions about what you as a therapist consider to be 'normal', 'abnormal' or 'problematic'. For example, Spence cautions against seeing orgasm as an overvalued goal, and encourages awareness of how phrasing of questions can be important in conveying openness and curiosity about a client's experience. So the question 'do you *manage* to *achieve* orgasm every time you have sex?' conveys the assumption of the 'normality' of orgasm as the goal of sex and something to be 'achieved'. An alternative question might be 'What is it you want to experience during sex?', or 'what are your goals during sex?'. These opening questions can lead on to discussion of clients' expectations of sex, their assumptions about what 'normal' sex is, and how they are making sense of their own perceived difficulties with sex and sexuality.

FINDING AN AGREED LANGUAGE

Lack of a vocabulary to describe subjective or physical experiences of sex can mean that clients and therapists may need to be supported to find a comfortable language to have conversations about sex. Finding and using an agreed language familiar to clients is a way to enhance both comfort and clarity in such discussions.

Depending on their backgrounds clients will have diverse experiences of sexual language, terminology and familiarity with particular words and phrases. Some clients may well be more familiar than you are with certain culturally derived sexual terms e.g. frottage, bondage (terminology and definitions of such culturally sexual terms will shift and change with time and place, so a 'definitive list' of such definitions is neither possible nor appropriate). You may or may not be familiar with these, but either way it will be important to show non-judgemental curiosity about the meaning of the terms, even if you think you know them. Feel free to clarify their meaning with your clients by asking about the language that they are familiar with and feel comfortable to use. Be transparent if you are not familiar with their language; this is preferable to getting it 'wrong'.

Furthermore, consideration of the meanings communicated through language use is very important. Lynne Ellis (1997) suggests that sexual identities are constituted out of a complex web of moral, legal, political and economic discourses that shift over time and place. Words can be seen as reflections of these wider values and have symbolic meaning. Therefore, the language we use with clients in the consulting room will be important for how meaning (and hence problems) are constructed and how our values and those of our clients are communicated. Consideration of language use and terminology can often be the key to opening up or closing down therapeutic discussions.

Exercise 2.7 Getting comfortable with language.

1   List all the words you can think of in common language for:

- sexual acts
- female body parts and genitalia
- male body parts and genitalia.

Write the words down, say them out loud. Note the words you feel most and least comfortable with and why.

2   Consider the following situations in pairs or small groups:

  a   You have a client who refers to a vagina or penis or sexual intercourse using a word you think is inappropriate or offensive (e.g. cunt, cock).

   - Do you avoid using the word, or do you use it and make yourself uncomfortable?
   - Do you agree to use it, or try to find another term that you are both comfortable with?

  b   You have a client who uses the phrase 'down there', you assume they are talking about their genitals but they are vague and seem to be embarrassed. What might you do or say in this situation?

If there is a particular term that you personally feel uncomfortable using, you might want to consider talking about the use of that word with your client and discussing its meanings. You might want to talk about how it is used, by whom and for what purpose, its connotations, and share the dilemma about whether to use it in therapy or not.

As far as possible try to be direct and discuss language openly with your client. If you are having a discussion about sex, check out the different terms that you may use and discuss with your client which terms you both agree on. If you can demonstrate by your attitude that you are comfortable with a whole range of terms and language, then you may find your client much more enabled to have a conversation with you about sex.

If you are working with a client who expresses sexist or homophobic language, consider how you might manage this. Is it possible to challenge sexism or homophobia while staying engaged with the client? It may be useful to stay curious about the person and why they may be saying this to you at that moment and to consider what they might be trying to communicate. Consider your client's previous experiences that have led them to that position, or perhaps a lack of experience meaning that their ideas have never been challenged before, or they may have not had the opportunity before to think differently. You could see this as an opportunity rather than a challenge, and be open to the idea that your client's ideas may not be set in stone, but may reflect the dominant discourses that they have been exposed to with their family and culture about sexuality. Consider also that the meaning of sexist language might be different given the gender of the client and therapist.

WHEN ENGLISH IS NOT THE CLIENT'S FIRST LANGUAGE.

If using an interpreter, having conversations about sex and sexual issues can be more sensitive or complex. Interpreters will vary widely in their level of comfort and experience in talking about sensitive and confidential issues such as these (Butler, 2008). As with other similar issues it may be helpful to talk with your interpreter before the session about the possibility of such conversations arising. You may want to ask about the language they may feel comfortable to use or to avoid. If appropriate, you might be able to use your interpreter as a cultural advocate to discuss different attitudes and beliefs about sex. For example, a married Muslim female Bengali client may feel empowered by a conversation with a female interpreter about the teachings of the Koran in relation to sex within marriage. Of course the opportunities to have such conversations will depend greatly on the knowledge, experience and comfort level of the interpreters you are working with and if it is appropriate within the service for them to take on this role. It will be useful to spend time with the interpreter to explore these possibilities before you open up conversations with clients. It can be helpful to reiterate conversations about confidentiality and professional boundaries, especially if your client and interpreter are from small communities who may meet outside of the session in some context. Feelings of shame, fear of stigma or concerns about confidentiality may be more acute if an interpreter is from the same community. The gender of the interpreter is also likely to be important to consider. It may be necessary to have more explicit conversations with client and interpreter together about what might make it easier or more comfortable for both of them to have these conversations. Some clients may prefer not to use an interpreter due to issues of embarrassment or fears about confidentiality. These wishes should be respected, although the work may take longer or not be possible in the same way. It is also important to check out the meanings of words used by both you and the client, and spend time building a common language. If your client speaks another language, ask them what these words are in that language and which ones they would like to use (Tribe & Ravel, 2002).

CONFIDENTIALITY

This is an important consideration in all areas of therapeutic practice; however, in the area of sexual behaviour clients may well need more reassurance that any information they share will be treated confidentially. As therapists we need to be clear with our own confidentiality policies. Ensure you have your client's permission before writing anything in a letter that might go to a general practitioner (GP) or to their home address where others may live.

ASSESSMENT AND TAKING A SEXUAL HISTORY

How much information is relevant or appropriate to obtain for the purposes of having comfortable discussions about sex in most therapeutic settings? Useful reflexive questions to aid ethical practice in this area might include the following.

- Who is this conversation for?
- What is the purpose of gathering information? What will I/we do with it?
- What does the client need/want to tell me? What do they hope for, would find useful in this conversation?
- Is there anything in my formulation so far to indicate any issues related to sex, sexuality, etc?
- If I have asked about relationships, did I ask about sex? If not why not? Am I avoiding asking or is it really not relevant to ask?
- If my client had any issues related to sex, would they feel comfortable asking me? How would I know?
- How will I know if I am being intrusive or inappropriate in my questions? Will my client be able to let me know and will I pick up the signals?

Remember you can check with your client at any point in the session if they feel comfortable with the questions, explore how the conversation is going for them and clarify the rationale behind the questions you ask.

Here are some specific assessment questions related to sexual issues you may want to consider.

1   What is the nature of the sexual issue?
2   Who is aware of the problem? Who is most concerned? Who is this a problem for? (Sexual issues often, though not always, occur in the context of relationship(s), therefore it is useful to explore where the problem is located.)
3   How long has it been a problem? Is it a new problem or has it occurred before?
4   Is this a problem of sexual functioning e.g. erectile problems, sexual pain or difficulties achieving orgasm?
5   Is this a new problem, specific to a current situation or relationship, for example not achieving orgasm after having a baby (secondary problem)? Has it always been a problem, for example never having achieved an orgasm (primary problem)?
6   What was the context of the individual's life and relationships at the time the problem started and have these contexts changed?
7   What are the client's feelings, attitudes and expectations about sex and sexuality?

If the aim is to provide psychosexual therapy for specific problems with sexual functioning such as erectile problems, sexual pain or anorgasmia (unable to have an orgasm) then it is appropriate to take a full sexual history. For a fuller discussion of how to take a sexual history, with a view to psychosexual therapy, see Spence (1991), Hawton (1985), Watson (2002), Kaschak and Teifer (2002).

DEVELOPING FURTHER CONVERSATIONS ABOUT SEX

Once you have put sex on your agenda in therapy, what next? What conversations might be possible or useful to your client once you've opened up the possibility of talking about sex or sexuality? In the first instance this could be a useful question to explore directly with a client, particularly if this is the first time they have told anyone about their concerns. If they were previously unaware that such a conversation might be available to them, then they may need some time to reflect on what it is they would find helpful. It might be useful to consider how sexual issues may be related to any other presenting concerns. Working within a CBT framework, a case formulation (Tarrier & Calam, 2002) might be usefully shared with a client that includes the sexual issues. If sex and sexuality has been included in the formulation then it is likely that a richer and more complete understanding of the client and their concerns may be reached. Then, when planning treatment based on this formulation, therapist and client prioritise which of the presenting issues to address (Beck, 1995).

If a client identifies specific sexual dysfunction it may be appropriate to refer them to local sexual health services if this should fall outside of your area of expertise. Alternatively, see Spence (1991) or Hawton (1985) for further guidance on treating specific sexual problems and providing sex and relationship therapy for couples or individuals.

There are so many possible conversations to have with clients on these topics and it is beyond the scope of this chapter to explore them all in any detail beyond pointing the reader in the direction of useful further resources. Some ideas may include the following.

- Discussion of where ideas, messages, values, assumptions regarding sex, gender, sexuality, sexual mores, attitudes may originate. Does the client's family, culture, wider society, religion, wider media etc., shape them? *A New View of Women's Sexual Problems* (Kaschak & Tiefer, 2002) provides an excellent guide to exploring the social and contextual issues in construction of women's sexual problems.
- What ideas do they have about femininity, masculinity, sexual desirability, and what do they consider to be 'normal'? Explore sexual myths

and provide reassurance if necessary through discussion about breadth of the concept of 'normal' sexuality.

- Explore attitudes, assumptions, beliefs and expectations about sex, perhaps using a sexual genogram to 'map' them (Hof & Berman, 1986). Who shares these ideas in the family, who has different ideas?
- Explore the client's preferred ideas or values about sex, especially if these are different from their family or culture. What values do they want to keep, re-evaluate or reject?
- Is there pressure to conform or fit to expectations? Where is this pressure coming from? Is it possible to do things differently?

One useful perspective to hold in mind during such conversations is that there is no single 'right' way to have sex or to be sexual, but that the social messages our clients and we receive about sex and sexuality exert huge influence on how we appraise and judge sexual behaviour and performance. As discussed by George (1993: 255) in a chapter on gay men's relationships in the AIDS era:

> The expectation to be entirely happy and fulfilled via a sexual relationship is both pervasive and persuasive in society, for straight and non-heterosexual people. Many people seem to feel a burden of responsibility to be happy (in a one to one relationship) and successful (in sex).

TALKING ABOUT ASPECTS OF SEX AND SEXUALITY THAT MAY FEEL DIFFICULT OR UNCOMFORTABLE

As in many other areas of practice, talking about sex and sexuality may evoke feelings and responses in the therapist. The earlier sections of this chapter explored self-reflective exercises on personal feelings and attitudes about talking about sex in general. This section looks in more detail at particular scenarios that may arouse certain feelings.

Exercise 2.8 Case examples

Consider the following scenarios. For each of them consider:

1   How might you personally feel about what your client is telling you?
2   How might you respond to your client?
3   How might your own feelings impact on what subsequent conversations you have or don't have with this client?

Scenario 1: a heterosexual, married male client tells you that he visits commercial sex workers (prostitutes) regularly.

Scenario 2: a gay male client tells you that he has multiple casual sexual partners, many of whom he meets in saunas and clubs and some of whom are completely anonymous.

Scenario 3: a female client tells you she has fantasies about sado-masochistic sex where she is tied up and spanked.

Scenario 4: a female client tells you she has a number of casual sexual partners of both genders, outside her relationship with her female partner. Her female partner does not know about these other partners and your client does not want to tell her in case it upsets her.

Scenario 5: a male client tells you he was repeatedly raped by a group of men. Later in the session he tells you it was at a sex party where he and others were taking a lot of drugs and alcohol.

You can use other scenarios drawn from your clinical experience to continue this exercise or to address issues specific to your service context. There are no clear 'right' responses to the above generic scenarios. The object of this exercise is to reflect on your own feelings about being told stories such as these, and how these feelings might lead you to open up or close down conversations. How might your responses affect your work? What might enable you to manage these feelings in order to work effectively with your client? Are there some client groups that you would not feel comfortable talking to about sex?

If you hold religious views or strong moral stances about sex that are divergent from your clients you need to take these to supervision as you would with other behavioural choices your clients may make that challenge you personally. You will need to think through your responses in light of your therapeutic model and your professional duty of care to your clients. If you really struggle with these issues then it may be appropriate to consider not working with a particular client or client group (Davies, 1998). However, it may be that you can develop empathic understanding of your client's position and choices, or find out more about the practice or identity, or look at your own issues in relation to them. By doing so you may be able to address your own feelings, while remaining curious, open and non-judgementally available to your client.

Clifford (2000) encourages self-reflection on personal feelings that might provoke moral judgements in the therapist. She suggests that working with such feelings is an interesting part of clinical work, encouraging reflection on every feeling, and that nothing should be taken at face value. She reflects that sometimes it is as though moral judgements are made about feelings considered good and others that appear less than worthy. However, it is not easy to control our feelings, so we should not feel shame when they are not as we expect them to be. Clifford (2000) suggests that recognition of feelings is the key to skill development. The process of recognition of uncomfortable feelings, examination of them, curiosity about whether such feelings are one's own or perhaps a reflection of a client's feelings, can be a key tool in therapeutic work. Once this reflection is done, then a choice can be made about a useful response.

WORKING WITH AROUSAL AND ATTRACTION IN THE THERAPEUTIC RELATIONSHIP

Boundaries are important in all areas of practice, but in this area perhaps more than any other client–therapist boundaries need to be carefully considered and communicated in order for clients to feel comfortable to disclose information. Having conversations about sex can feel like one is crossing a boundary, especially if as a therapist you find yourself becoming embarrassed, or even aroused. Depending on your therapeutic model, you may look at the process issues involved in the session. You will need to consider how your responses to your client might be influenced by your own feelings.

If sexual arousal occurs for client or therapist and this is identified or acknowledged in some way, then the first consideration is to be clear in one's own mind as a therapist, about the implications of this for the therapeutic relationship. It is also important to be clear on professional guidelines about boundaries regarding physical contact. Frequent conversations about sex are more likely to provide stimulus for triggering sexual arousal for therapist and client than other topics and therefore there may be increased temptation to act on these feelings. It is stressed by all authors in this area that the position of trust, influence and power of the therapist means that there is no such thing as informed consent in the case of therapist–client sexual contact and therefore that this always is exploitative (Spence, 1991; Plaut, 2008).

Maintaining appropriate boundaries, therapists may allow more freedom to acknowledge and not deny the feelings that are being evoked, as it is clear that they will not be acted upon. Orbach (1999: 17) suggests that: 'an erotic transference encourages a therapist to act on rather than analyse erotic feelings which can lead to an abuse of the therapeutic situation'. She suggests that therapists should not deny or side-step their own feelings of arousal because of fear of such feelings, because such suppression could increase the chance of inappropriate sexuality being unwittingly enacted in the therapy. Rather she encourages the therapist to think about erotic feelings for a patient, and most importantly what they signify, without fear of censure. 'A therapist might best help her patient if, when she finds herself aroused, she can become less afraid of her responses and keep herself consciously aware of them long enough to think about them privately, rather than banish them prematurely' (Orbach, 1999: 17).

In relation to a client becoming aroused in therapy, psychoanalytic models of transference offer perspectives on the mechanisms at work. Daines and Perrett (2000: 204) suggest that: 'sexuality and desire can be acted out in the transference through disowning and projecting of sexual thoughts and impulses. Erotic [. . .] and idealized thoughts and feelings can take the shape of intense feelings directed towards the therapist'. They discuss the need to acknowledge, analyse and work with what else might be being communicated. Reaching an understanding of a client's desire for the therapist may be a means by which the therapist can further understand the client's struggles, perhaps with love, intimacy and relationships. For further help on working with these issues in the therapeutic relationship from a psychodynamic perspective see Daines and Perrett (2000), Orbach (1999) and Mann (1997).

SPECIFIC ISSUES OF POWER AND DIFFERENCE

As already discussed, there is an inherent power differential in the therapist–client relationship, which can be further influenced by issues of gender, age, culture and sexual orientation. Therefore it is important to develop awareness of how such power differentials may impact on the availability of particular conversations and clients' power to ask for or decline to talk about particular topics. Gender issues are likely to be a significant consideration in this area of work, and clients may feel more comfortable with a matching gender therapist to talk about these issues. Power differences between the genders may make it more difficult for, for example, a female client to tell a male therapist that she feels uncomfortable answering questions about sex. It is important to have frank conversations about difference, and as the therapist, to name these process issues and make it clear that your client can choose not to answer questions and that refusal will not compromise therapy or that they can request to see a therapist of another gender, if this is possible in your service. However, a note of caution; remain curious about any possible power differences and previous experiences that underpin clients' responses to you as a therapist. Although social and political power is typically more likely to lie in the hands of a White male therapist, in fact people's lived experiences of feeling powerful and powerless may not be as simple as this. Although statistically it may be the case that sexist behaviour, sexual coercion and sexual abuse are more likely to happen to a woman and be perpetrated by a man, it is also the case that men can be on the receiving end of unhelpful and abusive sexual stereotyping, and sometimes sexual abuse, from women and other men. For example, dominant discourses of masculine heterosexual sexuality often overvalue certain aspects such as penis size and virility and undervalue emotional expression, which can lead to men feeling sexually inadequate and inexperienced in managing their own or others' emotional needs.

Liddle (1997) found that gay men and lesbian clients are more likely to seek gay male/lesbian therapists than heterosexual therapists. This finding may be explained by them selecting therapists who offered sexuality affirmative therapy, perhaps because they assume that they will not have to explain issues to do with sex or sexuality (for a detailed explanation of this see Chapter 4). As with any other issues related to difference and diversity, either visible or invisible, between therapist and client, it may be important to name and discuss what relevance the differences have to the nature of the therapeutic conversation you are able to have. The language you use, and curiosity and open-minded attitude you communicate may go a long way to enabling your client to feel comfortable discussing issues with you and challenging any preconceived ideas they may have about your ability to discuss their concerns with them.

TALKING ABOUT SEXUAL ISSUES IN SUPERVISION

Potentially all the areas discussed in this chapter could arise in clinical supervision as supervision is an important arena for exploration of difficulty and process issues that come up in therapy with clients. However, some of the same concerns may be present within the supervision process itself.

The following are some ideas to consider when having conversations about sexual issues with your supervisor.

- Ask about your services usual approach to exploring sex and sexual issues.
- Address language use in supervision sessions, e.g. what language will both of you feel comfortable using to talk about these issues?
- If you are able to do so, you may want to name and address some of the sensitivities and difficulties in talking about the issues. Ask your supervisor how they manage to work with these feelings of embarrassment etc? This may be especially relevant if your supervisor is more uncomfortable talking about sex than you are!

If you are a supervisor, here are some ideas on how to encourage a supervisee or junior member of staff to talk about sex.

- Be transparent about some of the difficulties and invite discussion of solutions to make it easier.

- Address language as you might with a client: what words might feel most/least comfortable to use?
- Think about issues of difference e.g. if the supervisor and supervisee are different genders, how might this impact on the conversation? Might it make it more or less comfortable and why?
- If your supervisee is visibly uncomfortable talking about these issues, as the typically more powerful party, you may need to enable your supervisee to guide the conversation to a large extent and not to feel under pressure to talk about things that are embarrassing. However, do not avoid these issues where they are appropriate. There is a balance between addressing complex issues and rapport and trust building. It is often the case that you need to build the latter before you can address the former.
- You could introduce examples from your own practice – modelling your own difficulties and discomfort and how you worked with them.

CONCLUSION

This chapter has been written as an introductory guide in developing self-reflective practice for putting sex and sexuality on the agenda in therapy with clients. It has been based on the assumption that many clients who come into therapy may value the chance to talk about these issues and to make sense of their experiences. The opportunities to talk openly and explore our personal concerns about sex are often quite rare. Faced with media and cultural messages about what is 'good sex', sometimes alongside other cultural mores about sex as shameful, taboo, or indeed omnipresent, can leave many confused about sex, ashamed or uncertain whether their sexual experiences, feeling, desires are 'normal'. Normal sex is a myth – human sexuality is diverse, ever changing, affected by a multitude of factors including age and health, as well as psychosocial processes such as how we construct it, perceive it and judge it. A therapeutic space can be an opportunity for clients to name concerns, explore ideas, take different perspectives and learn that 'normal' sex is very varied, and to judge or measure themselves more compassionately and fairly against these perceived standards. As a therapist you may be in a unique position to facilitate a client's thinking about the sort of sex they want, name when sex is not OK or is not wanted. You can also help with how to talk with partners more openly about sex, to understand changing sexuality as a result of age or illness, changing sexual desires, understanding our bodies, our fantasies, desires and urges. All these conversations and more are possible. The aim may be to find ways to express sexuality that feel healthy for us and our clients as individuals and respectful of others and ourselves.

FURTHER READING

American Psychiatric Association (2000). Guidelines for psychotherapy with lesbian, gay and bisexual clients. *American Psychologist*, 55 (12), 1440–1451.

Basson, R., Brotto, L.A, Laan, E., Redmond, G. & Utian, W. (2005). Assessment and management of women's sexual dysfunction: Problematic desire and arousal. *The Journal of Sexual Medicine*, 2 (3), 291–297.

Davies, D. & Neal, C. (eds) (2000). *Pink therapy 2: Therapeutic perspectives on working with lesbian, gay and bisexual clients*. Buckingham: Open University Press.

Erskine, A. (1994). The initial contact: Assessment for counselling in the medical context. In A. Erskine & D. Judd (eds), *The imaginative body: Psychodynamic therapy in healthcare*. London: Whurr Publishers.

Liddle, B.J. (1996). Therapist sexual orientation, gender, and counseling practices as they relate to ratings of helpfulness by gay and lesbian clients. *Journal of Counseling Psychology*, 43, 394–401.

Ramage, M. (1998). ABC of sexual health: Management of sexual problems. *British Medical Journal*, 317, 1509–1512.

Ratigan, B. (1995). Inner world, outer world: Exploring the tension of race, sexual orientation and class and the internal world. *Psychodynamic Counselling*, 1 (2), 173–186.

Ritter, K.Y. & Terndrup, A.I. (2002). *Handbook of affirmative psychotherapy with lesbian and gay men*. London: Guilford Press.

Rollnick, S., Miller, W. & Butler, C. (2008). *Motivational interviewing in healthcare: Helping patients change behaviour*. London: Guilford Press.

Weeks, J. (1981). *Sex, politics and society: The regulation of sexuality since 1800 – Themes in British social history*. London: Longmans.

REFERENCES

Annesley, P. & Coyle, A. (1995). Clinical psychologists' attitudes to lesbians. *Journal of Community and Applied Social Psychology*, 5, 327–331.

Bartlett, A., King, M. & Phillips, P. (2001). Straight talking: an investigation of the attitudes and practice of psychoanalysts and psychotherapists in relation to gays and lesbians. *British Journal of Psychiatry*, 179, 545–549.

Beck, J. (1995). *Cognitive therapy – The basics and beyond*. New York: Guilford Press.

Boyd Franklin, N. (1989). Therapist use of self and value conflicts with black families. In *Black families in therapy: A multi-systems approach*. New York: Guilford Press.

Butler, C. (2008). Speaking the unspeakable: Female interpreters' response to working with women who have been raped in war. *Clinical Psychology Forum*, 192, 14–18.

Clifford, D. (2000). Developing psychosexual awareness. In D. Wells (ed.), *Caring for sexuality in health and illness*. London: Churchill Livingstone.

Daines, B. & Perrett, A. (2000). *Psychodynamic approaches to sexual health*. Buckingham: Open University Press.

Dardick, L. & Grady, E.G. (1980). Openness between gay persons and health professionals. *Annals of Internal Medicine*, 93 (1), 115–119.

Davies, D. (1998). The six necessary and sufficient conditions applied to working with lesbian, gay and bisexual clients. *The Person Centred Journal*, 5 (2), 111–124.

Denham, C. (2004). *Sexuality: A biopsychosocial approach.* London: Palgrave Macmillan.

George, H. (1993). Sex, love and relationships: Issues and problems for gay men in the AIDS era. In J. Ussher & C.D. Baker (eds), *Psychological perspectives on sexual problems.* London: Routledge.

Hawton, K. (1985). *Sex therapy: A practical guide.* Oxford: Oxford University Press

Hitchcock, J.M. & Wilson, H.S. (1992). Personal risking: Lesbian self-disclosure of sexual orientation to professional health care providers. *Nursing Research*, 41 (3), 178–183.

Hof, L. & Berman, E. (1986).The sexual genogram. *Journal of Marital and Family Therapy*, 12, 39–47.

Hook, A. & Andrews, B. (2005). The relationship of non-disclosure in therapy to shame and depression. *British Journal of Clinical Psychology*, 44, 425–438.

Kaschak, E. & Tiefer, L. (2002). *A new view of women's sexual problems.* New York: Routledge.

Liddle, B.J. (1997). Gay and lesbian clients' selection of therapists and utilization of therapy. *Psychotherapy*, 34, 11–18.

Lynne Ellis, M. (1997). Who speaks? Who listens? Different voices and different sexualities. *British Journal of Psychotherapy*, 13 (3), 369–384.

McGoldrick, M. (1994). Culture, class, race and gender. *Human Systems: The Journal of Systemic Consultation & Management*, 5, 131–153.

Mann, D, (1997). *Psychotherapy: An erotic relationship: Transference and counter-transference passions.* London & New York: Routledge.

Markovic, D. (2007). Working with sexual issues in systemic therapy. *Australian & New Zealand Journal of Family Therapy*, 28 (4), 200–209.

Miller, D. & Green, J. (eds) (2002). *The psychology of sexual health.* Oxford: Blackwell Publishing.

Milton, M., Coyle, A. & Legg, C. (2005). Countertransference issues in psychotherapy with lesbian and gay clients. *European Journal of Psychotherapy, Counselling and Health*, 7 (3), 181–197.

Orbach, S. (1999). *The impossibility of sex.* London: Penguin Books.

Padesky, C. (1995). *Clinician's guide to mind over mood.* New York: Guilford Press.

Plaut, S.M. (2008). Sexual and nonsexual boundaries in professional relationships: principles and teaching guidelines. *Sexual and Relationship Therapy*, 23 (1), 85–94.

Reder, P. & Fredman, G. (1996). The relationship to help: Interacting beliefs abut the treatment process. *Clinical Child Psychology and Psychiatry*, 1 (3), 457–467.

Spence, S.H. (1991). *Psychosexual therapy: A cognitive-behavioural approach.* London: Chapman & Hall.

Tarrier, N. & Calam, R. (2002). New developments in cognitive behavioural case formulation: Epidemiological, systemic and social context: An integrative approach. *Cognitive and Behavioual Psychotherapy*, 30, 311–328.

Tribe, R. & Ravel, H. (2002). *Working with interpreters in mental health.* London: Brunner-Routledge.

Waterhouse, J. & Metcalf, M. (1991). Attitudes towards nurses discussing sexual concerns with patients. *Journal of Advanced Nursing*, 16, 1048–1054.

Watson, J. (2002). Taking a sexual history. In D. Miller & J. Green (eds) *The psychology of sexual health*. Oxford: Blackwell Publishing.

Wells, D. (2000). *Caring for sexuality in health and illness*. London: Churchill Livingstone.

Yalom, I. (1989) *Love's executioner and other tales of psychotherapy*. London: Penguin Books.

Chapter 3

Health, disability and sex

Catherine Butler

> There is always some madness in love. But there is also always some
> reason in madness
>
> Nietzsche

To start with what this chapter is not: it is not a chapter about sexual
dysfunction and psychosexual interventions. It is also not a chapter that
lists specific diseases, categories of mental illness or sensory and physical
impairments and how sex relates to these. Other books have specialised in
these areas in more depth and will be mentioned through this chapter.
What this chapter considers is how sex and sexuality interact with the lives
of individuals who do not fit within the social 'norm' of good health. This
social norm is that which is portrayed whenever sex or sexuality is used in
advertising or films: it belongs to those who are fit, young, healthy, able-
bodied, mentally well, high-achievers (how else could they afford to
purchase the designer product being sold with the help of their bodies?).
This chapter considers commonalities in issues of sex and sexuality for
people who fit outside this box and suggests interventions at both the
individual and community level, i.e. to the environments that impose on
people's sexuality (e.g. ward or residential settings).

Although sex and sexuality have always been an integral part of the lives
of disabled and chronically ill people, it is only recently that therapists,
health and rehabilitation professionals have started to address this
(Williams, 1993). More often disabled people are viewed as asexual and
ungendered, and the literature on disability mainly ignores the issue of
sexuality (Shakespeare, 1997). Finger (1992) argues that this is because
disability movements tend to be run by men and so issues of employment,
education and equal access dominate and issues of relationships, sex and
reproduction take second billing.

Earlier attempts at addressing sexuality adopted a 'deficit' model for
disabled people, with an emphasis on deviations from the social norm.
Resisting these negative or asexual images of sexuality for disabled or
chronically ill people is essential for well-being, for example, as a means of

giving and receiving pleasure and in maintaining intimacy and closeness with a partner (Anderson & Wolf, 1986). However, disabled people may lack the confidence or language to discuss sex, stemming from a lack of sex education and the low expectations of professionals, family or friends (Shakespeare, 1997).

This chapter will start by considering different definitional models of disability and how these may impact on sex and sexuality. It goes on to reflect on common myths about disabled people's sexuality and shared concerns, including the impact on sexuality of holding a stigmatised identity, of living in care systems and the issue of pregnancy. Differences specific to certain populations are then explored, namely those with a chronic illness, learning disabilities and people with mental health problems. Different aspects of socio-cultural diversity and their interaction with disability and sexuality are then described. Finally the painful issue of abusive sex is raised and institutional responses addressed. Throughout this chapter the term 'disabled people' will be used to describe those with sensory, intellectual, physical impairments and long-term mental health problems, whether present from birth or acquired in later life (e.g. through accident or chronic illness).

DEFINITIONS OF DISABILITY

Before moving on to the body of this chapter, different models of disability (physical, sensory, intellectual and long-term mental health) will briefly be explored and related to sex. If teaching these models to a class, the case examples used in the following exercises could be given to small groups so that the same case is considered from each different model of disability and it is possible to observe what different formulations and interventions are suggested by using the different approaches to disability.

The medical model

The medical model of disability has shifted dramatically in the last 25 years. The model used to take the view that an individual's impairment results in disability; the social context was considered in that this is where the individual's impairment results in 'handicap'. Classification systems of disability were developed to clarify terminology and to inform British medical and social policy (Bury, 1996). The World Health Organization (WHO) used this model in the *International Classification of Impairments, Disabilities and Handicaps* (ICIDH):

• *impairment*: any loss or abnormality of psychological, physiological, or anatomical structure or function;

- *disability*: any restriction or lack (resulting from an impairment) of ability to perform an activity in the manner or within the range considered normal for a human being;
- *handicap*: a disadvantage for a given individual, resulting from an impairment or a disability, that limits or prevents the fulfilment of a role that is normal (depending on the age, sex, social and cultural factors) for that individual (WHO, 1980: 27).

Exercise 3.1a Using the medical model

This exercise illustrates how using the medical model provides a frame for understanding sexual problems. It can be used for self-development or in training, with small groups taking each example and feeding back.

How might you understand the follow difficulties faced by disabled people from the position of the medical model and what interventions might you suggest?

- Ahmed has a moderate learning disability and lives in a residential home, attending a day centre three days a week. Ahmed has been in the home for nine years, over which time on three occasions he started to become sexual with another resident. On all these occasions this behaviour was discouraged by staff and he was prevented from continuing. He was recently found in the bedroom of a woman resident. Staff have asked you to attend to address this 'challenging behaviour'.
- Jenny has been internet dating in the hope of meeting a partner. She has been emailing one person in particular and he has suggested meeting up for a drink in a lively bar. Jenny is hard of hearing and knows that she will be unable to have a conversation in this venue, but does not want to broach the subject of her impairment at this point.
- Mark has not worked for the last three years because of ongoing depression, which has put a strain on his marriage. He has little motivation to do anything, including have sex, and becomes irritable when his wife tries to discuss this. He attends a men's group in a local day hospital but the issue of sex has never been brought up and he worries people will think him less of a man if he raises it.
- Lyn received a diagnosis of multiple sclerosis (MS) two years ago. This diagnosis was welcomed by her and her husband, Peter, as it explained her early symptoms of increasing weakness, reduced motor control and blurred vision. However, the diagnosis also brought fear of what will happen in the future, and Lyn is

particularly concerned about being a burden to Peter. The MS has already had an impact on their sex life, in that some positions they used to enjoy are now unsustainable, and Lyn's self-image has dropped so that she has started to avoid sexual contact.

Using the medical model as a frame to understand the above examples might elicit formulations and interventions such as the following.

- Ahmed is experiencing sexual feelings and he wants to express these with other residents. He could be taught how to masturbate to reduce his 'challenging behaviour'.
- Jenny's hearing impairment means she will have trouble meeting her date in the suggested bar; she could ask her doctor for a hearing aid.
- Mark has a lowered libido because of his depression, he could be prescribed antidepressants (selecting ones that do not lower libido as a side-effect) and referred for sex therapy.
- Lyn's MS means that some sexual positions are no longer possible and so she could be taught some new positions to try.

These explanations focus on the individual; they place the level of intervention at helping the individual to change and this can come about through 'expert' intervention by a health professional.

Bury considers the distinction in experience provided by the three categories of impairment, disability and handicap as important, but he recognised that they can be hard to disentangle in everyday life as disability is often relational between the person and their environment (Bury, 1996). Of concern is that these original WHO classifications positioned those with disabilities as being 'abnormal' human beings: 'People become individual objects to be "treated", "changed", "improved", made more "normal" . . . the overall picture is that the human being is flexible and 'alterable' whilst society is fixed and unalterable' (Mason & Rieser, 1992: 13).

The medical model provides no recognition that two people with the same level of impairment may have totally different experiences shaped by their environment and the attitudes and support of others (Morris, 1997). For example, French (1994) suggested four additional factors that may influence a person's experience of impairment:

- at what age the impairment was acquired;
- how visible the impairment is;
- whether people can understand the impairment;
- whether there is also an illness present.

If we relate these points to sex, the importance of good communication with a sexual partner is paramount. For example, Katy experiences chronic back pain that is not visible. This has been present since her car accident two years ago; she is still finding ways to help other people understand it. She has been dating Rob for some months and although he knows about her accident and the pain, they have not been in situations where it is particularly bad and he would notice (e.g. dancing for hours in a club). He is coming for dinner this evening and Katy imagines they will go to bed for the first time. She knows that many sexual positions will bring pain to her back. However, she has done some research via BackCare and learnt a position she thinks will be OK. She is nervous about how to bring this up or instruct Rob in this as she worries that reminding him of her pain will turn him off or that he might not understand the importance of this care and try a painful position anyway.

WHO (2001) further developed their use of the medical model in ICIDH and renamed it the *International Classification of Function and Disability* (ICF). This reworking took account of the social, cultural and environmental contexts and how these interact with the psychology and physiology of the individual; this revised form constitutes a biopsychosocial model. The emphasis is now on functioning, rather than on the medical reason for the impairment. The ICF replaced the term disability with 'activity limitation' and handicap with 'participation restriction' in 'life situations' (for example, self-care, domestic life, communication). A more major shift in the classification system is the inclusion of 'environmental factors', such as societal attitudes, support and relationships, living arrangements etc. The inclusion of this latter category was from the major influence of the social model.

The social model

The social model of disability grew in strength through the 1980s and 1990s and remains the predominant model of disability used in British disability rights organisations. A key writer in this area is the disabled activist and academic Mike Oliver (1990; 1996a; 1996b). This model takes the position that it is not an individual's impairment or the ability to function with such an impairment that causes disability, but instead it is social barriers that restrict and oppress people who are living with impaired abilities. Hence disability is defined by Disabled People International (1982, cited in Oliver 1996a: 41) as:

- *impairment*: the functional limitation within the individual caused by physical, mental or sensory impairment;
- *disability*: the loss or limitation of opportunities to take part in the normal life of the community on an equal level with others due to physical and social barriers.

In 2008 this model was used by the charity Leonard Cheshire Disability in an advertising campaign to remind the public that disabled people are sexual. The charity used the voices of young disabled people and animated them using the 'creature comfort' characters in a series of television and poster campaigns. For example, a female rabbit says 'it's not the wheelchair that gets in the way of sex, it's the barriers in people's mind'.

Exercise 3.1b Using the social model

This exercise used the framework of the social model to change the understanding of the problems previously presented in Exercise 3.1a.

1   Reconsider the scenarios in Exercise 3.1a and reformulate them using the social model.
2   What differences does this new formulation bring in terms of opportunities or constraints for:
   •   disabled people;
   •   health professionals;
   •   carers and partners.

Again, there are no correct answers to this exercise but some suggested examples of formulating and intervention using the social model might be as follows.

•   The residential home does not seem equipped to address the sexual needs of clients. Staff in the residential home could attend training on the sexual rights of residents and if residents were interested in developing a sexual relationship this could be supported by staff and a double bed provided.
•   The bar is not designed to be accessible to those with hearing impairments. In the longer term, if the bar suggested for the meeting was a local bar that Jenny would like to attend she could get help from a local lobbying group who could campaign to provide a quieter area in the bar.
•   The day hospital where Mark attends could have a special focus day on sex to encourage discussion and/or start a new group addressing sexual issues and removing sexual myths and expectations (as covered later in this chapter).
•   Links with national MS groups might address a wider poster campaign that encourages sex to be viewed as a regular part of the lives of people with MS.

However, the social model has been criticised for ignoring specific cultural and experiential dimensions of different conditions (Thomas, 1999). Some impairments have very specific impacts on the daily lives of those who live with them. For example, little is written about its use with mental health problems (e.g. Abberley, 1997; Crow, 1996; Hughes & Paterson, 1997) or deafness (e.g. Corker, 1998). In addition, the social model does not comment on groups who face double discrimination because of other areas of social difference (as discussed later in this chapter).

The social relational model

Thomas espouses the social relational model as it highlights the unequal relationship within society between those with and those without impairment; this 'manifests itself through exclusionary and oppressive practices – *disablism*' (1999: 40). The model also accounts for how disablism is expressed differently over time and place; for example, locking someone away in asylums with appalling conditions because they were experiencing a mental health problem would not be tolerated in Britain today; however, modern means of exclusion include difficulties in finding employment after a break due to mental health difficulties (Cobb, 2006).

Thomas separates restrictions in activities as a result of disablism from those that she terms 'impairment effects' (1990: 43). With the latter, a specific impairment may result in a restriction in activity (in her case she refers to the inability to hold objects in her left hand), however, this will not become a disability unless disablism makes it so in a social relational sense (following on from her example, if social policy deemed that being unable to hold things in her left hand meant she should not work in certain jobs or be a parent). Hence, Thomas provides a frame for understanding the lives of disabled people by focusing on the interaction between the socially determined (by disablism) disability and the specific impairment effects.

Exercise 3.1c Using the social relational model

This exercise views the same problems as previously discussed in Exercise 3.1a through the frame of the social relational model.

1 Reconsider the scenarios in Exercise 3.1a and reformulate them using the social relational model.
2 What differences does this new formulation bring in terms of opportunities or constraints for:
 • disabled people;
 • health professionals;
 • carers and partners?

Formulations and interventions of the cases using a social relational approach might include the following.

- An assessment of ability to consent could be given to Ahmed and the female resident and if they both wished to pursue a sexual relationship they could be provided with sex education, a double bed, privacy and ongoing support if needed.
- Jenny is aware of the disablist attitude she might meet from a new acquaintance and so she could suggest a quieter bar in which to meet.
- Mark and his partner could be offered therapy to discuss how they communicate about sex to avoid arguments and increase understanding. Day hospital staff could also be trained to raise the issue of sex in the men's group.
- Staff at Lyn's MS service could be trained to discuss sex with all their patients as a matter of routine and write/give out information booklets offering suggestions and further resources (such as the MS Society website at http://www.mssociety.org.uk), as well as cushions/supports that may help with certain positions.

Anderson and Wolf (1986) take a social relational approach in their consideration of how sexual behaviour is influenced by both the individual's psychological and physiological processes, the manifestation of their health condition and the influences of the socio-cultural milieu. They represent this in Figure 3.1.

Exercise 3.2 Case example

This exercise allows a chance to map out a case example using a social relational model.

Use Figure 3.1 to map out the various influences on Vincent, a 55-year-old man who has begun to experience problems with getting an erection. The doctors informed Vincent that these difficulties are due to damage to his peripheral nerves and small blood vessels in his penis as a result of his diabetes. Since this has started happening, Vincent has felt increasingly anxious about sexual encounters and has started to go out less. He tells himself this is because of the lethargy he can experience as a result of the diabetes, although he also describes how as a gay man there is pressure to have a perfect body and the ability to always get an erection. He is feeling down and frustrated by his current lack of sex and social contact that he feels his diabetes is imposing on him.

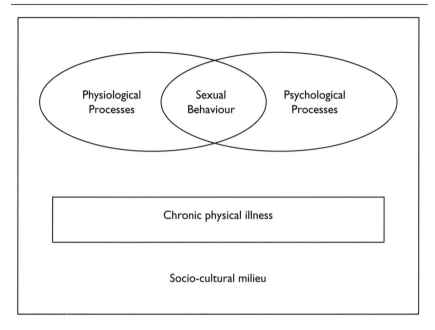

Figure 3.1 Model of chronic illness and sexual behaviour.

Source: Reproduced from Anderson, B.J. and Wolf, F.M. (1986: 169) Chronic physical illness and sexual behaviour: Psychological issues. *Journal of Consulting and Clinical Psychology*, 54(2).

Although there are no right or wrong answers for this exercise, some of the points that might be considered for Vincent include:

- physiological processes – his diabetes has resulted in damage to his peripheral nerves and small blood vessels in his penis;
- psychological processes – he has started to feel anxious about sexual encounters. He is also feeling low in mood, which might impact on his sexual desire and ability to get an erection;
- sexual behaviour – his sexual encounters are with strangers and this might make it difficult to discuss his difficulties;
- chronic physical illness – his relationship with his diabetes has become one of frustration and he sees this as the main reason why he is not being as sociable or sexual;
- socio-cultural milieu – he experiences pressure from gay culture to have a fully functioning penis. Sex is also linked to social contact and an avenue to socialise.

All these points will combine to provide an overarching formulation of Vincent's current problems. They could all be shared with Vincent to agree the area to focus on first.

This chapter attempts to take account of both the social and cultural contexts that shape and limit the lived experience of disabled people, before focusing in on some specific issues of both disablism and impairment effects.

COMMON MYTHS ABOUT HEALTH, DISABILITY AND SEX

Society perpetuates numerous myths about sex, disability and illness. These myths can impact both upon the psyche and functioning of disabled people, as well as those who treat and care about them.

Exercise 3.3 Myths about disability and illness

This exercise generates and unpicks some of the common myths surrounding disability.

1   Ask the group to generate all the ideas about sex, disability and illness they can come up with.
2   After completing the list, discuss how these myths might affect the motivation, behaviour and mood of:
   • a disabled person;
   • their partner;
   • carers/residential staff;
   • health care professionals including GPs, staff in sexual health clinics, hospital consultants;
   • society in general.

Common myths you may wish to include on the list are:

• disabled people are not sexual;
• disabled people are incapable of having 'proper' sex;
• sex saps strength and so should not be engaged in if already unwell;
• if you are predisposed to heart attacks or stroke, these could be brought on by sex;
• people with mental health problems and learning disabilities are oversexed;
• all gay men are at risk of AIDS;
• the radiation used in cancer treatment is contagious.

Obviously myths such as these, and resulting discrimination, will have a direct impact on the development of sexual confidence and a positive body image for disabled people. This might be a developmental issue for those born disabled, or may be faced later in life if the impairment is acquired over the life course.

COMMON CONCERNS

Asexual/devalued identities

Disabled people are not valued as potential partners (Griffiths *et al.*, 1989), as is evidenced by their invisibility in the media, and reinforced by rehabilitation manuals who assume the disabled person's partner is non-disabled, and hence the main caregiver and in charge of the relationship. Many illnesses and impairments carry stigma, as well as sexual difficulties themselves being stigmatised, associated with shame at not performing as a 'real man' or 'receptive woman'. Sontag (1978) explains this stigmatisation of illness and impairment as representing existing or potential limitations and is linked to negative images and myths. Fife and Wright (2000) note that stigma attaches itself particularly strongly to conditions where the person can be 'blamed', where the condition is visible, and where it results in impaired ability. This is notable with HIV and AIDS, with its association with other stigmatised identities and behaviours: sex workers, injecting drug users and anal sex. Such stigma is reinforced by global institutional discrimination, such as being denied entry into the United States if HIV positive, or in the criminalisation of HIV transmission. Living with stigma makes disclosure about illness and impairment difficult and so limits avenues for support and potential resources.

Living in care

Disabled people may spend some or much of their lives living in the 'care' of paid caregivers. Morris (1997) reports that those who live in care as children (when sexual identity is formed) often continue to do so as adults due to a lack of options, low expectations of others, and a lack of role models of disabled people living independently (and with active sex lives). Care environments frequently do little to enhance or encourage the sex lives of their residents, issues of sexuality and sex often being viewed as incon-venient rather than natural (Carolan, 1984). Consequently, there is rarely privacy or assistance (e.g. double beds) in expressing sexuality in a way taken for granted by non-disabled adults. In addition, when sexual advice is given it tends to have a medical focus and not be discussed in a relationship context (Yoshida, 1994). Alternatively, a romantic relationship might be encouraged, but the practical sexual side of it ignored: 'The couple saw their most immediate need as being privacy in which to embark on a sexually active courtship, not what level of cooker would best suit them' (Milner, 1986: 86).

Exercise 3.4 Considering an inpatient setting

This exercise helps the reader, or training participant, consider formulating about sexual difficulties at a systems level. If used in training it can be worked on in small groups.

An adult inpatient ward for people experiencing acute mental health problems has residents stay for up to six months. Residents are of various ages and socio-cultural backgrounds, as are staff, many of whom are ever-changing agency nurses. Many residents are medicated with psychotropic drugs, which are reviewed in multidisciplinary ward rounds. Visiting times for partners and families are for four hours every evening. Residents sleep in gender-segregated wards of four single beds, with curtains to pull around them for privacy when washing or dressing.

- What might be the challenges for residents or staff in raising issues of sex?
- What would be the issues for couples in relation to sex?

Zilbergeld (1979) formulates three main reasons why staff in care environments avoid issues of sex and sexuality:

1   The primary task is viewed as recovery (in the case of chronic illness and mental health problems) and the maintenance of good health, and so sex is viewed as secondary to this.
2   Staff may not feel confident or competent to work with clients on these issues.
3   The dominance of the medical model places any difficulties with sex as within the individual and so the barriers placed by the environment can be ignored.

Brown (1994) asserts that the role of care environments for those with learning disabilities is to regulate and control their sexuality. People with learning disabilities are viewed as either innocent, and therefore asexual and in need of protection, or else oversexed and in need of control. As a consequence, men and women with learning disabilities live in atypical groups of adults with little privacy or recognition of their gender and sexuality (Brown, 1994). Brown (1987) found that parents of people with learning disabilities tend to align themselves with the idea of their children's innocence and so expect institutions to protect their child from both sexual expression as well as abuse.

Pregnancy

A loss of fertility may become an issue with some health conditions. In addition, disabled people may fear that if they have a child they may die before the child has grown up or they may be unable to care for them sufficiently (Anderson & Kornblum, 1984). If their condition is known to be genetic, such as sickle cell disease, this may influence whether couples choose to have children, with potential mourning of future plans and hopes if this is not achieved. Although these may be genuine concerns for the couple, these ideas also reflect societal prejudices applied to all disabled women: that they make bad parents or could pass on 'defective' genes (Hwang, 1997). These fears may therefore have been internalised by both or either member of the couple. Tragically, such discrimination has lead to a greater number of sterilisations and hysterectomies than in non-disabled populations (Brecker, 1993). Counter to this oppression, Smith (1989) provides evidence that disabled mothers are no less effective at parenting than non-disabled mothers. For a lesbian, gay, bisexual or transgendered (LGBT) disabled parent, these prejudices may be further compounded by homophobia in that people may fear their custody rights may be jeopardised (Rights of Women, 1984).

History and the eugenics movement also witnessed the direct control of procreation for men and women with learning disabilities, with segregated institutions for men and women and enforced sterilisations (Burns, 1993). Even today, men and women are supported as individuals but rarely as a couple, with the chance of a family only being 'rewarded' if the couple meet criteria that demonstrate 'independence skills and financial autonomy' (Brown, 1994: 127).

SPECIFIC DIFFERENCES

Chronic illness

The majority of disabilities occur as a result of chronic illness, mostly occurring in later life (and hence why there tend to be more women registered disabled), as opposed to disability as a result of trauma or early life conditions (Bury, 1997). Sex can become an issue for people with numerous chronic health concerns, including spinal cord injury, multiple sclerosis, stroke, arthritis, diabetes, cardiac and pulmonary disease and some cancers (particularly of the reproductive organs). Henshaw (2001) provides details of exactly how neuroendocrine, vascular and musculoskeletal conditions impact upon sexual functioning.

Some chronic illnesses have a direct impact on how people feel about their gendered and sexual selves; for example, women who have lost a breast and/or have extensive scarring as a result of breast cancer treatment can lose self-confidence in their sexuality given the societal emphasis on breasts being 'sexy' (Akkerman, 1999). HIV also has an obvious direct impact on sexuality, i.e. in terms of the fear of infecting others through sex.

It is beyond the scope of this chapter to go into detail about the specific concerns of each health condition in relation to sex, as well as the details of help and advice that can be given. Instead the reader is directed to the following books which have in-depth chapters on different chronic health conditions, including sexual positions to minimise pain and topics to bring attention to when conducting an assessment or intervention.

- M. Sipski and C. Alexander (1997). *Sexual function in people with disability and chronic illness: A health professional's guide.* Maryland: Aspen.
- H. Heath and I. White (2002). *The challenge of sexuality in health care.* London: Blackwell.

However, it should be noted that even these books fall into reinforcing some of the myths and stereotypes of disabled people: for example, in the recommendations for sexual positions in Sipski and Alexander (1997) the images always depict a physically-impaired person copulating with an able-bodied person.

There now follows some common sexual themes that arise for people with an acquired chronic health condition.

Medication

Many medications have been found to have side-effects that affect sexual functioning, these include antihypertensive and cardiovascular medications, as well as neuroleptic and antidepressant drugs (Weiner & Rosen, 1997). However, this relationship is not straightforward as other factors such as relationship quality, psychology and the effects of the underlying condition itself which will all contribute to sexual functioning. A thorough assessment of all these factors therefore needs to be conducted before changes in medication are considered, and this should always happen under medical supervision.

Additionally, some more invasive treatments, such as surgery and radiotherapy, may result in a loss of fertility for men and women. This will also have an impact on an individual's sense of their sexuality, so it is important that these risks are clearly discussed with people prior to and after such procedures are carried out.

Relationship adjustment

With the onset of serious physical illness or impairment, relationships must adjust to adapt to any resulting changes. Greengross (1976) reports that unfortunately many relationships break down if one partner become dependent on the other, this is particularly so if it is the woman who became dependent – perhaps because of the loss her original caregiving role. However, disabled women are still perfectly able to continue to be nurturing and caregiving (Hwang, 1997).

Exercise 3.5 Case vignette

Consider the following vignette and questions to highlight possible concerns for both members of a couple. If used for group work in training, participants could role play the conversation, after which each participant could feed back how it felt for them to be in the conversation.

Tony worked as a builder all of his life but had to retire aged 55 following a stroke. The stroke left him with reduced functioning down his left side, and although he can walk with a stick, he has lost the dexterity in his left had. Since being discharged from hospital five months ago, Tony and his wife Fiona have not had sex. Tony has no problem getting erections, but their previous patterns of sex saw Tony always initiating it and he reports no longer feeling 'in the mood'. With further questioning Tony talks about not feeling like a man any more as he has lost his strength, which he finds frustrating and he can often snap at anyone near him, and he does not feel physically attractive. Before the stroke Fiona would have time to herself during the day, but now Tony is always home she finds herself more irritable and they often row. In addition, Tony is now sleeping in the lounge because he cannot manage the stairs to their bedroom.

- How would you work with this case? As either individual or couple work?
- What interventions might you consider?

The onset and manifestation of a chronic health condition can break down established patterns for intimacy and sex. Partners may need to develop a language to talk about sex, with the disabled person needing to be clear and direct about their wishes. This may be particularly difficult for women who may not be used to taking a directive role during sex (Hwang, 1997).

Learning disabilities

The principles of 'normalisation' and 'social role valorisation' (Wolfens-berger, 1972, 1983) have been informing learning disability theory and practice since the 1970s. Issues of sex, sexuality and gender test and stretch these principles to their limit, and they fail. Instead, services regulate and control their clients' sexuality, justified as protection from pregnancy and abuse (Brown, 1997), with the underlying assumption that women with learning disabilities should not procreate and make bad parents, whereas men are seen as oversexed and out of control (both men with learning disabilities in general and non-disabled men who are sex offenders). Resist-ance to this asexual and ungendered positioning is discouraged and may hold negative consequences for those who try making themselves more visible rather than increasing their acceptance and integration (Brown, 1994). In addition, Brown (1994) points out then there is no 'norm' for anyone when it comes to sex, that this concept is based on what is 'respectable' in the current socio-cultural context, but people rarely measure up to this criteria.

Brown (1994) suggests what actively supporting people with learning disabilities to be sexual would look like:

- Include sexual and gender issues in care plans. This might include helping someone to meet a partner or maintain an existing relationship.
- Work with parents to support their child's sexuality within their cultural and religious traditions.
- Bring in specialist knowledge and training to support staff, not just in 'crisis' situations, but in developing a milieu that supports residents' sexuality.
- Consider interlinking networks that could support people, e.g. women's groups, LGB groups, survivors of sexual abuse etc.
- Consider alternative living arrangements. This may be either to create privacy, to enable couples to live together or to put people with learn-ing disabilities in contact with families and children with learning disabilities so they can act as role models.

When it comes to sex education for people with learning disabilities, Burns (1993: 134) points out that this education is more often than not a course on 'sex negation', with an emphasis on how to avoid sex and not do it, rather than on what to do. More often than not, no sex education is given, with O'Callaghan and Murphy (2002) finding that only 55 per cent of their sample of adults with learning disabilities had received any sex education, compared to 98 per cent of 16 year olds without learning disabilities. People with learning disabilities therefore lack important knowledge on issues such as conception, contraception and sexually transmitted infections (STIs); for example, only 60 per cent of O'Callaghan and Murphy's (2002) sample knew what AIDS was and only 18 per cent knew that using a condom could protect from catching it.

When sex education is taught it starts from the basis of no knowledge or experience, whereas many people with learning disabilities will already have some experience and understanding of sex, will have seen images of sex and sexuality in the media, as well as having witnessed the developmental changes of their own bodies (Burns, 1993). A preference would be to incorporate the existing knowledge and experience of participants within training to increase the personal relevance and learning potential.

Mental health

Mental health has a long established link with sexual functioning. Models of anxiety are the premise upon which psychosexual therapy is based (Hawton, 1985), and the last question in Beck's Depression Inventory asks directly about an increase or decrease in sexual desire. Disturbances in sexual functioning and sexual self-esteem have been documented for people also diagnosed with eating disorders (de Silva, 1993), psychosis (Lilleleht & Leiblum, 1993) and post-traumatic stress disorder (de Silva, 1999), among others. This established relationship between mental heath and sexuality is bi-directional: abusive or dysfunctional sex can lead to mental health issues, and mental health issues can lead to problems with sex. For example, childhood sexual abuse has been linked to later mental health difficulties such as self-harm, a diagnosis of borderline personality disorder (Silk *et al.*, 1995) and eating disorders (Oppenheimer *et al.*, 1985), and erectile dysfunction in men can lead to depression (Nicolosi *et al.*, 2004).

The manifestation of mental health problems in relationships is therefore likely to include a sexual dimension, which in turn could impact upon a partner's sexual self-esteem and mental well-being. It is therefore important for therapists and health care providers to raise the topic of sex and discuss/ work with concerns raised by clients. Chapter 2 considers how such conversations might be initiated and developed.

SOCIO-CULTURAL DIVERSITY

Holding dual or multiple identities may mean in different contexts different parts of the self are foregrounded or accepted. For example, a disabled gay man might feel 'more gay' in disabled group meetings, but more 'disabled' with other gay men. The subtle and direct effects of different forms of social prejudice (racism, heterosexism, disablism, sexism) can thus interact and play out in different ways in different contexts. Socio-cultural differences will now be considered in more detail.

Gender

Living with disability is always a gendered experience that affects men and women differently. Butler (1999) describes how gender is 'performed' based on socio-culturally constructed norms. For men, a strong message is to be strong, independent and practical; this includes being sexually dominant, having a strong sexual interest and skilful sexual prowess (Tepper, 1997). Whereas Zilbergeld (1992) describes how a man's identity is tied to the functioning of his penis, Tepper focuses this on disability and asks 'What happens if a man loses his ability to attain or maintain an erection or to ejaculate as a result of an acquired disability? What happens if a man loses sensation in his genitals, if he uses a catheter, or if he has physical limitations?' (1997: 138). Tepper (1997) goes on to suggest that if a man has an acquired disability, his memory of his sexual performance prior to this may be clouded by the fantasy model of sexual prowess generated and maintained by society. Some of the myths contained within this fantasy model make it even more difficult to surmount and act as a barrier to redefining and restabilising a good sex life. Examples of such myths include: that sex should be spontaneous and not planned, or that 'real men' do not talk about feelings and needs. Zilbergeld (1992) provides a comprehensive list of further myths that will limit men's ability to develop their sexual selves.

Tepper (1997) suggests that therapists and health care professionals can work with clients on the following:

- to deconstruct male sexual myths and re-educate men about their sexuality (including focusing on pleasure rather than performance);
- to explore any sexual functioning limitations as a result of their disability and possible solutions to these;
- to improve communication skills about sex and individual needs.

Women's bodies are socially constructed as belonging to society, to be constantly under scrutiny and their shape policed by social norms. This sexism influences the lived experience of disabled women. From childhood, disabled girls are treated differently than non-disabled peers (Brecker, 1993; Carolan, 1984): their sexual development and needs are ignored and they are overprotected.

Despite stories to the contrary, disabled women have sex! White *et al.* (1993) sent a questionnaire to women living in the community after a spinal cord injury. They found that 83 per cent had had sexual relationships since the injury. Hwang (1997) reports how a disabled woman activist who had quadriplegia challenged the view of disabled women being asexual by posing in *Playboy* (this was met with mixed reactions from feminists and other disabled activists). It is the length of time since an injury that is the most relevant factor with regards to sex, not the level of impairment (Hwang, 1997). However, when disabled women do pursue an active sex life, health services are often ill equipped to serve them; for example, gynaecological examination tables are difficult to use for wheelchair users (Brecker, 1993).

Ethnic minorities

Disabled people from ethnic minorities face racism and disablism from society, as well as racism and an ignoring of issues of race, culture and ethnicity from within the disability movement. The social model of disability emphasises the commonality of experience for disabled people, which negates important socio-cultural differences within the group, that can be viewed as 'optional extras' (Priestley, 1995). This lack of attention occurs in research, writing, policy and institutional practices, e.g. 'there has been very little analysis of the experience of black disabled people, or of the diverse and complicated issues which affect us' (Begum, 1992: 71).

Similarly, the importance of support from one's community to face up to racism is well known. However, community organisations that provide this support have been found to neglect issues of disability that may affect their members (Perkins, 1987).

This lack of attention is of concern as race and cultural expectations interact with disability in complex ways. For example, there may be strong cultural expectations for women to become mothers, but this might not be possible if someone has fertility problems as a result of their impairment. Similarly, African women who are HIV positive will be recommended not to breastfeed and have a caesarean section if their viral load is considered too high at the time of birth because of the risk of infecting their baby. However, breastfeeding is an important cultural practice and questions may be asked if a woman is not seen to be doing this, and so she may fear people will guess her HIV status. It is therefore important for therapists and health care professionals to discuss cultural expectations with clients and how their condition or its treatment may interact with these. More research is needed in this area to fill the dearth of literature.

Sexual and gender minorities

When a disabled person is acknowledged to be sexual, it is assumed their sexuality is heterosexual (Appleby, 1994). LGBT disabled people are either invisible or their rights denied. A well-publicised example of this (Thompson, 1992; Thompson & Andrzejewski, 1988) is in the case of Sharon Kowalski (Box 3.1).

Box 3.1 The Case of Sharon Kowalski

In November 1983, Sharon Kowalski was in a car crash that left her in a coma for months, after which she had impairments in her motor skills and communication. Sharon's father, Donald, was awarded legal custody on the condition that Sharon's partner, Karen, was allowed equal access to hospital records and visitation time. Sharon was able to communicate that she wished to return to her shared home with Karen, and medical staff reported that Sharon had progressed significantly because of Karen's consistent input. However, Donald Kowalski refused Karen visiting access and would not allow Sharon to live with Karen because of his homophobia.

Karen used her legal team, the Minnesota Civil Liberties Union and the St Cloud Handicap Services Association to campaign to become Sharon's legal guardian. Karen campaigned on national televised talk-shows and spoke in front of LGB groups and disabled organisations. A 'National Committee to Free Sharon Kowalski' was formed linking these organisations, which saw disability activists visiting Sharon in hospital for support and LGB activists fundraising to cover Karen's legal costs.

Eventually Karen was awarded legal guardianship and Sharon returned home to live with her partner in their shared home.

LGBT disabled people face discrimination and prejudice from heterosexual non-disabled people. A health crisis may result in LGBT people turning to their family for help, and possibly having to come out to them for the first time (as with Sharon Kowalski). They may be the only person in their family who is LGB or T and so they may not be met with support or understanding (Hillyer, 1993). Whereas other minority groups (e.g. if Jewish) may have been taught to feel pride in their minority membership and traditions, this is unlikely to be the message received from a family who are learning of their child's sexuality for the first time (Hillyer, 1993).

LGBT disabled people face homophobia within disability movements and disablism from LGBT groups. Some people may choose not to use the terms LGB or T because they already hold a stigmatised and devalued identity through being viewed as 'disabled', and so would not wish to take on another identity they know is discriminated against (Appleby, 1994). This is reinforced by messages to the disabled person to appear as 'normal' (i.e. able-bodied and heterosexual) as possible (Hillyer, 1993). When LGBT disabled people are viewed as asexual by their non-disabled LGBT peers it negates the courage it takes for LGBT disabled people to come out.

Davidson-Paine and Corbett (1995) interviewed gay men with learning disabilities who spoke of rejection from the disabled community when they came out. However, once out the gay community may also reject and negatively evaluate them, with its focus on near perfect bodies and fashion/style (Bennett & Coyle, 2001).

Appleby (1994) interviewed disabled lesbians about their understanding of why disablism might exist within LGBT communities, given that they are both discriminated against and so might have more strength in teaming up (such as in Box 3.1). One woman in Appleby's study thought it was because 'disability means weakness, and the whole focus on building a lesbian community is about women uniting in strength' (1994: 23). Hearn (1991: 37) suggests that the HIV epidemic has forced LGBT people to recognise, understand and account for 'human frailty'. However, there remains a lack of access for LGBT disabled people to LGBT communities, both in terms of physical access (e.g. with the presence of ramps or signers at events), but also in terms of acceptance, understanding and support (Appleby, 1994).

Interestingly, the argument has also been put that same-sex sexual relationships might actually be more tolerated, (a blind-eye turned rather than construed as a positive development), than heterosexual sexual relationships because of the lack of risk of procreation (Brown, 1994). However, other authors (e.g. Scotti *et al.*, 1996) found that staff more easily 'tolerated' masturbation, followed by heterosexual kissing and 'heavy petting', heterosexual oral sex, heterosexual intercourse and finally *anything* homosexual. Similarly, Jones (1995) found that only a third of the 150 staff she interviewed had discussed lesbian and gay sexuality with clients, even with clients believed to be lesbian or gay, compared with two-thirds who had discussed 'sexuality in general' (cited in Bennett & Coyle, 2001).

Age: adolescence

Twenty-five years ago, Coupey and Cohen (1984) found a total absence of information about sexual development and sexuality in rehabilitation and education programmes for adolescents with chronic ill health. Since then, Burns (1993) also reports that children growing up with disabilities are less likely to receive adequate sex education. And yet, at a time when adolescents have to adjust to numerous physiological changes as a result of puberty, it is essential to address the interaction with their disability and impairment of any treatment offered. For example, Coupey and Cohen (1984) found that teenage girls objected to wearing a body-brace that was required to help with their scoliosis because it visibly flattened their breasts. (Issues of mid life are covered throughout this chapter; those pertaining to older adults are discussed in Chapter 5, as well as in an excellent book by Zarb & Oliver, 1992.)

ABUSIVE SEX

Definitions of sexual abuse must take account of unequal power and its misuse (Brown & Turk, 1992). Without consent or in the presence of intimidation or force, sexual behaviours are abusive whether they involve direct contact or non-contact abuse, such as voyeurism, indecent exposure etc. (Sexual Offences Act 2003. More information about the classification of this is found in Chapter 1). Determining whether an individual has capacity to consent is central to this issue. There are three ways this can be done when it comes to people with learning disabilities: a diagnostic, outcome or functional approach. A diagnostic approach refers to an over-arching rule based on diagnosis – such as in Britain people with severe intellectual disabilities (an IQ less than 50) are considered 'incapable' of making a decision to consent to sexual behaviour. An outcome approach is based on a judgement about the decision the person made – the person may be judged 'incapable' because their decision was deemed 'irrational'. A functional approach judges whether someone has the capacity to consent based on the match between their ability and the demands of the task, in this case sex. So to be able to consent to sex a person has to be able to understand what sex is, the consequences of having sex (e.g. the risk of pregnancy and STIs), that they can choose freely whether to have it or not and that they are able to communicate their choice. In the UK this latter functional approach is most often used (Murphy, 2003) and is endorsed jointly by the British Medical Association (BMA) and the Law Society. However, this definition does not always stand up in court (see Box 3.2). Murphy (2003: 149) therefore proposes clear and precise points to represent the minimum amount of knowledge required by someone to be able to have capacity to consent to sex:

- that sex is different from personal care;
- that penetrative sex can lead to pregnancy;
- that penetrative anal sex is associated with a risk of HIV/AIDS;
- that people have a choice about whether to engage in sexual relationships.

The recommendations highlight the need for education about sex for people with learning disabilities.

Emotional, physical, sexual abuse and rape are unfortunate realities for many disabled people and vulnerable adults, with women being particularly vulnerable (Sobsey et al., 1995). The term 'vulnerable adult' refers to a person who is 18 years or older who receives or needs community care services because of 'mental or other disability, age or illness and who is or may be unable to take care of him or herself, or unable to protect him or herself against significant harm or exploitation' (Lord Chancellor's

Box 3.2 The case of R v. Jenkins

R was a young woman with severe learning disabilities who became pregnant by her support worker. The support worker admitted having had sex with her and he was charged with rape. R was assessed by an expert witness and deemed to not have the capacity to consent to sex following the guidance of the BMA and Law Society (1995), for example she could not name basic body parts, distinguish between pictures of sexual intercourse and other pictures and did not understand about her pregnancy. However, an expert witness for the support worker challenged this decision, suggesting that because R did not avoid the support worker and therefore seemed to like him, she did have capacity to consent to sex. The judge decreed that the guidance by the BMA and Law Society was therefore wrong, as R did not need to understand the implications of sex to be able to consent, she just needed an understanding of sex itself and because she was deemed capable of consenting to sex by the second expert witness the case against the support worker could not be held. The support worker's conviction was therefore quashed and he walked free (Murphy, 2000).

Department, 1997: Point 8.7). This definition can therefore include people with learning disabilities, with mental health problems, with physical disabilities or impairments and older people, especially if there are additional complications as a result of sensory impairments, physical frailty or chronic illness. Services are required to provide any necessarily assistance, support or protection to individuals classified as a 'vulnerable adult'; guidance on developing polices and procedure to do this are provided by the Department of Health *No Secrets* publication (Department of Health, 2000).

For people with learning disabilities, sexual abuse most commonly happens in the home or day placement of the victim or perpetrator (Brown *et al.*, 1995). It is extremely difficult for the abused person to speak out against the abuse or refuse to comply in relationships of power differentials where the abused is dependent on the abuser. Fear or shame can contribute to silence, resulting in most abuse going unreported (Ridington, 1989). This is particularly so for people with learning disabilities who have been encouraged to do as they are told and be 'good' and are dependent on others (Brown, 1997).

Perpetrators include partners, parents and service provides. For women with learning disabilities who have been abused, it is men with learning disabilities who form the largest group of reported perpetrators (Brown *et al.*, 1995), perhaps because of difficulties for these men in keeping abuse a secret (Brown, 1997). McCarthy (1991) found that many women with learning disabilities did not enjoy heterosexual sex because of an inability to describe and assert their desires, as well as ignorance about their own bodies (cited in Brown, 1994).

For disabled people who live with partners, domestic violence is thought to be as high as 60 per cent, compared with 33 per cent in the general population, and disabled girls are thought to be twice as likely as non-disabled girls to be sexually abused (Russell, 1995). Physical barriers can make it hard for disabled women to leave (such as 'safe houses' not being wheelchair accessible) and if the perpetrator is also disabled police may underestimate their ability to inflict violence and abuse (Russell, 1995).

Exercise 3.6 Assessing your service – a proposed audit

This exercise provides questions to consider how easily your service, or your training participants' service(s), is accessible for disabled people.

- How many disabled people use your service?
- Does this reflect the number of disabled people in the general population?
- What are the possible barriers in your service in making it accessible (include physical barriers, staff training, local knowledge that your service is accessible)?
- What action plan can be devised to address these barriers?
- What are the deadlines and who is responsible for each point of the plan?

Brown (1997) provides clear and concise advice and guidelines in addressing and preventing abuse for people with learning disabilities (both for victims and perpetrators). This includes advice that would apply to all people with impairment and disabilities of any kind:

- inform and educate disabled people about their sexuality, sexual rights and options (including heterosexual and LGBT choices);
- train staff to be able and confident in delivering this information;
- provide clear and unambiguous policies to guide staff in their work around sex and sexuality, and procedures to follow if abuse is reported;
- provide easy and accessible means for abuse to be reported;

- provide a balance between privacy and openness, for example have bathroom doors that lock but staff should know who is in the bathroom and for how long;
- make sexual health and contraceptive services available to all;
- relationships within staff teams themselves should reflect a respectful attitude towards gender and sexuality.

CONCLUSION

This chapter attempts to add to the emerging literature on sex, sexuality and disability. The chapter has taken a social relational approach, in that shared experiences of disability have been described, in addition to attention paid to separate and unique issues for certain groups. Disabled people will continue to flirt, have sex, become parents, live as gendered beings, although many factions of society still need to develop and to accept and adapt to this. Disabled people are adept at reading and adjusting to their bodies and societal responses, but society still needs to listen and learn from them. Society in turn can continue to support disabled people by protecting them from abuse and research and develop sexual understanding, language and any relevant aids and equipment (such as wheelchair accessible gynaecological couches). The balance between privacy, freedom and preventing abuse and invisibility must be struck. This starts in our attitudes, conversations, physical workplaces and the focus of staff teams. How will you take this forward?

RESOURCES

Ann Craft Trust

Formerly the National Association for the Protection from Abuse of Adults and Children with Learning Disabilities.
http://www.anncrafttrust.org

Sexuality Support Team (formerly known as Consent)

Sexuality training for people with learning disability.
Woodside Road, Abbots Langley, Hertfordshire WD5 0HT
Tel: 01923 670796. Email: ESU@hertspartsft.nhs.uk

Discern

Free counselling for disabled people on personal relationships and sexuality.
Chadburn House, Weighbridge Road, Littleworth, Mansfield NG18 1AH
Tel: 01623 623732

Enabledalready.com

A free dating and friendship site for disabled people.
http://www.enabledalready.com

BackCare

Formerly known as the National Back Pain Association.
http://www.backcare.org.uk

Regard

Lesbian and gay disability organisation.
http://www.regard.org.uk

REFERENCES

Abberley, P. (1997). The limits of classical social theory in the analysis and trans-
formation of disablement. In L. Barton and M. Oliver (eds), *Disability studies:
Past, present and future*. Leeds: The Disability Press.
Akkerman, D. (1999). *Breast cancer, sexuality and self-esteem*. ACCCIS database.
Victoria: Anti-cancer Council of Victoria, Australia.
Anderson, B.F. & Kornblum, H. (1984). The family environment of children with a
diabetic parent: Issues for research. *Family Systems Medicine*, 2, 17–27.
Anderson, B.J. & Wolf, F.M. (1986). Chronic physical illness and sexual behaviour:
Psychological issues. *Journal of Consulting and Clinical Psychology*, 54 (2),
168–175.
Appleby, Y. (1994). Out in the margins. *Disability and Society*, 9 (1), 19–32.
Begum, N. (1992). Disabled women and the feminist agenda. *Feminist Review*, 40,
Spring, 70–84.
Bennett, C. & Coyle, A. (2001). A minority within a minority: Identity and well-
being among gay men with learning disabilities. *Lesbian and Gay Psychology
Review*, 2, 9–15.
Brecker, L.R. (1993). Women with disabilities struggle for a healthy view of their
sexuality. *ADVANCE for physical therapists*, 18, 11–12 and 23.
British Medical Association and Law Society (1995). *Assessment of mental capacity:
Guidance for doctors and lawyers*. London: British Medical Association.
Brown, H. (1987). Working with parents. In A. Craft (ed.), *Mental handicap and
sexuality: Issues and perspectives*. Tunbridge Wells: Costello.
Brown, H. (1994). 'An ordinary sexual life?': A review of the normalisation principle
as it applies to the sexual options of people with learning disabilities. *Disability
and Society*, 9 (2), 123–144.
Brown, H. (1997). Sexual rights and sexual wrongs in the lives of people with
intellectual disabilities. In R.I. Brown (ed.), *Quality of life for people with
disabilities* (2nd edn). Cheltenham: Stanley Thornes.

Brown, H. & Turk, V. (1992). Defining sexual abuse as it affects adults with learning disabilities. *Mental Handicap*, 20, 44–55.

Brown, H., Stein, J. & Turk, V. (1995). Report of a second two year incidence survey on the reported abuse of adults with learning disabilities, 1991 and 1992. *Mental Handicap Research*, 8, 1–22.

Burns, J. (1993). Sexuality, sexual problems, and people with learning difficulties. In J.M. Ussher & C.D. Baker (eds), *Psychological perspectives on sexual problems: New direction in theory and practice*. London: Routledge.

Bury, M. (1996). Defining and researching disability: Challenges and responses. In C. Barnes and G. Mercer (eds), *Exploring the divide: Illness and disability*. Leeds: The Disability Press.

Bury, M. (1997). *Health and illness in a changing society*. London: Routledge.

Butler, J. (1999). Gender trouble: Feminism and the subversion of identity. London: Routledge.

Carolan, C. (1984). Sex and disability: 'Handicap – Less important than loving'. *Nursing Times*, 80 (39), 28–30.

Cobb, A. (2006). *Guide to surviving working life*. London: MIND.

Corker, M. (1998). *Deaf and disabled, or deafness disabled?* Buckingham: Open University Press.

Coupey, S.M. & Cohen, M.I. (1984). Special considerations for the health care of adolescents. *The Paediatric Clinics of North America*, 31 (1), 211–219.

Crow, L. (1996). Including all of our lives: Renewing the social model of disability. In C. Barnes and G. Mercer (eds), *Exploring the divide: Illness and disability*. Leeds: The Disability Press.

Davidson-Paine, C. & Corbett, J. (1995). A double coming out: Gay men with learning disabilities. *British Journal of Learning Disabilities*, 23, 147–151.

de Silva, P. (1993). Sexual problems in women with eating disorders. In J.M. Ussher & C.D. Baker (eds), *Psychological perspectives on sexual problems: New directions in theory and practice*. London: Routledge.

de Silva, P. (1999). Sexual consequences of non-sexual trauma. *Sex and Marital Therapy*, 14 (2), 143–150.

Department of Health (2000). *No secrets: Guidance on developing and implementing multi-agency polices and procedures to protect vulnerable adults from abuse*. London: Department of Health.

Fife, B.L. & Wright, E.R. (2000). The dimensionality of stigma: A comparison of its impact on self of persons with HIV/AIDS and cancer. *Journal of Health and Social Behaviour*, 4, 50–67.

Finger, A. (1992). Forbidden fruit. *New Internationalist*, 233, 8–10.

French, S. (1994). *On equal terms: Working with disabled people*. Oxford: Butterworth-Heinemann.

Greengross, W. (1976). *Entitled to love*. London: Malaby Press.

Griffiths, D., Quinsey, V. & Hinsburger, D. (1989). *Changing inappropriate sexual behavior: A community based approach for persons with developmental disabilities*. Baltimore, MD: Brookes.

Hawton, K. (1985). *Sex therapy: A practical guide*. Oxford: Oxford University Press

Hearn, K. (1991). Disabled lesbians and gays are here to stay! In T. Kaufmann & P. Lincoln (eds), *High risk lives*. Bridport: Prism Press.

Henshaw, P.C. (2001). Sexual aspects of physical disability. In P. Kennedy (ed.), *Psychological management of physical disabilities*. Hove: Routledge.

Hillyer, B. (1993). *Feminism and disability*. Norman: University of Oklahoma Press.

Hughes, B. & Paterson, K. (1997). The social model of disability and the disappearing body: Towards a sociology impairment. *Disability and Society*, 12 (3), 325–340.

Hwang, K. (1997). Living with a disability: A woman's perspective. In M.L. Sipski & C.J. Alexander (eds), *Sexual function in people with disability and chronic illness: A health professional's guide*. Maryland: Aspen.

Jones, V. (1995). *Heterosexism and homosexual oppression in the provision of services to support the sexuality of people who have a learning difficulty* (unpublished manuscript). King Alfred's College, Winchester.

Lillelehet, E. & Leiblum, S.R. (1993). Schizophrenia and sexuality: A critical review of the literature. *Annual Review of Sex Research*, 4, 247–276.

Lord Chancellor's Department (1997). *Who decides? Making decisions on behalf on mentally incapacitated adults*. London: HMSO.

McCarthy, M. (1991). *I don't mind sex, it's what the men do to you: Women with learning disabilities talking about their sexual experiences*. MA dissertation, Middlesex Polytechnic.

Mason, M. & Reiser, R. (1992). The medical model and the social model of disability. In M. Mason & R. Reiser (eds), *Disability equality in the classroom: A human rights issue*. London: Disability Equality in Education.

Milner, J. (1986). *Social work and sexual problems*. Buckingham: Pepar.

Morris, J. (1997). Gone missing? Disabled children living away from their families. *Disability and Society*, 12 (2), 241–258.

Murphy, G.H. (2000). Justice denied. *Mental Health Care*, 3, 256–257.

Murphy, G.H. (2003). Capacity to consent to sexual relationships in adults with learning disabilities. *Journal of Family Planning and Reproductive Health Care*, 29 (3), 148–149.

Nicolosi, A., Moreira, E.D., Villa, M. & Glasser, D.B. (2004). A population study of the association between sexual function, sexual satisfaction and depressive symptoms in men. *Journal of Affective Disorders*, 82 (2), 235–243.

O'Callaghan, A.C. & Murphy, G.H. (2002). *Capacity to consent to sexual relationships in adults with learning disabilities*. Final Report to the Nuffield Foundation. Kent: Tizard Centre, University of Canterbury.

Oliver, M. (1990). *The politics of disablement*. London: Macmillian.

Oliver, M. (1996a). *Understanding disability*. London: Macmillian.

Oliver, M. (1996b). A sociology of disability or a disablist sociology? In L. Barton (ed.), *Disability and Society: Emerging issues and insights*. Harlow: Longman.

Oppenheimer, R., Howells, K., Palmer, R.L. & Chaloner, D.A. (1985). Adverse sexual experience in childhood and clinical eating disorders: A preliminary description. *Journal of Psychiatric Research*, 19, 357–361.

Perkins, N. (1987). Disability in the Afro-Caribbean communities. In GLAD, *Disability and ethnic minority communities – A study in three London Boroughs*. London: Greater London Association of Disabled People.

Priestly, M. (1995). Commonality and difference in the movement. *Disability and Society*, 10 (2), 157–169.

Ridington, J. (1989). *Beating the 'odds': Violence and women with disabilities.* Position Paper 2. Toronto, Canada: DisAbled Women's Network.

Rights of Women (1984). *Lesbian mothers on trial, a report on lesbian mothers and child custody.* London: Rights of Women.

Russell, M. (1995). Piercing the veil of silence: Domestic violence and disability. *New Mobility*, 6 (26), 44–49 and 53.

Scotti, J., Slack, B., Bowman, R. & Morris, T. (1996). College student attitudes concerning the sexuality of persons with mental retardation: Development of the perceptions of sexuality scale. *Sexuality and Disability*, 14, 249–263.

Shakespeare, T. (1997). Researching disabled sexuality. In C. Barnes & G. Mercer (eds), *Doing disability research.* Leeds: The Disability Press.

Shakespeare, T., Gillespie-Sells, K. & Davies, D. (1996). *The sexual politics of disability: Untold desires.* London: Cassell.

Silk, K.R., Lee, S., Hill, E.M. & Lohr, N.E. (1995). Borderline personality disorder symptoms and severity of sexual abuse. *American Journal of Psychiatry*, 152 (7), 1059–1064.

Smith, I. (1989). Shattering the myths: Sexuality in rehabilitation for spinal cord injury. *Rehabilitation Management*, 2, 28–34.

Sobsey, D., Wells, D., Lucardie, R. & Mansell, S. (eds) (1995). *Violence and disability: An annotated bibliography.* Baltimore, MD: Paul H. Brookes.

Sontag, S. (1978). *Illness as metaphor.* New York: McGraw-Hill.

Tepper, M.S. (1997). Living with disability: A man's perspective. In M.L. Sipski & C.J. Alexander (eds), *Sexual function in people with disability and chronic illness: A health professional's guide.* Maryland: Aspen.

Thomas, C. (1999). *Female forms: Experiencing and understanding disability.* Buckingham: Open University Press.

Thompson, K. (1992). Karen Thompson talks about the case that never should have had to happen. *Disability Rag*, 3 (2), 20–21.

Thompson, K. & Andrzejewski, J. (1998). *Why can't Sharon Kowalski come home?* San Francisco: Spinsters/Aunt Lute.

Weiner, D.N. & Rosen, R.C. (1997). Medications and their impact. In M.L. Sipski and C.J. Alexander (eds), *Sexual function in people with disability and chronic illness: A health professional's guide.* Maryland: Aspen.

White, M.J., Rintala, D.H., Hart, K.A. & Fuhrer, M.J. (1993). Sexual activities, concerns and interests of women with spinal cord injury living in the community. *American Journal of Physical Medicine and Rehabilitation*, 72 (6), 372–378.

Williams, D. (1993). Sexuality and disability. In J.M. Ussher & C.D. Baker (eds), *Psychological perspectives on sexual problems: New directions in theory and practice.* London: Routledge.

Wolfensberger, W. (1972). *The principle of normalization in human services.* Toronto: National Institute of Mental Retardation.

Wolfensberger, W. (1983). Social role valorization: A proposed new term for the principle of normalization. *Mental Retardation*, 21, 234–239.

World Health Organization (1980). *International Classification of Impairments, Disabilities and Handicaps: A manual for classification relating to the consequences of disease (ICIDH).* Geneva: World Health Organization.

World Health Organization (2001). *International Classification of Functioning, Disability and Health (ICF).* Geneva: World Health Organization.

Yoshida, K.K. (1994). Institutional impact on self-concept among persons with spinal cord injury. *International Journal of Rehabilitation Research*, 17 (2), 95–107.

Zarb, G. & Oliver, M. (1992). *Ageing with disability: The dimensions of need.* London: Thames Polytechnic.

Zilbergeld, B. (1979). Sex and serious illness. In C.A. Garfield (ed.), *Stress and survival: The emotional realities of life-threatening illness*. St Louis: Mosby.

Zilbergeld, B. (1992). *The new male sexuality*. New York: Bantam Books.

Chapter 4

Sexual and gender minorities: consideration for therapy and training

Catherine Butler

> Alice could not help her lips curling in a smile as she began, 'Do you know. I always thought Unicorns were fabulous monsters too! I never saw one alive before!' 'Well, now that we have seen each other', said the Unicorn, 'If you'll believe in me, I'll believe in you. Is that a bargain?' 'Yes, if you like', said Alice.
>
> Lewis Carroll

Lesbian and gay men are frequent users of therapy (Bieschke *et al.*, 2000) and transsexual clients need to see a therapist as a requirement to gain access to gender reassignment treatments, as well as for numerous other reasons (Hovell & Davidson, in press). However, training in issues relevant to lesbian, gay, bisexual or transsexual (LGBT) people, and guidance on how to work with them in a respectful and enabling way, is only now beginning to develop within psychology, counselling and psychotherapy (Shaw *et al.*, 2008). In addition to this, even less is written or researched into heterosexual sexuality (with the exception of Denman, 2004) as the dominant sexual group, which remains predominantly uncritiqued or explored. Within this group, gender roles are taken as fixed and stable (discussed in depth in chapter 1) and so therapists rarely think about those who fall outside these dominant heterosexual or gender norms.

Census data suggests that 6 per cent of the UK population identify as lesbian or gay (Department of Trade and Industry, 2006), which equates to 3.6 million people. This figure does not include those who identify as bisexual or who may have same-sex sexual experiences but identify as heterosexual. It also does not include transgender people who may not classify themselves within male and female, and so may not fall within the category of 'heterosexual', sometimes preferring the label 'queer'. This chapter will focus on sexual and gender minority identities, providing useful information that can be used in teaching or with clients, as well as self-reflective exercises to develop one's understanding and practice.

The chapter begins with exploring the contexts that influence LGBT lives, before moving on to discuss therapy specific topics. This broad introductory stance is taken because it is essential that therapists have explored their own beliefs, attitudes and feelings about sexuality and expectations of gender before working with LGBT clients (Godfrey *et al.*, 2006). This self-reflection applies to both heterosexual and non-transsexual therapists in order to work 'cross-culturally' (as with working across race, religion, gender etc.), as well as LGBT identified therapists to avoid assumptions of knowledge or similarity. Roberts (2005) proposed that such self-reflection is essential to address the power differentials within the therapeutic relationship and the potential positions of privilege or oppression in the lives of therapist and client.

The topics in this chapter reflect those suggested for training about sexual and gender minority issues as recommended by the British Psychological Society (BPS) Division of Clinical Psychology (2007):

- addressing attitudes and myth busting;
- heterosexism and homophobia/biphobia/transphobia;
- therapies aimed at changing sexual orientation/conversion therapies;
- theories of sexuality and transgender;
- working with LGBT clients;
- sexual and gender minority therapy;
- legislation;
- issues for LGBT therapists;
- useful resources.

ADDRESSING ATTITUDES AND MYTH BUSTING

As mentioned previously, before working with LGBT clients it is important to have explored one's own attitudes and beliefs about sexuality and gender. Based on the premise that 'prejudiced attitudes are grounded in misinformation' (Peel, 2002: 259), it is hoped that by 'exposure to realities of lesbian and gay lives, people's prejudices and fears can be overcome' (Peel, 2002: 255).

Experiential exercises are a useful way to put oneself in the shoes of the 'other', to move beyond abstract conceptualisations of what this would be like and instead engage participants' emotions as to what it would *feel* like. Such exercises encourage individualised active learning, where the participant is struck by points that are pertinent to them. 'Homoworld' and 'The Heterosexual Questionnaire', described below, provide useful tools for therapists or trainers to self-reflect and draw out their attitudes and beliefs about LGB lives for examination.

Homoworld

Homoworld (Butler, 2004) is written as a day-in-the-life story about a heterosexual who lives in a world where the majority of people are lesbian or gay. While reading or listening, the following questions could be considered as a guide.

- What surprised or struck you?
- Did anything make you feel uncomfortable?
- What forms of support might you have employed?
- What issues did it reveal to you that people from sexual minorities may face (emotionally, socially, politically)?
- What issues did it bring up regarding sexuality generally?

Homoworld is provided in Appendix 1 of this chapter. It has also been adapted into a film and is available free of charge from the Doctorate in Clinical Psychology at the University of East London, London.

The Heterosexual Questionnaire

This questionnaire was developed by Rochlin (1992) and asks questions to heterosexual people that are often asked to LGB people. Readers can thus experience what emotions it raises to be asked these questions and if any questions seem particularly absurd or intrusive.

The Heterosexual Questionnaire

1 What do you think caused your heterosexuality?
2 When and how did you first decide that you were heterosexual?
3 Is it possible that your heterosexuality stems from a neurotic fear of members of the same sex?
4 Isn't it possible that all you need is a good gay lover?
5 If heterosexuality is normal, why are a disproportionate number of mental patients heterosexual?
6 Who have you disclosed your heterosexuality to? How did they react?
7 The great majority of child molesters are heterosexuals (95 per cent). Do you really consider it safe to expose your children to heterosexual teachers?
8 Heterosexuals are noted for assigning themselves and each other to narrowly restricted, stereotyped sex roles. Why do you cling to such an unhealthy form of role playing?
9 Why do heterosexuals place so much emphasis on sex?
10 There seem to be very few happy heterosexuals. Techniques have been developed that you might be able to use to change your sexual

orientation. Have you considered aversion therapy to treat your sexual orientation?

11 Why are heterosexuals so promiscuous?

12 Why do you make a point of attributing heterosexuality to famous people? Is it to justify your own heterosexuality?

13 If you've never slept with a person of the same sex, how do you know you wouldn't prefer that?

14 Why do you insist on being so obvious and making a public spectacle of your heterosexuality? Can't you just be what you are and keep it quiet?

Source: Rochlin, M. (1992). In W.J. Blumenfeld (ed.), *Homophobia: How we all pay the price*. Copyright © 1992 Warren J. Blumenfeld. Reproduced with permission of Beacon Press, Boston.

Challenging, and hopefully changing, negative attitudes can also sometimes require the direct provision of alternative accurate information to dispel negative beliefs and stereotypes. The follow sections provide useful information and resources to address such a challenge.

Heterosexual/gender privilege

Heterosexual/gender privilege refers to things that heterosexual or non-trans people might take for granted, but which are actually awarded them because of their heterosexuality or non-trans status. Examples include:

- seeing yourself represented in advertising as a model of 'normality';
- knowing that your sexuality or gender will be unquestioned, accepted and will not raise any eyebrows, or worse, provoke hostility;
- not having to think twice about talking about your partner;
- being comfortable with your gender of birth;
- having a developmental and established sense of your 'performance' of your gender (e.g. fashion, gesture, etc.).

Are there other examples that you could think of? If this exercise is used in training it can provide an opportunity to give an update on how things have changed in more recent years (for example, same-sex couples can now adopt (Adoption and Children Act, 2002), same-sex partnerships can now be legally recognised (Civil Partnership Act, 2005), you can change your gender on your birth certificate (Gender Recognition Act, 2004) etc.).

The use of films

Films provide a gentle way of challenging negative stereotypes if chosen carefully. A list of suggested films is provided in Appendix 2. Film clips can be used in training as a way of emphasising prejudice depicted in the film, which can also lead onto a discussion of how things may have moved on.

Quiz

The quiz below is one way to test your knowledge and beliefs about LGBT issues. If you are using such a quiz in training, participants can keep their answers to themselves to avoid any pressures of being seen as not knowing in the wider group.

Questions

1   What is the age of consent for lesbians?
2   What percentage of LGBT people have children?
3   How many homosexuals are estimated to have died in Nazi concentration camps during World War II?
4   In what year was gay male sex no longer criminalised?
5   In what year was homosexuality no longer considered a mental illness?
6   What was Section 28?
7   Under the Gender Recognition Act (2004) what criteria must someone meet to have his or her acquired gender legally recognised?

Answers

1   There isn't one! The age of consent for gay men and heterosexual men and women is 16 since 2001.
2   Thirteen per cent of gay, bisexual and transgender men and thirty-one per cent of lesbian, bisexual and transgender women (Morgan & Bell, 2003).
3   Over 50,000.
4   1967 in England and Wales, 1980 in Scotland.
5   1973 in the *Diagnostic and Statistical Manual of Mental Disorders (DSM)* and 1992 in the *International Classification of Mental and Behavioural Disorders (ICD)* used by the World Health Organization.
6   A law that made it illegal to 'promote' homosexuality, this was relevant for sex education in schools. It became law in 1988 until 2003.
7   Transgender people must live in their acquired gender for at least two years and this be approved by a psychologist or psychiatrist.

Lesbian and gay timeline

Stonewall (http://www.stonewall.org.uk) provide a detailed and regularly updated timeline of events that have an impact on LGB people; an adapted version is provided in Appendix 3 but this will need updating. The information contained in the timeline gives a good overview of the changes in the law and key events that have shaped the socio-cultural context of LGB people. Older clients will have been directly affected by some of these events, which might impact upon their openness in discussing their sexuality with therapists. This timeline does not provide any information on trans issues, but these could be added with information found on trans sites listed in the resources section.

If you use this timeline in training it can be given out to participants, asking them to skim through it for five minutes and then report back on what struck them. Alternatively, some of the significant events can be pointed out, e.g. the Wolfenden Report (Committee on Homosexual Offences and Prostitution, 1957) stated that 'private morality is not the law's business,' which began the process of decriminalising homosexuality.

Naming stereotypes

Stereotypes might be the first ideas somebody has about the sexuality and gender they think they might be: this could delay or make it confusing to come out as LGBT or seek out others if they feel they do not fit the stereotype. Stereotypes are culturally and historically dependent and so will shift over time and place. Asking participants to generate stereotypes highlights current cultural ideas and provides an opportunity to voice some of the less 'politically correct' ideas or beliefs they may have come across, hold, or wish to check out. It is better that these ideas are voiced so they can be discussed, and challenged, openly.

Participants are asked to generate stereotypes of the labels listed in Table 4.1, which can be drawn up on flip chart paper. Participants can work either as a large group or in small groups with each group taking a different label. It is important to note that transgender labels used by the medical profession include FTM – female to male, and MTF – male to female. However, these assume binary gender categories and so it is more correct to use the terms 'trans man' and 'trans woman' respectively (there are more on these definitions in Chapter 1).

Write participants' answers on a flip chart and once completed invite comments. For example, lesbians often have very few positive stereotypes whereas gay men sometimes attract some superficially positive ones. Stereotypes are often based on aspects of traditional heterosexual gender roles and so deviations from this are named (e.g. lesbians wearing 'comfortable shoes' or gay men being 'camp'). Damaging stereotypes, sometimes displayed in films such as Sharon Stone's murderous lesbian girlfriend in *Basic Instinct*, include that sexual minorities are perverted, sexually deviant, mentally ill or spreaders of sexually transmitted diseases. Again, the exercise provides an opportunity to challenge some of these; for example, although there are high

Table 4.1 Generating stereotypes

Gay men	Lesbians	Bisexual men	Bisexual women
e.g. dress well	e.g. man-haters	e.g. promiscuous	e.g. highly sexual

Heterosexual men	Heterosexual women	Transgendered men	Transgendered women
e.g. like sport	e.g. emotional	e.g. butch	e.g. glamorous

rates of HIV in gay male populations, there have been more heterosexuals living with HIV in the UK since 1999 (http://www.hpa.org.uk). It is also interesting to ask participants which aspects of the stereotypes they agree or disagree with in regard to those that were generated to fit themselves, and how do they feel about these.

Providing statistics

Although it is more than ten years old, Long's 1996 paper provided a challenge to many stereotypes that pervade society, examples of which are given below. The range of figures is broad enough that they probably still apply today.

- Gay men and lesbians do not desire and are not capable of permanent relationships. Forty-five to eighty per cent of lesbians, forty to sixty per cent of gay men are in steady relationship at any given time.
- Gay and lesbian relationships are less satisfactory than heterosexual relationships. No difference has been found and there is some evidence for greater sexual satisfaction.
- Lesbians and gays are not effective parents. No differences have been found between lesbian and heterosexual mothers in terms of maternal interests or child-rearing practices (limited research into gay fathers).

- Children raised by gay or lesbian parents will be psychologically damaged in some way (poor social adjustment, sexual identity confusion). No difference has been found in peer group popularity, social adjustment/competence, behavioural problems.
- In lesbian and gay couples, one partner usually plays the traditional feminine role and the other usually plays the traditional masculine role (butch/femme role division). Most lesbians and gays reject traditional masculine–feminine roles as a model for relationships. Most couples are in 'dual-worker' relationships and in relation to household tasks, decision-making processes and sexual behaviour roles seem to be based on skills or interest.

Diversity and sexual identity

There is no one way to be gay, lesbian, bisexual or transgender, just as there is no one way to be heterosexual, a man or a woman. Diversity within sexuality labels can be in some of the following areas and a useful exercise can be to ask participants to generate what the issues might be under each of the following headings.

Gender

The lives of lesbians and gay men are very different; there are different meeting places, socio-cultural norms and sexual practices. Same-sex venues are important for socialising, networking and meeting partners. Lesbians are less visible in the public eye than gay men, and perhaps because of this 'lesbian visibility' has been important, for example lesbians cutting their hair short to be recognisable to each other and perhaps as a political statement to wider society (Clark & Turner, 2007). However, the 1990s saw increased visibility of lesbians fitting more mainstream feminine presentations, with 'lipstick lesbians' or 'lesbian chic'. Today lesbians present in a wide variety of ways compared with the butch/femme dichotomies of the 1950s.

Race/ethnicity

People are likely to notice variation in race before they notice variation in sexuality. In a racist world, protection from this racism is essential from one's own community. To declare oneself as from a sexual minority within that community could potentially limit the support available to handle racism. For this reason, 'coming out' has been considered a White privilege. However, not being out can be associated in the LGBT community with shame, and racism within this community can limit support against homophobia. People from sexual and ethnic minorities therefore can face the potential for double discrimination on the basis of racism and homophobia from mainstream society (this is further discussed in Chapter 6). There are different ethnic and cultural traditions around gender and sexuality roles and expectations. So for example, in Asian communities where arranged marriages are practised it can be extremely difficult to live and be accepted as LGBT. In Iran it is illegal to be lesbian or gay because it is no longer a mental illness, but because transsexuals are categorised under 'Gender Identity Disorder' (a psychiatric condition), trans people can receive medical assistance and care by the state.

Chapter 6 explores culture and sexuality in detail, but specific to LGB communities, same-sex sexual behaviour is found in many cultures although it might not be labelled 'homosexuality'

- Latin/Arab – the 'active' insertive sexual partner is viewed as heterosexual;
- Melanesian – the manhood ceremony involves young adolescents ingesting the semen of older men through fellatio to ingest 'manhood' and come of age;
- USA – A 'Boston marriage' in the nineteenth century involved two women who lived together like husband and wife to financially support each other, although this relationship was not necessarily sexual;
- over 30 African populations (including Nigeria, South Africa, The Sudan) have the concept of a female husband, similar to the Boston marriage above.

Similarly, trans people are accepted and have an honoured place in some societies (Denman, 2004):

- male Krishna devotees may imagine themselves to be female and sometimes dress in female clothing;
- hijra in India are considered a third-gender role that is neither male or female, so they may wear female clothing but have a beard. They often have sexual relationships with men but distinguish themselves from homosexuals;
- two-spirit people in Native American Indian societies are men or people with a Disorder of Sex Development (more on this in Chapter 1), living as women and honoured as shamans;
- Xanith in Oman occupy a position between men and women, wearing indeterminate clothing and so being able to be among women in purdah but go unaccompanied as men do.

In the West, such gender fluidity is viewed as a problem and constructed as a medical (e.g. Disorder of Sex Development) or mental (e.g. Gender Identity

Disorder) disorder that requires medical and/or psychiatric treatment, including surgery and hormone therapy.

Religion

Most of the world religions have been interpreted to prohibit same-sex sexual practices, or practices such as anal sex, and see them as sinful. For a religious client, their faith and sexuality may be in conflict. Fortunately, many LGB faith groups exist as a resource (see the resources section at the end of this chapter). In more rural communities alternative venues to bars clubs, which may conflict with religious practices such as not drinking alcohol, may not be available.

Age

Across the lifespan there are specific issues for LGBT people (D'Augelli & Patterson (1994) go into these issues in depth). These range from 'coming out' (described in more detail later in this chapter); parenting issues in mid-life; or being an older adult who lived in a time when their sexuality was considered criminal and a mental illness. In addition, LGB social spaces tend to be geared towards those under 50 years old. This makes it more difficult for older LGBT people to meet friends or partners, particularly if they came out or transitioned later in life (perhaps after children and marriage) and so might not have a social network. (Sex and sexuality across the lifespan in general is discussed further in Chapter 5).

Class

Class may influence having the funds to access resources such as Pride events, the confidence and verbosity to speak about one's sexuality and expecting to be accepted, and seeing oneself represented in LGB media will all be influenced by class. However, in other ways visiting the only gay bar in the town cuts across class barriers as having sexuality in common brings people together. Keogh et al. (2004) describe how working class men are more likely to face discrimination because of their sexuality at work, but are less likely to attend LGB community events – where they might gain a sense of belonging and support. For trans people, being in a low socio-economic group may also affect access to funds to pay for procedures not covered by the NHS (e.g. electrolysis), the option to be seen in a private clinic (which may not insist on an all or nothing transition which the NHS might), or the risk of unemployment (e.g. due to prejudice while living as the preferred gender prior to any medical interventions to assist this transition such as hormone treatment).

Sexuality

There are further minority sexualities and sub-cultures within LGBT communities, such as the sadomasochism community (Langdridge & Barker, 2007). These individuals can face prejudice and rejection from the wider LGBT community. There is also a debate about whether trans issues should be grouped together with LGB issues, as although a transsexual person's sexuality label might change if they change gender, as might their partner's, this change might have no meaning or be rejected by those involved (so a heterosexual partner of a trans woman may not consider herself to now be in a lesbian relationship). The connection between sexuality and trans-sexuality is a complex consideration of development, definition, association, perspective etc. Whereas sexuality is increasingly been seen as fluid (especially with identities such as 'queer' being available), this is less the case when it comes to gender. And yet there is a huge range of both behavioural gendered characteristics, as well as biological variation (e.g. women who have facial hair, men who develop some breast tissue etc.).

Rural/urban

The environmental contexts of rural and urban settings will impact upon other people's exposure to LGBT lives and so their reaction to such things as someone in the community 'coming out', same-sex partners living together or moving into the area, or someone transitioning gender. For LGBT people, access to supportive communities or places to socialise and meet friends and partners might be limited in rural settings.

Ability

Meeting friends and partners if an LGBT person has a physical or learning disability can be a challenge. There are some LGB disability specialist groups, such as for people who are deaf, but by and large the social network is geared to able-bodied people, which in extreme can be body fascistic (for examples pick up a copy of the gay male press to be met by bulging muscles and six packs on nearly every page). Cambridge (1997) reports that LGB people with learning disabilities are less likely to have their support needs met and men are at a higher than average risk of contracting HIV. Trans people might have difficulty being heard and responded to if they have a learning disability, particularly when their expressions of gender and sexuality have been controlled and policed by carers or residential staff.

HETEROSEXISM AND HOMOPHOBIA/BIPHOBIA/ TRANSPHOBIA

This section starts with some important terminology; in training sessions participants can be asked to give examples to ensure understanding:

- homophobia: an irrational fear of homosexuality;
- biphobia: an irrational fear of bisexuality (by heterosexuals or homosexuals);
- heterosexism: a world view, a value-system that prizes heterosexuality, assumes it is the only manifestation of love and sexuality and devalues all that is not heterosexual (Herek, 1986).

The term 'homophobia' was first used in 1869 by Dr Benkert in Hungary and introduced to the English language in the 1890s by the sexologist Havelock Ellis. It has since been criticised (e.g. Kitzinger & Perkins, 1993) because it individualises and depoliticises the oppression of LGB people. Alternatively, 'heterosexism' places such oppression within a socio-cultural context that is learnt and sanctioned by the dominant culture. As yet, there is not an equivalent term in use with regards to trans people, but the term 'transphobia' is used (Whittle, 2006). Examples of heterosexism and transphobia in psychology include normative theories of development (which exclude or pathologise LGBT experiences) or the invisibility of LGBT issues and lives in teaching and writing.

- Sexual prejudice: all negative attitudes based on sexual orientation, whether the target is homosexual, bisexual, or heterosexual (Herek, 1999).

This term is used increasingly in psychological literature (Hegarty, 2006) and widens the lens of oppression again to include all those engaging in non-mainstream sexual practices (and so would include heterosexuals who have non-monogamous relationship or practice sadomasochism).

THERAPIES AIMED AT CHANGING SEXUAL ORIENTATION/CONVERSION THERAPIES

An issue to discuss during training is how would you respond if a client asks for help to change their sexual behaviour? There might be various reasons why someone might ask this: it could be because they are not happy with the kinds of sex they are having, the type of partner they are having it with or the context in which it occurs. It is worth exploring with the client why they consider their sexual behaviour to be a problem, when it first started to be constructed as problematic, and who else might agree or disagree with this view? It is important that the therapist's ideas of what is 'appropriate' sexual behaviour do not guide the therapy, and supervision can be helpful for expressing beliefs about sex and sexuality held by the therapist. There may be some circumstances where helping the client address an aspect of their sexual behaviour is entirely appropriate; for example a client may struggle to use condoms when taking recreational drugs and want to find strategies to prompt him to do so. However, any therapy that is based on heterosexist prejudices, internalised by the client or therapist, should never be conducted.

Therapy aimed at changing sexual orientation was routinely offered when homosexuality was viewed as a mental illness before *DSM-III* in 1973 (American Psychiatric Association). 'Cures' for homosexuality included medical 'treatments' such as surgical interventions (including sterilisation, lobotomy, clitoridectomy), chemical interventions (including hormone injections, sexual depressants), psychological interventions (including hypnosis, aversion therapy using emetics and shock) and other procedures (such as cold sitz baths and 'homo-anonymous' which was similar to Alcoholics Anonymous) (Kutchins & Kirk, 1999). Criticism of these approaches came from the Gay Liberation Movement and from within the profession, with the likes of Kinsey *et al.* reporting the frequency and hence 'normality' of same-sex sexual practices for men (1948) and women (1953). In 1979, Masters and Johnson's book *Homosexuality in Perspective*, also refuted homosexuality as a mental illness, however, unfortunately they claimed to be able to change the sexual preferences of homosexuals to a 'normal' heterosexual pattern. In general, criticisms have centred on how these approaches harm clients, the prejudice inherent in their theoretical basis, their violation of human rights and evidence that they have minimal effectiveness in helping to change sexual orientation. A comprehensive description of the issues around conversion therapy is provided by Shidlo *et al.* (2002).

Since 1973, conversion therapy is not available on the NHS, however it is still researched, taught and offered, particularly in the USA. The main proponent of this approach is Nicolosi (1991) who offers 'reparative therapy' that is based on psychodynamic theory and the premise that non-heterosexual adjustment is never a satisfactory resolution of sexual identity development. The National Association for Research and Therapy of Homosexuality offers 'evidence' and 'treatment' to support this approach. The film *But I'm a Cheerleader* offers a comical insight into what happens in conversion 'camps', and examples of the rules for such places are on the Love In Action website (http://www.loveinaction.org), which opposes reparative therapy.

The American Psychiatric Association (1998) has issued a position statement on conversion therapies:

1   Homosexuality is not a diagnosable disorder and any therapy based on this premise is unethical.
2   As a general principle a therapist should not determine the goal of treatment to changing sexuality coercively or through subtle influence.
3   Reparative therapy uses theories and methods that make it difficult to find scientific evidence for its effectiveness.

The Australian Psychological Society (2000a) has produced a similar statement.

Exercise 4.1 Case study

Mahmod is a 30-year-old Kurdish man who presents asking to change his sexual behaviour from having casual sex with men to dating women. He has been in the UK for three years and has no friends or family in this country and is unemployed. He comes from a large family where he did not feel emotionally supported, was criticised by his father and found relationships and intimacy with women difficult. Since he came to the UK he found that he could find casual sex with men easily but felt shame and guilt at this as he wanted to have a family and succeed as he believed it would gain his father's and family's approval.

How would you work with this client? On the one hand, there might be the argument that for religious, personal or family reasons a therapist should assist him to change his sexual behaviour as it causes him distress; on the other, there is the argument that such assistance to change his sexual behaviour should never be encouraged as a therapeutic goal and encouraging self-acceptance may be more helpful. How might you negotiate reformulation if you held a different view to him on the goal of changing his sexual behaviour?

THEORIES OF SEXUALITY AND TRANSGENDER

When teaching theories of sexuality or gender, it first needs to be asked why are we curious about this? People do not ask why are people heterosexual or the gender they are, so putting LGBT people under the microscope hints at an unspoken assumption that it is questionable or dubious to identify this way. There is also a moral agenda that such theories would indicate either that people do not choose their sexuality or degrees of gender, or else that they do, and could be 'treated' or reformed. However, clients may be

Table 4.2 Poles of the theories of sexuality and gender

Essentialist	Social Constructionist
• Nature: innate	• Nurture: choice
• Fixed and immutable	• Fluid and changeable
• Occurs across cultures, species and throughout history	• Shaped by cultural and temporal norms
• Provides a 'cause'/linear explanation	• Complex, multifaceted explanation

genuinely curious about why they are LGBT, and to explore this with them it is useful to know some of the theories of sexuality and transgender to validate or challenge their views, depending on what would be more helpful. Theories of sexuality and gender tend to fall into two camps, set out in Table 4.2.

With regards to sexuality, essentialist views could be used to pathologise homosexuality as a 'mutation' or non-adaptive. Alternatively, social constructionist views could be used to pathologise and offer conversion therapy. Gender tends to be constructed as fixed, based on essentialist unquestioned assumptions and so social constructionist ideas of gender are more hidden.

Biological explanations

Biological explanations suggest there are genetic or anatomical differences between heterosexual people and gay men or lesbians. For example, research has found differences in brain structure, prenatal exposure to androgens, fraternal birth order, differences in finger length and linked homosexuality to left-handedness. A comprehensive review of these theories is provided by Wilson and Rahman (2005). Socio-biological theories also exist to explain the social advantages of a biological predisposition to homosexuality for the group. These are based on the assumption that LG people do not have children, for example, LG people provide an extra pair of hands to help or there is a reduction in competition for mates. Denman (2004) describes these theories in more detail. For trans people, biological explanations are politically important, as trans people must convince psychiatrists that they have always felt in the wrong gender, that it is innate and not a conscious choice, and so be allowed access to gender reassignment surgery and procedures.

Psychiatric explanations

Psychiatry historically pathologised homosexuality as a mental disorder under various different titles:

- *DSM-I* (APA, 1952) 'sociopathic personality disorder'.
- *DSM-II* (APA, 1968) 'sexual orientation disorder'.
- *DSM-III* (APA, 1973) 'egodystonic homosexuality'. The criteria for this classification were:

> 1. The individual complains that heterosexual arousal is persistently absent or weak and significantly interferes with initiating or maintaining wanted heterosexual relationships
> 2. There is a sustained pattern of homosexual arousal that the individual explicitly states has been unwanted and a persistent source of distress.
>
> (APA, 1973)

There is no question raised about why an individual might be distressed at being homosexual on a socio-political level, instead, understandable distress generated by prejudice and oppression was pathologised.

- *DSM-III-R* (APA, 1987) 'egodystonic homosexuality' was removed and this is the only version of DSM where homosexuality is not pathologised;
- *DSM-IV* (APA, 1994) 'sexual disorder not otherwise specified'. The criteria for this being similar to that of egodystonic homosexuality: 'sexual disturbances including persistent and marked distress about sexual orientation'.

Detailed information about the changing fate of homosexuality in the *DSM* is provided by Kutchins and Kirk (1999). It is worth noting that the World Health Organization did not declassify homosexuality as a mental disorder until 1992 with *ICD-10*, which retains the classification of egodystonic sexual orientation.

Trans people are viewed as having the mental disorder 'Gender Dysphoria' in *ICD* and 'Gender Identity Disorder' in *DSM*. In Britain, to obtain gender reassignment surgery on the NHS individuals must live as their acquired gender for two years and be assessed by a psychiatrist. This medicalised approach is in contrast to how other cultures may view transgender mentioned earlier.

Psychological explanations

It would be a book in itself (and it has been, e.g. Davies & Neal, 2000) to try to list every psychological theory's consideration of homosexuality. However, the main theories relating to the psychology are detailed below.

Learning theory

Classical learning theory suggests that a resulting homosexual orientation will arise from exposure to adverse heterosexual experiences and positive homosexual ones. This theory has been use to justify 'treatments' such as the use of emetics to make a patient feel nauseous and vomit when viewing homosexual images (often porn). However, there is no substantive evidence to support this theory. Learning theory in relation to trans involves parental encouragement of 'other' gender behaviour and discouragement of matching gendered play, or the individual's wish to avoid homosexuality (e.g. Bancroft, 1989). There is no evidence to support these views.

Psychoanalytic theory

Psychoanalytic theories have had the most to say about sexuality; some useful examples include Drescher (1999) and Drescher *et al.* (2003). Freud did not label homosexuality as mental illness but considered that we are all born bisexual. However, he proposed that this would change to heterosexuality with normal development, and so in his Oedipus Complex theory homosexuality was viewed as a perverse orientation, or a developmental disorder or arrest. Later theories have viewed homosexuality as pathological (e.g. Socarides, 1963), justifying exclusion of openly homosexual people to train as analysts (which has only changed in the last 25 years). This meant all psychoanalytic writing was about clients and not personal experience, a situation that has changed in latter years (e.g. O'Connor & Ryan, 1993). This has caused many splits in recent psychoanalytic theories, e.g. between those who still view homosexuality as pathological and those who do not. Psychoanalytic theorists also have developed theory about transsexuals. However, sadly this theory has also been used to pathologise, e.g. involving unresolved separation anxiety from the mother (e.g. Person & Ovesey, 1978), which again has no evidence. However, recent developments (e.g. Di Ceglie, 2000) have taken a less pathologising, although still psychiatric, view.

Systemic theory

Systemic theories have ignored sexuality, however early models (e.g. structural therapy or *The Family Life Cycle* by Carter & McGoldrick, 1980) assume that heterosexuality is the norm. The definition of 'family' is often taken as blood relatives in a nuclear family structure. Historically the marriage bond was privileged in the use of genograms. Such a view can create one way of seeing relationships and families, a 'universe', as opposed to the 'multiverse' that Maturana and Varela (1986) place at the centre of

systemic theory, particularly with the strong influence that social constructionism has played in later developments. However, there is a small amount
of literature about lesbian and gay lives applying this theory (e.g. Malley &
Tasker, 1999). In general, this approach does not work with the notion of
pathology in the individual but explores how problems arise in socio-
cultural contexts. It can therefore help to challenge oppressive social
discourses and address issues of power, as well as explore alternate perspectives on gender and sexuality.

Cognitive Behavioural theory

Beckian cognitive behavioural therapy also ignores sexuality in its theor-
ising, but it does take account of environmental influences and so could be
used to address experiences of heterosexism and transphobia, and case
studies have been published doing this (e.g. Padesky, 1989). Used inappro-
priately, clients' experiences of heterosexism or transphobia could be
viewed as 'negative automatic thoughts' to be corrected or newer methods,
such as Acceptance and Commitment Therapy, could also depoliticise
heterosexist and prejudicial experiences. Ellis, the main proponent of
Rational Emotive Therapy, labelled people who were exclusively homosexual as abnormal (1965), even psychotic, which he later retracted (1976,
2001). Behavioural therapy has also been used to desensitise clients of their
same-sex sexual responses on the premise that these responses were due to
faulty learning (Barlow, 1973). Martell *et al.* (2004) write about how to use
this approach ethically with LGB clients.

Contemporary theory

Psychology overall has recently shifted away from researching and explain-
ing the cause of homosexuality, to examining the assumptions that underlie
the construct of heterosexuality, e.g. patriarchy and enforcing gender roles.
There has also been a move to examine the origin of LGBT hostility, e.g.
that it violates established gender codes. Along with this have come the
critiques of the construct of homophobia, in favour of heterosexism,
heterosexual privilege and sexual prejudice. This shift has been heavily
influenced by post-modernism and feminism. Two other influential theories,
queer theory and continuum theories, are detailed below.

Queer theory

Queer theory considers identities such as gender and sexuality as not being
fixed. In addition, there are no fixed groups with common characteristics
or interests e.g. 'women' or 'lesbians'. Instead, identities are *performed*
(Butler, 1990) based on prevailing socio-cultural norms. Those with power

categorise and regulate the lived experiences of minority peoples, positioning them as 'the other', deviating from the dominant, and thus 'desirable', norm (Foucault, 1972). Queer theory tends to reside in academia and has not been taught or adopted by many practising psychologists. However, social constructionism, as a close cousin not specifically about sexuality, is widely taught and so there is a space for queer theory to move into. Butler and Byrne (2007) give examples of the usefulness of this theory in their work.

Continuum theories

These started with Kinsey who said:

> Not all things are black nor all things white. It is a fundamental of taxonomy that nature rarely deals with discrete categories. Only the human mind invents categories and tries to force facts into separated pigeon-holes. The living world is a continuum in each and every one of its aspects. The sooner we learn this concerning human sexual behaviour the sooner we shall reach a sound understanding of the realities of sex.
>
> (Kinsey et al., 1948: 639)

Kinsey et al. (1953) created a seven-point continuum of sexual behaviour ranging from exclusively homosexual to exclusively heterosexual (for more information visit www.kinseyinstitute.org). Klein (1983) and Klein et al. (1985) developed the construct of sexuality beyond just sexual behaviour and proposed it was made up of seven components: sexual behaviour; emotional preference; sexual fantasies; sexual attraction; social preference; life style; social world and community; self-identification. Klein suggested a continuum existed for each of these components that will change if considered in the past, present or image of the ideal.

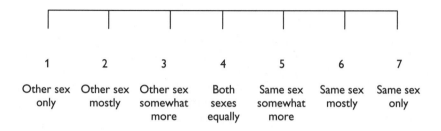

1	2	3	4	5	6	7
Other sex only	Other sex mostly	Other sex somewhat more	Both sexes equally	Same sex somewhat more	Same sex mostly	Same sex only

Figure 4.1 Klein Sexual Orientation Scale. Produced with data from Klein, F. (1993). *The bisexual option* (2nd edn). New York: Haworth Press.

Exercise 4.2 The Klein Scale

Print numbers 1–7 and the scale descriptors on pieces of A4 paper and put them together on the floor in a line from one side of the room to the other. Ask participants to line up behind the number that best represents them in response to the following questions.

- Social preference: with members of which sex do you socialise?
- Lifestyle preference: what is the gender ratio of the places where you choose to socialise?
- Emotional preference: members of which sex do you love and like mostly?
- Sexual identity: with which group do you identify your sexual identity?
- Sexual fantasies: who are your sexual fantasies about?
- Sexual attraction: to whom are you sexually attracted?
- Sexual behaviour: with whom have you actually had sex?

Note: these questions are ordered loosely in descending order of privacy. The trainer needs to judge whether asking the latter questions will be appropriate for participants, for example, on an ongoing course participants may not want to reveal their sexual fantasies to each other. However, you can still ask the question and ask participants to sit down when they wish, then ask them why it was they might have felt uncomfortable revealing this. Also, ask participants if they would have stood somewhere different if the exercises had been done five years ago or if they could imagine standing somewhere different in future. What do they learn from this?

These scales are in relation to sexuality but scales can also be developed in relation to gender to emphasise the fluidity of gender as well. This is an interesting way to draw out gender role stereotypes and how people position themselves in relation to these. To do this as a lineal scale (as with sexuality) from male to female would mean that as one moved towards the female pole, aspects of a masculine identity would have to be given up, when in fact these two aspects of identity might exist simultaneously (for example, a woman who likes servicing her motorbike and wearing heels when she goes out for a night). A better model would be to represent masculinity and femininity on a graph (Figure 4.2).

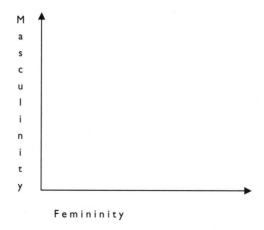

Figure 4.2 Gender identity graph.

Exercise 4.3 A scale of gender

Place yourself, or ask participants to place themselves on the above graph to represent how masculine and feminine they feel. Consider how this might change in different contexts: e.g. at work, on a night out, in bed, on a dance floor, driving?

To conclude about theories of sexuality – our understanding of the nature and origins of sexuality develops as a function of:

- the questions we ask;
- the methods by which we seek the answers;
- how we interpret the data;
- all further limited by the cultural context in which we work and the lens through which we see the world.

Exercise 4.4 Reflection on theories of sexuality

Having considered the theories, where would you position your work? Which of the theories do you think are essentialist or social con-structionist? Which theories might be helpful to your clients? Which do you feel more comfortable with?

WORKING WITH LGBT CLIENTS

This section is often the 'point' of doing teaching in this area. Both LGBT and heterosexual therapists can develop skills in working with clients who are different from themselves in terms of sexuality or gender. However, there are issues specific to heterosexual therapists and LGBT therapists; issues pertaining to the former are now considered, issues pertaining to the latter are discussed at the end of this chapter.

Heterosexual therapists may have a number of concerns in working with LGBT clients, some of which are discussed by Spellman (1999) and Accoroni (2006). Such issues might include not knowing how to raise the issues of sexuality or gender variance, who has responsibility to raise it (the therapist or the client) and not feeling knowledgeable about relevant LGBT issues. Feeling a lack of knowledge, inexperience, and hence feeling deskilled, can be compounded by the lack of teaching on LGBT issues and integration into training curricula. It is important to position LGBT training as part of an ongoing process that requires revision, expansion and updating. In his sexuality training, Dominic Davies (personal communication) has adapted suggestions from Blumenfeld (1992) to suggest heterosexual therapists conduct 'homowork' to understand how it might feel to be lesbian or gay in today's society, including:

- buying a gay or lesbian magazine and reading it in public;
- wearing a pro-LGBT T-shirt or badge;
- holding hands with someone of the same sex in public;
- keeping your heterosexuality in 'the closet' for a week by not discussing it with anyone, e.g. if talking about what you did at the weekend do not mention your partner's name or gender.

You might also like to try out the following in relation to gender:

- go shopping in your local supermarket while cross-dressed;
- try something on the other end of the stereotypical gender spectrum you have never done before, e.g. if you are very feminine go paint-balling, if very masculine get your nails manicured.

What do LGBT clients want their therapist to know? Long et al. (1993) (cited in Long, 1996) interviewed LGB clients and identified the following areas, which can also apply to transgender:

- awareness of 'invisibility' in society;
- 'coming out' as a continual process;
- social and political history of LGBT;

- awareness of effects of homo/transphobia, including the impact of violence.

What is important to emphasise is that when working with LGBT clients, the therapist should be alert to whether their sexuality/transgender *per se* is the problem and if so *who* is it a problem for?

If sexuality is problematic for LGB clients, some of the psychological pressures they may present with include the following:

- Dealing with heterosexism:
  - internal: heterosexism/homophobia might have been internalised to cause low self-esteem, self-harm or thoughts of suicide (this is sometimes referred to as 'internalised homophobia', e.g. Wagner *et al.*, 1996);
  - external: having to cope with bullying, verbal or physical abuse, heterosexual privilege etc.;
  - institutional: having to cope with prejudice and discrimination, in health, education, mental health systems etc. (e.g. McFarlane, 1998);
  - difficulty accessing services (e.g. McFarlane, 1998; King *et al.*, 2003).
- The influence of LGB culture and sub-cultures: alcohol and drugs (there are higher rates of drug and alcohol use than in the general population, Hughes & Eliason, 2002), the prevalence of HIV in gay male communities, the pressures of body image.
- Increased suicide and self-harm in youth (Rivers, 1997).
- Negotiating sexual relationships within relationships.
- Considering issues related to wanting children and parenting.
- Support in illness and old age.
- Employment issues such as discrimination at work.
- 'Coming out.'

Issues to do with coming out deserve a particular mention; they connect to other areas in this chapter and are also discussed in Chapter 5 and in Chapter 6 in relation to Black and ethnic minority LGB people. Coming out, disclosing one's sexual identity to others, can happen for the first time at any point in a person's life and from then on it is a repeatable process as new environments and people are encountered (Cowie & Rivers, 2000). Some research suggests that gay men come out on average at a younger age than lesbians (Savin-Williams, 1990). Numerous models of the process of coming out have been developed, e.g. Cass (1979), Woodman and Lenna (1980), Coleman (1982), D'Augelli (1994) and Rivers (1997) to name a few. Cass's six-stage model is one of the most widely known (Ritter & Terndrup, 2002) and so is described below as an example.

- Identity confusion: the individual begins to question whether they are heterosexual as they realise they have thoughts, feelings or behaviours that might be classified as homosexual.
- Identity comparison: the individual considers the consequences of what it might mean to be homosexual in relation to their former sense of self and begins to develop a new meaning system.
- Identity tolerance: the individual begins to recognise that they might be homosexual and seeks out contact with other homosexual people to compensate for feelings of alienation in heterosexual society.
- Identity acceptance: the individual will prefer homosexual social contact to heterosexual as they feel supported and a sense of belonging and start to selectively disclose their identity.
- Identity pride: the individual may experience anger with wider society because of heterosexism and homophobia and so split the world into supportive homosexuals and oppressive heterosexuals, contact with other homosexuals is maximised.
- Identity synthesis: the individual no longer draws a clear line between homosexuals and heterosexuals, can recognise similarities between the two and their sexuality is reduced to just one part of their identity among others.

However, these models have been criticised because they assume a one-off lineal progression through stages and that someone is either heterosexual or gay (therefore not accounting for if someone is bisexual or their sexuality or gender changes over time – Davies, 1996). In addition, they do not differentiate male and female experiences, consider the influences of a person's social environment or recognise that all the stages do not fit with the experience of large numbers of LG people (Langdridge, 2007).

Transgender clients might present in therapy with the following specific psychological issues:

- dealing with stigma, discrimination and prejudice;
- rejection from the gendered group that has been reassigned;
- experiencing verbal and physical aggression;
- lack of funds due to the expense of treatments and difficulty working because of discrimination;
- not wanting surgery, only some kinds of medical intervention, but only being offered all or nothing;
- post-operative regret tends to be caused by poor surgical outcome or unrealistic expectations of the surgery (Denman, 2004);
- adjusting to changes in relationships with partners and friends.

Giving participants case examples to work on in small groups is a good way to consider how they would feel, think and what they would do if working with LGBT clients. It is good to include scenarios that reflect the clients that participants will be working with, so for example, with clinical psychology trainees include scenarios that cover older adults, learning disabilities, adolescence (including issues of coming out) and someone from an ethnic minority. It is also useful to include trans clients so that participants can consider the medical and societal oppression and prejudice that these clients face day-to-day. After working on the role plays for 20–30 minutes, have participants feed back from each different scenario and invite the rest of the class to comment or add to points raised. This is another opportunity to provide resources, information and do some myth busting.

SEXUAL AND GENDER MINORITY THERAPY

Gay Affirmative Therapy (GAT) was a term that grew during the 1980s and 1990s indicating that the therapist affirms an LGB identity as equally positive in experience and expression as a heterosexual identity. It is not a new form of therapy but an adjunct to existing therapy models that takes the above stance. Whole books have been written on the subject, e.g. Ritter and Terndrup (2002) and Kort (2007). GAT developed because of evidence of harmful therapeutic practice (Milton, 1998), including a lack of knowledge of LGB concerns and consequential reliance on stereotypical assumptions about LGB people, viewing them as 'pathological', overemphasising the relevance of their sexuality in assessing their presenting problems and underestimating the effects of prejudice and discrimination on clients' lives.

Gabriel and Davies (2000) extended the term to 'sexuality affirmative therapy' to include lesbian, bisexual and queer identities. There have been critics of both these terms (e.g. Simon & Whitfield, 1995) questioning what is being affirmed, and whether the therapist has the authority to decide this and they ask instead what meaning the client might make of their sexuality? Davies (personal communication) has since further extended the term to 'sexual and gender minority therapy' to also include transsexuals and remove the concept of 'affirming'.

The basic principles of this approach, drawn from commonalities across the literature and which fit in any therapeutic model, are:

- the therapist should to be aware and comfortable with their own sexuality;
- the therapist should respect the client's sexuality, lifestyle and culture, attitudes and beliefs;
- the therapist should be aware of the pervasiveness of heterosexism/homophobia and the effects of this on clients' lives;
- the therapist should be aware of the socio-political history of LGBT people and the diversity within LGBT communities.

There are other principles that are recommended by different authors, which might not fit with every therapeutic approach, e.g. 'the therapist should support the development of a positive self-identity and LGBT network' (Davies, 1996) which might not fit with less directive therapeutic modalities.

Perhaps one of the most definitive guidelines for working with LGB clients is from the American Psychological Association's Division 44 (the lesbian and gay section) (http://www.apa.org/pi/lgbc/publications/guidelines.html) and for trans clients the World Professional Association for Transgender Health's *Standards of Care for Gender Identity Disorders* (http://www.wpath. org/Documents2/socu6.pdf). In addition, the Australian Psychological Society (2000b) has produced *Ethical guidelines for psychological practice with lesbian, gay and bisexual clients* and the British Association for Counselling and Psychotherapy (BACP) has produced a review of research on counselling and psychotherapy with LGBT clients (King et al., 2007). At the time of writing, the British Psychological Society was in the process of developing a similar guide for LGBT clients in a British context. A measure of how 'gay affirmative' a therapist's practice is has been developed by Crisp (2006) and Dillon and Worthington (2003).

When including these principles in training, you can ask participants to come up with how they will show respect and awareness with clients. This sometimes leads to discussions about disclosure of one's own sexuality if asked by a client, which is covered in the section for LGBT therapists later.

LEGISLATION

The importance of therapists being aware of the historic context and current legislation has been cited by LGBT clients, and is one way of demonstrating an interest and some knowledge of factors affecting LGBT lives. The lesbian and gay timeline produced by Stonewall (pp. 126–128 this chapter) is an easy way of accessing legislative history, but not for trans people. Recent legislative amendments in the UK that are important to mention include:

- 2001 age of consent for gay men lowered to 16 (17 in Northern Ireland) to be equal with heterosexuals;
- 2002 same sex couples allowed to apply for joint adoption (still banned in Scotland);
- 2003 Section 28 repealed (since 1988) which prohibited the 'promotion' of homosexuality;
- 2004 buggery and gross indecency was removed from the Sexual Offences Act.

There has also been new legislation that affects the lives of LGBT people.

- The Civil Partnership Act 2004 – This came into force on 5th December 2005. It allows a legal partnership between two people regardless of gender, having parity of treatment with spouses, including survivor pensions, immigration, equal tax treatment, protection against domestic violence and next of kin rights.
- The Gender Recognition Act 2004 – This allows transgender individuals recognition of their acquired gender and protection under discrimination through the Sex Discrimination Act (1975).
- Equality Act (Sexual Orientation) Regulations 2007 – This came into force on 30th April 2007, prohibiting sexual orientation discrimination in the provision of goods, facilities and services. A consequence of this is that sexuality should now be included in all diversity training provided by employers (the Department of Health (2006) has produced standards for this training for the NHS).

However, despite all these excellent recent changes, there are still ongoing problems for LGBT people living in a discriminatory society.

- Hate crimes against LGBT people remain a common occurrence, e.g. the 1999 Admiral Duncan pub bombing aimed at the gay community; in October 2005, Jody Dobrowski was murdered for being gay. A comprehensive consideration of the heterosexist culture that can support and generate these hate crimes is provided by Herek and Berrill (1992).
- For under 18-year-old LGBTs, Stonewall (Hunt & Jensen, 2006) report that 65 per cent have experienced homophobic bullying in schools (rising to 75 per cent in faith schools), yet only 23 per cent of pupils report that their school gives the clear message that homophobic bulling is wrong. Of those bullied, 92 per cent experienced verbal abuse, 41 per cent physical abuse, 17 per cent had received death threats, 13 per cent threatened with a weapon and 12 per cent sexually assaulted. However, only 58 per cent reported this bullying, and of these reported cases 62 per cent of the time nothing was done. Rivers (2000) writes about the long-term consequences of such bullying at this early, informative age. O'Loan et al. (2006) have produced a comprehensive report about homophobic bullying in Scotland and provide clear guidelines on dealing with this.
- Seventy countries still criminalise same-sex relations, punishment includes the death sentence. Amnesty International campaign against this and have produced various country reports documenting the ill-treatment of LGBT people around the world (http://www.amnesty.org.uk/content.asp?CategoryID=876).

ISSUES FOR LGBT THERAPISTS

LGBT therapists face unique issues when working with LGBT clients. These include clients holding high expectations that the therapist will understand them, as well as the possibility that the clients' fears, anxieties and concerns may be similar to those of the therapist. On a practical level, LGBT communities are small, particularly outside large cities, and so therapists may run into clients at community events (such as film festivals or Pride gatherings). This may lead therapists to feel like they are 'living in a fishbowl', where their best behaviour is expected at all times as their personal life and professional credibility may be linked. Therapists may feel they have to restrict their social life or behaviour at social events, which could lead to resentment and frustration. The importance of preparing for such eventualities is essential, openly discussing with clients the likelihood of running into each other socially and a plan for if this happens.

However, having a plan may require the therapist to disclose their sexuality. There are numerous views on whether this is advisable. One view is that therapists have an ethical responsibility to disclose if a client asks directly. Another view is to find out what difference it will make to the client if the answer is one thing or another, and then decide together if the therapist should disclose. Some therapists, particularly those who work psychoanalytically, suggest that one should never disclose, so that the client can project their own fantasies onto the therapist and these can be worked with. However, more recent psychoanalytic writers have rejected this view and encourage disclosure (e.g. Isay, 1989).

A related point is whether to disclose one's sexuality when doing training. If the trainer is LGBT, they risk feeling exposed or the participants feeling resistant in sharing or checking out ideas that they fear might be prejudiced or incorrect. However, research indicates that contact, or 'exposure', to LGBT individuals is an effective way of reducing prejudice and providing credible information (Peel, 2002). If the trainer is heterosexual, it gives the message that these issues are important for everyone to be aware of, and not just those with a 'vested interest'. Ultimately it is up to the comfort of the trainer to decide, but modelling 'coming out', and doing so at the start of the training, can create an atmosphere of trust and openness to sharing.

Given the smallness of LGBT communities, LGBT therapists may find themselves in dual relationships with clients, defined by the BACP as:

> Dual relationships arise when the practitioner has two or more kinds of relationship concurrently with a client, for example client and trainee, acquaintance and client, colleague and supervisee. The existence of a dual relationship with a client is seldom neutral and can have a powerful beneficial or detrimental impact that may not always be easily foreseeable. For these reasons practitioners are required to consider the

implications of entering into dual relationships with clients, to avoid entering into relationships that are likely to be detrimental to clients, and to be readily accountable to clients and colleagues for any dual relationships that occur.

(BACP, 2007: 5)

Despite these concerns, there might also be some advantages to holding dual relationships with clients. Laura Brown (1984: 15) suggests that this position allows for 'ethics that flow with our interdependencies rather than values that create false dichotomies'. We can therefore be human and real with our clients, although a clear sense of our own boundaries is necessary to remain our professional selves. If running a workshop with LGBT therapists, ask participants what might be some of the complications that dual relationships pose, as well as the advantages? Further exploration of the issue of dual relationships is provided by Gabriel (2005).

USEFUL RESOURCES

LGBT history month is in February each year and is supported by the Department of Health. It recognises and celebrates the contribution of LGBT people in history. (http://www.lgbthistorymonth.org.uk).

The Department of Health has set up a Sexual Orientation and Gender Identity Advisory Group that has commissioned and produced the following resources:

- *Real Stories, Real Lives: LGBT People and The NHS* – a DVD to be used as a practical tool in training staff and raising awareness;
- *An introduction to working with Lesbian, Gay and Bisexual people*;
- *Core Standards for training on Sexual Orientation*;
- *Monitoring of Sexual Orientation in the Health Sector*;
- *Harassment and Sexual Orientation in the Health Sector*;
- *A guide for young trans people in the UK.*

All of these and further resources are found on: http://www.dh.gov.uk/ EqualityAndHumanRights.

Further reading

Feinberg, L. (1996). *Transgender warriors: Making history from Joan of Arc to Dennis Rodman*. Boston: Beacon Press.
Hutchins, L. & Kaahumanu, L. (eds) (1991). *Bi any other name*. Boston: Alyson.
Mole, S. (1995). *Colours of the rainbow: Exploring issues of sexuality and difference. A resource for teachers, governors, parents and carers*. London: Camden Health Promotion Service.

Pierce Buxton, A. (1994). *The other side of the closet: The coming-out crisis for straight spouses and families*. New York: John Wiley & Sons.

Smith, A. & Calvery, J. (2001). *Opening doors: Working with older lesbian and gay men*. London: Age Concern.

Useful websites

Lesbian and Gay

- LGBT Health website
  http://www.healthwithpride.nsh.uk
- PACE
  http://www.pacehealth.org.uk
- Stonewall
  http://www.stonewall.org.uk
- Regard. An organisation for disabled LGBT people.
  http://www.regard.org.uk
- Broken Rainbow. Domestic violence support.
  http://www.broken-rainbow.org.uk
- *LGBT Religious groups*
  Jewish: http://www.jglg.org.uk
  Muslim: http://www.imaan.org.uk/
  Christian: http://www.lgcm.org.uk
  Catholic: http://www.questgaycatholic.org.uk/home.asp
  Buddhist: www.sgi-uk.org/

Transgender

- Gender Trust
  http://www.gendertrust.org.uk
- Press for Change
  http://www.pfc.org.uk
- Beaumont Society
  http://www.beaumontsociety.org.uk
- FTM Network
  http://www.ftm.org.uk
- Gires (Gender Identity Research and Education Society).
  http://www.gires.org.uk

Young people

- Albert Kennedy Trust. LGB youth.
  http://www.akt.org.uk

- Gay Youth UK
  http://www.gayyouth.org.uk
- Mermaids. Trans youth.
  http://www.mermaidsuk.org.uk/

Older people

- Polari
  http://www.casweb.org/polari/
- Age Concern LGBT Project
  http://www.ageconcern.org.uk/AgeConcern/openingdoors.asp

Handout for clients

The following may be useful questions for a client to ask a potential therapist to assess their ability to work in an affirming way with sexual and gender minority clients (adapted from Bettinger, 2001):

- Do you believe that sexual orientation can or should be changed?
- What work have you done to understand your own anti-homosexual bias?
- What specific training have you done to work with sexual or gender minority clients?
- What reading have you done about LGBT psychology/therapy?
- When did you last attend a workshop/seminar on working with sexual or gender minority clients?
- Have you worked with other sexual and gender minority people?

Questions to ask yourself after an initial meeting might be:

- Did you feel a need to hide anything?
- Were you honest?
- Did you need to explain anything about your life to the therapist and how did they receive this? How comfortable were you doing this?
- Do you look forward to talking with the therapist again?

REFERENCES

American Psychiatric Association (1952). *Diagnostic and statistical manual of mental disorders* (1st edn) (DSM-I). Washington, DC: APA.
American Psychiatric Association (1968). *Diagnostic and statistical manual of mental disorders* (2nd edn) (DSM-II). Washington, DC: APA.

American Psychiatric Association (1973). *Diagnostic and statistical manual of mental disorders* (3rd edn) (DSM-III). Washington, DC: APA.

American Psychiatric Association (1987). *Diagnostic and statistical manual of mental disorders* (3rd edn – Revised) (DSM-III-R). Washington, DC: APA.

American Psychiatric Association (1994). *Diagnostic and statistical manual of mental disorders* (4th edn) (DSM-IV). Washington, DC: APA.

American Psychiatric Association (1998). *Reparative therapy* [Position statement]. Washington, DC: APA.

Accoroni, A. (2006). On being straight in LGB places. *The Psychologist*, 19 (1), 20–21.

Australian Psychological Society (2000a). *Position statement on the use of therapies that attempt to change sexual orientation.* Melbourne: Australian Psychological Society.

Australian Psychological Society. (2000b). *Ethical guidelines for psychological practice with lesbian, gay and bisexual clients.* Melbourne: Australian Psychological Society.

Bancroft, J. (1989). *Human sexuality and its problems* (2nd edn). Edinburgh: Churchill Livingstone.

Barlow, D. (1973). Increasing heterosexual responsiveness in the treatment of sexual deviation: A review of the clinical and experimental evidence. *Behaviour Therapy*, 4, 655–671.

Bettinger, M. (2001). *It's your hour: A guide to queer-affirmative psychotherapy.* New York: Alyson Books.

Bieschke, K.J., McClanahan, M., Tozer, E., Grzegorek, J.L. & Park, L. (2000). Programme research on the treatment of lesbian, gay and bisexual clients: The past, the present and the course of the future. In R.M. Perez, K.A. DeBord & K.J. Bieschke (eds), *Handbook of counseling and psychotherapy with lesbian, gay and bisexual clients.* Washington, DC: American Psychological Association.

Blumenfeld, W.J. (1992). *Homophobia: How we all pay the price.* Boston: Beacon Press.

British Association for Counselling and Psychotherapy (BACP) (2007). *Ethical framework for good practice in counselling and psychotherapy.* Leicestershire: BACP.

Brown, L.S. (1984). The lesbian feminist therapist in private practice and her community. *Psychotherapy in Private Practice*, 2 (4), 9–16.

Butler, C. (2004). An awareness-raising tool addressing lesbian and gay lives. *Clinical Psychology*, 36, 15–17.

Butler, C. & Byrne, A. (2007). Queer in practice: Therapy and queer theory. In L. Moon (ed.), *Feeling queer or queer feelings? Radical approaches to counselling sex, sexualities and genders.* London: Routledge.

Butler, J. (1990). *Gender trouble: feminism and the subversion of identity.* New York and London: Routledge.

Cambridge, P. (1997). How far to gay? The politics of HIV in learning disability. *Disability and Society*, 12 (3), 427–453.

Carter, E. & McGoldrick, M. (1980). *The family life cycle: a framework for family therapy.* New York: Gardner Press.

Cass, V.C. (1979). Homosexual identity formation: A theoretical model. *Journal of Homosexuality*, 9, 105–126.

Clarke, V. & Turner, K. (2007). Clothes maketh the queer? Dress, appearance and the construction of lesbian, gay and bisexual identities. *Feminism & Psychology*, 17 (2), 267–276.

Coleman, E. (1982). Developmental stages of the coming out process. *Journal of Homosexuality*, 7, 31–43.

Committee on Homosexual Offences and Prostitution (1957). *Report of the Committee on Homosexual Offences and Prostitution*. London: HMSO.

Cowie, H. & Rivers, I. (2000). Going against the grain: Supporting lesbian, gay and bisexual clients as they 'come out'. *British Journal of Guidance & Counselling*, 28 (4), 503–513.

Crisp, C. (2006). The Gay Affirmative Practice Scale (GAP): a new measure for assessing cultural competence with gay and lesbian clients. *Social Work*, 51 (2), 115–126.

D'Augelli, A.R. (1994). Identity development and sexual orientation: toward a model of lesbian, gay and bisexual development. In E.J. Trickett, R.J. Watts & D. Birman (eds), *Human Diversity: Perspective on people in context*. San Francisco: Jossey-Bass.

D'Augelli, A.R. & Patternson, C.J. (eds) (1994). *Lesbian, gay and bisexual identities over the lifespan*. New York: Oxford University Press.

Davies, D. (1996) Working with people coming out. In D. Davies & C. Neal, (eds), *Pink therapy: A guide for counsellors and therapists working with lesbian, gay and bisexual clients*. Buckingham: Open University Press.

Davies, D. & Neal, C. (eds) (1996). *Pink therapy: A guide for counsellors and therapists working with lesbian, gay and bisexual clients*. Buckingham: Open University Press.

Davies, D. & Neal, C. (2000). *Pink therapy 2: Therapeutic perspectives on working with lesbian, gay and bisexual clients*. Buckingham: Open University Press.

Denman, C. (2004). *Sexuality: A biopsychosocial approach*. Basingstoke: Palgrave Macmillan.

Department of Health (2006). *Core training standards for sexual orientation: Making national health services inclusive for LGB people*. London: Department of Health.

Department of Trade and Industry (2006). *Departmental Report*. Norwich: Department of Trade and Industry.

Di Ceglie, D. (2000). Gender identity disorder in young people. *Advances in Psychiatric Treatment*, 6, 458–466.

Dillon, F.R. & Worthington, R.L. (2003). The Lesbian, Gay and Bisexual Affirmative Counseling Self-Efficacy Inventory (LGB-CSI): development, validation and training implications. *Journal of Counseling Psychology*, 50 (2), 235–251.

Division of Clinical Psychology (DCP) (2007). *Good practice guidelines for the training and consolidation of clinical psychology practice in HIV/sexual health settings*. Leicester: British Psychological Society.

Drescher, J. (1999). *Psychoanalytic therapy and the gay man*. New York: Haworth Press.

Drescher, J., D'Ercole, A. & Schoenberg, E. (eds) (2003). *Psychotherapy with gay men and lesbians: Contemporary dynamic approaches*. New York: Haworth Press.

Ellis, A. (1965). *Homosexuality: Its causes and cure*. New York: Lyle Stuart.

Ellis, A. (1976). *Sex and the liberated man*. New York: Lyle Stuart.

Ellis, A. (2001). *Sex without guilt in the twenty-first century*. New Jersey: Barricade Books.

Foucault, M. (1972). *The archaeology of knowledge and the discourse on language*. New York: Pantheon.

Gabriel, L. (2005). *Speaking the unspeakable: The ethics of dual relationships in counselling and psychotherapy*. Hove: Routledge.

Gabriel, L. & Davies, D. (2000). Management of ethical dilemmas. In C. Neal & D. Davies (eds), *Pink therapy 3: Issues in therapy with lesbian, gay, bisexual and transgender clients*. Buckingham: Open University Press.

Godfrey, K., Haddock, S.A., Fisher, A. & Lund, L. (2006). Essential components of curricula for preparing therapists to work effectively with lesbian, gay and bisexual clients: a Delphi study. *Journal of Marital and Family Therapy*, 32 (4), 491–504.

Hegarty, P. (2006). Where's the sex in sexual prejudice? *Lesbian & Gay Review*, 7 (3), 264–275.

Herek, G.M. (1986). On heterosexual masculinity: Some psychical consequences of the social construction of gender and sexuality. *American Behavioral Scientist*, 29, 563–577.

Herek, G.M. (1999). AIDS and stigma. *American Behavioral Scientist*, 42 (7), 1105–1103.

Herek, G.M. & Berrill, K.T. (eds) (1992). *Hate crimes: Confronting violence against lesbians and gay men*. London: Sage.

Hovell, L. & Davidson, S. (in press). Constructions of gender identity: Dilemmas in health settings. *Journal of Health Psychology*.

Hughes, T.L. & Eliason, M. (2002). Substance use and abuse in lesbian, gay, bisexual and transgender populations. *Journal of Primary Prevention*, 22 (3), 263–298.

Hunt, R. & Jensen, J. (2006). The school report: The experiences of young gay people in Britain's schools. London: Stonewall.

International Commission of Jurists & International Services for Human Rights (2007). *The Yogyakarta Principles on the application of international human rights law in relation to sexual orientation and gender identity*. http://www.yogyakarta-principles.org.

Isay, R. (1989). *Being homosexual: Gay men and their development*. New York: Avon Books.

Keogh, P., Dodds, C. & Henderson, L. (2004). *Working class gay men: Redefining community, restoring identity*. London: Sigma Research.

King, M., McKeown, E., Warner, J., Ramsay, A., Johnson, K., Cort, C., Wright, L., Blizard, R. & Davidson, O. (2003). Mental health and quality of life of gay men and lesbians in England and Wales: controlled, cross-sectional study. *British Journal of Psychiatry*, 183, 552–558.

King, M., Semylen, J., Killaspy, H., Nazareth, I. & Osborn, D. (2007). *A systematic review of research on counselling and psychotherapy for lesbian, gay, bisexual & transgender people*. Leicestershire: BACP.

Kinsey, A.C., Pomeroy, W.B. & Martin, A.C. (1948). *Sexual behaviour in the human male*. Philadelphia: W.B. Saunders.

Kinsey, A.C., Pomeroy, W.B. & Martin, A.C. (1953). *Sexual behaviour in the human female*. Philadelphia: W.B. Saunders.

Kitzinger, C. & Perkins, R. (1993). *Changing our minds: Lesbian feminism and psychology.* London: Onlywomen Press.

Klein, F., Sepekoff, B. & Wolf, T. (1985). Sexual orientation: A multi-variable dynamic process. *Journal of Homosexuality,* 11, 35–49.

Klein, F. (1993). *The bisexual option* (2nd edn). New York: Haworth Press.

Kort, J. (2007). *Gay affirmative therapy for the straight clinician.* New York: Norton.

Kutchins, H. & Kirk, S.A. (1999). *Making us crazy: DSM – The psychiatric bible and the creation of mental disorders.* London: Constable.

Langdridge, D. & Barker, M. (2007). *Safe, sane and consensual.* Basingstoke: Palgrave.

Langdridge, D. (2007). Are you angry or are you heterosexual? In L. Moon (ed.), *Feeling queer or queer feelings?* London: Routledge.

Long, J.K. (1996). Working with lesbians, gays and bisexuals: Addressing heterosexism in supervision. *Family Process,* 35, 377–388.

McFarlane, L. (1998). *Diagnosis: Homophobic.* London: PACE.

Malley, M. & Tasker, F. (1999). Lesbians, gay men and family therapy: A contradiction in terms? *Journal of Family Therapy,* 21 (1), 3–29.

Martell, C.R., Safren, S.A. & Prince, S.E. (2004). *Cognitive-behavioural therapies with lesbian, gay and bisexual clients.* New York: Guilford Press.

Masters, W.H. & Johnson, V.E. (1979). *Homosexuality in perspective.* New York: Bantam Books.

Maturana, H & Varela, F. (1986). *Tree of knowledge: Biological roots of human understanding.* London: Shambhala Publishers.

Morgan, L. & Bell, N. (2003). *First out . . . findings of the beyond barriers survey of lesbian, gay, bisexual and transgender people in Scotland.* Glasgow: Beyond Barriers.

Milton, M. (1998). *Issues in psychotherapy with lesbian and gay men: A survey of British psychologists.* Occasional Paper, Vol. 4. Leicester: BPS Division of Counselling Psychology.

Nicolosi, J. (1991). *Reparative therapy of male homosexuality: A new clinical approach.* Northvale, NJ: Jason Aronson Inc.

O'Connor, N. & Ryan, J. (1993). *Wild desires and mistaken identities: Lesbianism and psychoanalysis.* London: Virago.

O'Loan, S., McMillan, F., Motherwell, S., Bell, A. & Arshad, R. (2006). Guidance on dealing with homophobic bullying. Edinburgh: Scottish Government. http://www.scotland.gov.uk/Publications/2006/05/25091604/0.

Padesky, C. (1989). Attaining and maintaining positive lesbian self-identity: A cognitive therapy approach. *Women and Therapy,* 8, 145–156.

Peel, L. (2002). Lesbian and gay awareness training: challenging homophobia, liberalism and managing stereotypes. In A. Coyle & C. Kitzinger (eds), *Lesbian and gay psychology: New perspectives.* London: Blackwell.

Person, E. & Ovesey, L. (1978). Transvestism: New perspectives. *Journal of the American Academy of Psychoanalysis,* 6 (3), 301–323.

Ritter, K.Y. & Terndrup, A.I. (2002). *Handbook of affirmative psychotherapy with lesbians and gay men.* New York: Guilford Press.

Rivers, I. (1997). Lesbian, gay and bisexual development: Theory, research and social issues. *Journal of Community & Applied Social Psychology,* 7, 329–343.

Rivers, I. (2000). Long term consequences of bullying. In C. Neal & D. Davies, *Pink therapy Vol 3: Issues in therapy with lesbian, gay, bisexual and transgender clients.* Buckingham: Open University Press.

Roberts, J. (2005). Transparency and self-disclosure in family therapy: dangers and possibilities. *Family Process*, 44 (1), 45–63.

Rochlin, M. (1992). The heterosexual questionnaire. In W.J. Blumenfeld (ed.), *Homophobia: How we all pay the price*. Boston: Beacon Press.

Savin-Williams, R.C. (1990). *Gay and lesbian youths: Expressions of identity.* Washington, DC: Hemisphere.

Shaw, E., Butler, C. & Marriot, C. (2008). Sex and sexuality teaching in UK clinical psychology courses. *Clinical Psychology Forum*, 187, 7–11.

Shidlo, A., Schroeder, M. & Drescher, L. (2002). *Sexual conversion therapy: Ethical, clinical and research perspectives*. New York: Haworth Medical Press.

Simon, G. & Whitfield, G. (1995). *A discourse-in-progress: Gay affirmative practice and a critical therapy*. Paper presented at the Association of Lesbian, Gay and Bisexual Psychologies conference, University of Nottingham.

Socarides, C.W. (1963). The historical development of theoretical and clinical concepts of overt female homosexuality. *Journal of American Psychoanalytic Association*, 11, 386–414.

Spellman, D. (1999). To boldly know . . . and not know, about heterosexual dominance. *Journal of Family Therapy*, 21, 55–59.

Wagner, G., Brondolo, E. & Rabkin, J. (1996). Internalised homophobia in a sample of HIV+ gay men, and its relationship to psychological distress, coping, and illness progression. *Journal of Homosexuality*, 32 (2), 91–106.

Whittle, S. (2006). *Transphobia – what it is and what is its impact*. Address to the Transgender Pre-Conference of the 23rd ILGA World Conference. http://www.pfc.org.uk/node/1265.

Wilson, G. & Rahman, Q. (2005). *Born gay: The psychobiology of sex orientation.* London: Peter Owen.

Woodman, N.J. & Lenna, H.R. (1980). *Counseling with gay men and women*. San Francisco: Jossey-Bass.

World Health Organization (1992). The ICD-10 Classification of Mental and Behavioural Disorders: Clinical Descriptions and Diagnostic Guidelines. Geneva: WHO.

APPENDIX 1: HOMOWORLD

First printed in *Clinical Psychology Forum* (2004), 36, 15–17 (reprinted with permission by the British Psychological Society).

You wake up to the sound of your radio alarm dedicating songs to same sex couples:

- Jolene, please don't take my woman;
- When a man loves a man . . .

As you sit to have breakfast you gaze blankly at the cereal packet depicting the bonuses of its vitamins and minerals as played out by a family running through a cornfield: two dads, their son and a red setter. You briefly flick on Breakfast TV to catch the end of Richard and Jimmy discussing the latest face make up available for drag queens.

You leave for work, passing some of your neighbours saying goodbye on the way: Melissa and Iris and further down the street John and Mike. As you sit on the tube you look around you at the ads to pass the time: cheaper travel insurance for same-sex couples, the wonderbra ad: 'Come on girls'. At the next stop a man enters the tube and something about him you can't put your finger on makes you suspect he is also heterosexual. He glances over and spots you and smiles the smile of recognition. You think 'I can tell you're straight too, but maybe no one else here has noticed!'. You might laugh to yourself and enjoy the exclusivity of the contact.

Arriving at work, one of the admin staff is showing pictures of her holiday she just took with her girlfriend in Lesbos. As you join the group to look at the photos you get asked 'Where did you take your last holiday?' Do you admit it was Corfu, a destination well known for its heterosexual holidays, and do you say who you went with?

You start your working day and see your first client. During the session the client discusses her excitement at having found a sperm donor through one of the many agencies set up to match potential parents with similar outlooks on parenting. Can you relate to this and share her joy? She makes the comment: 'you know what it's like, it takes so much thought, time and testing to find the right match. Finally I found someone who wants to be there to talk through decisions but agrees to let me have the final word'. How do you feel admitting to yourself that you don't fundamentally know what its like, that for you it would just be a case of stopping using birth control? The thought rekindles the awkwardness you felt finding one of only two clinics in London set up to provide birth control. The stigma you might have felt walking towards it through the hospital grounds, surely everyone must know that's where the heteros go? The condescending looks of the receptionist as she asks you loudly whether you have used the service before and would you prefer your GP not to be informed. You might find these thoughts and memories interrupting your session. Do you take this to supervision? Does your supervisor even know that you are straight? Do you know what your supervisor's personal feelings are about it? Do you fear your supervisor might be secretly pathologising you? These thoughts make you remember that you will be changing placements in a few months. You briefly hope the next team will be more accepting.

At the end of the day people are going for a drink at the nearest gay bar on the corner. Some are bringing partners. Do you invite yours, knowing there will be staff there you are not out to? Staff whose response to your heterosexuality you cannot be sure of. Or do you go for a few hours and then leave to travel into central London and the straight ghetto of Old Brompton Street? But maybe you just want a quiet drink as you are tired and you know Old Brompton Street will be full of pumping Celine Dion and boozed pint drinkers. With no real alternative, you decide to head home. Just as you have made the decision your partner texts to say he will meet you at the tube as he is leaving for home now too. As you smile a member of staff you don't know well catches your eye and says, 'That from your girlfriend? What's her name?' Do you come out, lie or say you're much too busy to be in a relationship? You wonder what their response would be if you did come out:

- full acceptance;
- a total lack of interest and changing the subject due to embarrassment;
- or else they might imagine they now have licence to ask you a list of overtly personal questions because 'some their best friends are straight' and they've even been in a straight bar so they really don't have a problem with it, e.g.
  'So how long have you known you were straight?'
  'What a waste, I would never have guessed you were straight.'
  'Do your parents know?'
  'Is the sex better?'
  'What do you actually do in bed anyway?'

Finally you reach your home tube station and as promised your boyfriend is there to meet you. You feel a flood of relief at seeing him, realising how tired you are. But do you greet him with a kiss with all these people still around? As you walk home you both have to walk down a quiet street. You start to hold hands, glad of the contact. However, unexpectedly a group of youths rounds the next corner and you let go. Did they see the contact? Are they going to say anything, heckle you? Worse still, is this a potentially violent situation? You both stare at the floor as you walk past.

Safe behind closed doors at last, you decide to order a pizza. Your partner is in the kitchen when the doorbell rings and doesn't realise you've already opened it. He shouts 'I'll get that darling' and you notice the pizza delivery boy trying to hide a laugh as your boyfriend bounds into the hall behind you.

As you curl up on the sofa you flick on the TV to see if anything is on. Nothing matches your mood:

- BBC1: the film *When Harry met Henry*.
- BBC2: A review of the contemporary version of *Romeo and Jonathan* at the Young Vic.
- ITV: American funniest home videos special on commitment ceremonies.
- CH 4: *Big Brother*, the episode where the straight person comes out to a fanfare of questions.
- CH 5: *Better Gay Sex*.

You flick through a copy of *The Blue Paper* (the free 'straight' paper about the scene), which you remembered to pick up last time you were in the centre of town as you can't get it locally. You are amused by the rally to join a kiss-in protest after a straight couple were asked to leave the airport lounge following their public display of affection. However, you become disheartened as you read that Clause 29 has once more not been voted out by the House of Commons, their fear being that if straight relationships are even acknowledged to exist by schools it might result in young girls wanting to experiment with older men, or boys with older women. 'This country needs to uphold the same-sex values that made it strong' and are reflected in its tax benefits.

You finally decide to turn in, deciding not to read any more of your Mary Sheldon novel which you bought excitedly because it actually featured a straight character in its subplot. However, you've gone off the book since you found the character was a shallow representation of straight clichés.

The end of another day in Homoworld!

APPENDIX 2: FILMS TO CONSIDER USING IN TRAINING

If These Walls Could Talk 2

Three lesbian stories are shown in different time periods in the same house. The first is set in the early 1960s and shows the devastating impact of the death of a woman whose family do not accept her lesbian relationship, and so the surviving woman is threatened with losing their shared home in addition to her partner. The second story is set in the early 1970s and illustrates the politics of butch/femme dichotomies pertinent to feminism at that time. The final story is a light-hearted modern day yarn of a lesbian couple trying various ways to have a baby.

The Gay Rock and Roll Years

This film shows how lesbians and gays have been represented in films through out the history of cinema. Early footage of lesbians and gay men in distress or being blackmailed because of their sexuality can illustrate how things have changed.

TransAmerica

The film starts with a description of the expensive and complex body modification procedures that male to female transexuals undertake before they have gender reassignment surgery. It demonstrates the need for psychiatric approval to undergo the surgery and how disempowered this can make clients feel. Later in the film a family's response to a transitioning woman is depicted and her difficulty in being accepted in her new gendered identity.

Boys Don't Cry

This film is about a young woman living as a man in mid-country America without access to transsexual communities or surgery. The film shows the hatred that gender variant people can experience from others, which results in extreme violence and murder.

Brokeback Mountain

This film also depicts mid-America but through the experiences of two male cowboys who fall in love. Both men marry to try and live a heterosexual lifestyle but continue to meet regularly at Brokeback Mountain. The film contains many touching scenes and speeches of the intensity of their feelings for each other within a context that makes it impossible to be together.

But I'm a Cheerleader

This film is about an American high school student whose friends know she is a lesbian before she does. The start of the film has excellent examples of lesbian stereotypes (e.g. being vegetarian) that they confront her with to make their point. The latter part of the film shows a conversion therapy centre.

APPENDIX 3: SEXUAL MINORITY TIMELINE

1 **1935** Freud normalises homosexuality and bisexuality in therapy.
2 **1948** Alfred Kinsey publishes *Sexual Behaviour in the Human Male* and *Sexual Behaviour in the Human Female*, suggesting a continuum between homosexuality and heterosexuality.
3 **1954** In the UK the Home Secretary appoints the Wolfenden Committee and this reports in 1957 and recommends that homosexual acts between consenting adults in private should no longer be illegal based on arguments that the law was impractical rather than not immoral and the age of consent set at 21. Supported by the Archbishop of Canterbury, the British Medical Association and National Association of Probation Officers.
4 **1966** Martin Seligman uses aversion therapy to change sexual orientation.
5 **1967** Sexual Offences Act receives Royal Assent, partially decriminalises sex between men aged over 21 in England and Wales.
6 **1968** Charles Socarides uses psychoanalytic theory to promote reparative therapy.
7 **1969** Stonewall riots start gay rights movement in the USA.
8 **1969** Word 'homophobia' appears in print in American *Time* magazine.
9 **1970** The first meeting of London Gay Liberation Front.
10 **1973** The American Psychiatric Association removes homosexuality from a list of mental disorders.
11 **1979** Michael Foucault writes about anti-essentialist notions of sexual identity suggesting sexuality is socially constructed.
12 **1981** HIV first named and safer sex emerges.
13 **1982** Homosexual orientation decriminalised in Northern Ireland with the passing of a law reform in the House of Commons.
14 **1986** DSM and American Psychiatric Association removes all references to homosexuality as a psychiatric disorder.
15 **1987** In the UK Section 28 of the Local Government Act, preventing the 'promotion of homosexual orientation' by local authorities with help of Local Government Minister Michael Howard.
16 **1989** Stonewall lobbying group established in response to the introduction of Section 28.
17 **1990** Term 'queer theory' first used at a conference in California by Theresa De Laurentis.
18 **1990** Term 'heterosexism' coined by Herek.
19 **1992** Nicolosi, Socarides and Kaufman found National Association for Research and Therapy of Homosexuality.
20 **1992** WHO *ICD* drops classification of homosexuality as a mental disorder.

21 **1994** In the UK the age of consent between two men is reduced from 21 to 18. An amendment to reduce to 16 is defeated in the House of Commons.

22 **1996** *Pink Therapy* published in the UK, by Davies and Neal.

23 **1997** In the UK Government immigration policy recognises same-sex couples under certain conditions.

24 **1998** In the UK the age of consent for sex between two men is reduced to 16 in House of Commons but not Lords.

25 **1998** BPS Division of Counselling Psychology surveys its members' attitudes and practices of working with lesbian and gay clients.

26 **1999** In the UK the Law Lords rule that same-sex partners are entitled to the same tenancy rights as a heterosexual spouse.

27 **2000** The American Psychological Association produces guidelines for psychotherapy with lesbian, gay and bisexual clients.

28 **2000** The Australian Psychological Society produces *Ethical Guidelines for Psychological Practice with Lesbian, Gay and Bisexual Clients*.

29 **2000** In the UK a new code of conduct is introduced by the army following the removal of the ban on lesbian and gay men serving in the armed forces.

30 **2000** The Sexual Offences (Amendment) Act 2000 came into force, reducing the minimum age of consent from 18 to 16 in England and Wales, and making male rape a criminal offence.

31 **2002** *Handbook of Affirmative Psychotherapy* by Ritter and Terndrup published.

32 **2002** In the UK unmarried and gay couples are given the right through Parliament to adopt.

33 **2003** In the UK Section 28 of the Local Government Act is repealed after 15 years.

34 **2003** In the UK Employment Equality (Sexual Orientation) Regulations became law making it illegal to discriminate against lesbians, gay men and bisexuals in the workplace.

35 **2004** In the UK the Civil Partnerships Act receives Royal Assent.

36 **2004** In the UK the Gender Recognition Act provides transgender people with legal recognition in acquired gender, subject to some specified exceptions.

37 **2005** In the UK Section 146 of the Criminal Justice Act 2003 is implemented, empowering courts to impose tougher sentences for offences aggravated or motivated by the victim's sexual orientation.

38 **2005** In the UK the introduction of the Adoption and Children Act gives wide-ranging rights to same-sex couples wishing to adopt a child.

39 **2006** In the UK the Equality Act makes inclusion of LGB staff and user/patients within health and social care a requirement.

40 **2007** The Faculty of HIV/Sexual Health of the Division of Clinical Psychology (DCP) of the BPS write best practice guidance for the

training of clinical psychologists in sex and sexuality and surveys the training course provision.

41 **2007** BPS sets up a working party to develop guidelines for working clinically with sexual minority clients on request of the Faculty of HIV and Sexual Health of the DCP.

42 **2007** *The Yogakarta Principles on the Application of International Human Rights Law in Relation to Sexual Orientation and Gender Identity* is published (International Commission of Jurists & International Services for Human Rights).

43 **2008** Pink Therapy starts a certificate course in sexual minorities therapy.

Chapter 5

Sex and sexuality across the lifespan

Amanda O'Donovan

> The distinction between children and adults, whilst probably useful for some purposes, is at heart a specious one, I feel. There are only individual egos, crazy for love.
>
> Niccolo Macchiavelli

INTRODUCTION

Sexuality is present in one form or another from birth. Sexual impulses and responses are ubiquitous across all ages and ideas around sensuality, and our relationships with our bodies, begin to be formed in infancy and evolve throughout life. As with all areas of sex and sexuality, assumptions and prejudices can narrowly construct ideas of 'normal' functioning across the age ranges and can be limiting and unhelpful. This chapter provides an overview of issues of sex and sexuality at various points of the lifespan from childhood, adolescence and adulthood through to old age. It also aims to guide reflection on our own expectations about sex and sexuality at different life stages as well as exploring developmental influences that affect sexual identity. These understandings can usefully inform our therapeutic work and having an awareness of developmental and lifespan contexts can helpfully inform and enrich our conversations about sex and sexuality in the therapeutic context.

Sex and sexuality over the course of our own lifetimes

Before exploring ideas around developmental perspectives it may be useful to reflect on the contexts that have enriched and informed the narratives you hold currently about sex and sexuality. Meanings attached to sex and sexuality are shaped by age, gender, developmental stage, social and cultural contexts. These different contexts have varying levels of influence or dominance at different points in our lives.

During childhood in most Western societies, families, parents, carers and media are the most influential. In adolescence, the dominant influences on self and sexuality shift from being family-led to that of peers and friends. In adulthood, in addition to the wealth of previous experiences outlined above, partners, intimate relationships and expectations about social roles shape narratives about sex and sexuality.

The following exercise reflects on the influences that have shaped your ideas and expectations about sex and sexuality over different periods of your life. It may also be helpful to think about how broader societal beliefs and expectations may have shifted over your lifespan in similar or different directions to your own. Although focusing on the developmental context, as Davidson (2000: 168) observes 'it is important to keep in mind how these interact with other cultural and sub-cultural factors contributing to a person's overall sexual identity'.

Exercise 5.1 What influences our ideas about sex?

This exercise can be done either as individual self-reflection, or within small groups or pairs (given the sensitive nature of this topic it may not be appropriate to feed back to a larger group for discussion).

Consider what have been the main influences on your own sexuality and sexual development throughout your life.

1   Who or what were the main influences that shaped your ideas about your body, sensuality and sexuality: as a child? as a teenager? as an adult?
    You may want to think about different areas of sex and sexuality such as erotic fantasies, self-identification (e.g. sexual orientation), sexual attraction, sexual behaviour and preferences, primary relationships etc. For instance your views on relationships may be similar to those of your parents (i.e. committed monogamous heterosexual) but you may hold different ideas around sexual behaviours (i.e. erotic expression, sadomasochism, oral sex).

2   How have ideas about male/female sexuality changed over your lifetime? What have been the dominant discourses or assumptions about sex and sexuality over these decades? How are your ideas or experiences of sex and sexuality similar or different to these? (e.g. ideas from the 1950s about gender roles, feminist movement of the 1970s, Brazilian waxing and recreational pole dancing classes in the 2000s etc.).
    Identifying the main influences on our experiences of sex and sexuality at different periods of our lives can enrich and inform

the narratives we hold about sex and sexuality currently. Reflecting on our own sexuality and how it is positioned according to dominant cultural expectations about sex can be helpful in understanding experiences of normality and difference. Becoming aware of the cultural contexts that shape sexual behaviour can also be helpful in thinking about the use of diagnostic labels in the areas of sex and sexuality and how these too are products of particular social and historical contexts.

SEX AND SEXUALITY IN INFANCY AND CHILDHOOD

Babies are sensual creatures and experience and understand the world through their direct physical experience of it. Parents' and carers' touch and voices, along with the sensations of strong biological drives, powerfully shape our early experiences. As babies grow and develop a sense of self they begin to explore their bodies and learn to differentiate their physical body from the rest of the world through their senses of vision, taste and touch. Babies are tactile beings and desire physical closeness and affection and derive comfort from contact with parents and carers, fulfilling important developmental needs.

Concepts of sexuality that broadly encompass sensuality, experience of physical affection, emotional regulation and relationship to the physical body begin to be formed in infancy and evolve throughout life. Secure and affectionate relationships with caregivers are an essential part of the ability to form close and loving relationships as adults and sexual expression as an adult has been found to relate to attachment style (Davis et al., 2004; Birnbaum, et al., 2006; Horne & Biss, 2009). Attachment style is related to overall sexual motivation and motives for sex, with the exception of physical pleasure, which is ubiquitous across all attachment styles. As may be anticipated, adults with anxious attachment styles are more likely to seek sex to meet emotional needs such as intimacy and reassurance than are individuals with avoidant styles.

As babies grow into childhood, they continue to explore their bodies and this body and genital awareness is often accompanied by awareness of their parents' bodies at preschool age. Preschool children also develop knowledge around gender identity, genital differences and sexual body parts. Some small studies in Western settings have found that parental nudity and positive attitudes to sex and sexuality have been found to have some positive effect on children's long-term adjustment and sexual functioning (Lewis & Janda, 1988; Okami et al., 1998).

When babies explore and come to know their own bodies, they do not distinguish between exploration of their genitalia and exploration of other body parts. Masturbation, or seeking pleasurable feelings through touch, may begin as soon as an infant discovers his or her genitals. These behaviours may be met with alarm, embarrassment or disapproval by parents who may construct this as dirty or wrong. Children may come to internalise these negative feelings of shame or guilt that may then shape future sexual development or expression. However, this early exploration is part of developing a healthy sexuality and considered to be normal by therapists although it is frequently discouraged or punished in many cultures (Keighley, 2002).

Sexual feelings in children are normal and healthy. Becoming familiar with ideas linked to healthy expressions of sexuality in childhood is an important way of understanding our own sexuality and sexual experience, as well as those of our clients and enables richer conversations to be had about sex and sexuality in the early years of life. However, there are often many anxieties or difficulties in talking and thinking about childhood sexuality and it is often ignored, considered inappropriate or seen as a taboo subject. Currently, one of the most common contexts in which children and sex are discussed are pathological experiences such as child abuse and paedophilia. This problem-saturated focus is echoed in conversations about childhood sexuality that are limited to issues of risk and protection of children. Broader conversations about body exploration and positive accounts of sensual and sexual experience should be part of clinical and broader cultural conversations about childhood sexuality.

STAGES OF SEXUAL DEVELOPMENT

Our understandings of sexual development across the lifespan are informed by early work in this area. One of the most influential models of sexual development is Freud's account of psychosexual stages that closely linked the development of the sex drive (libido) to the formation of personality. Freud in 1905 described five of these psychosexual stages, which were centred on erogenous zones of the body (see Box 5.1). Freud theorised that the pursuit of pleasure and avoidance of pain drives the infant to explore his or her body and the world and in psychoanalytic explanations, seeking pleasure is perceived as inextricably linked to sexual gratification (Freud, 1962).

Although well known and widely referenced, these stages of development are only one conceptualisation of this process and many other positions question the fixed nature of the stages or the Freudian repressive hypotheses that underly them. Foucault (1978), among others, asserts that sex does not need to be 'investigated' in order to understand it, rather we

---

Box 5.1 Freud's psychosexual stages of development

1 **Oral phase** (birth to 2 years). The baby focuses on the tongue, lips, and mouth and derives gratification from breastfeeding and sucking, biting, swallowing and other oral exploratory activities. Weaning represents the first conflict between mother and infant.

2 **Anal stage** (2 to 4 years). The baby is aware of sensation and pleasure of the anus and bowel movements including defecating and retaining faeces. Toilet training may be the first time an infant receives disapproval from parents or carers.

3 **Phallic stage** (3 to 5 years). The genitals are the focus of pleasurable experience. Within the psychoanalytic framework these sensations are coupled with sexual desire directed at the opposite sex parent. The child competes with the same-sex parent for the desired parent's attention – boys compete for their mother's attention (Oedipal complex) and girls compete for their father's attention (Electra complex).

4 **Latent sexuality** (6 – puberty). The phallic stage is followed by 6 to 7 years of latent sexuality that is then rekindled in puberty. Children at this stage often engage in games of show and tell or exploration. Sexual impulses are sublimated and children engage in same-sex friendships.

5 **Genital phase** (adolescence). This stage is a period of physical growth and personal development. Sexual needs and impulses are reawakened. The adolescent and young adult invests sexual energy in, and seeks sexual gratification from, others. The child's own body is no longer the only source of sexual pleasure. This object-relatedness is sometimes referred to as 'mature love'!

---

should explore why we currently place so much emphasis on sexuality. This repressive power can be understood not as something that holds our desires down but rather it is responsible for setting the context and thereby creating these desires.

Developmental descriptions of psychosexual development emphasise the role of learning and socialisation (see Box 5.2). Along with the physical and emotional milestones that are reached in early development, important learning occurs in how we experience and relate to our bodies and how we form attachments to others. These relationships to self and others shape our experiences of intimacy and sex in later life. Although these key experiences can be conceived of as stages of sexual development, there is a huge amount of individual and cultural variation in how and when (and if) these experiences occur. Kohlberg (1966) applied Piaget's developmental

Box 5.2 Early psychosexual development

0–2 years. Gender assigned to infant. Physical intimacy and emotional attachment develop between parents/carers and infants. Positive physical sensations are associated with feeling loved and secure. Learning and curiosity about own body including touching and exploration of genitalia.

2–3 years. Awareness of difference between boys and girls. Development of gender identity as children start to identify as being male or female. Learning culturally defined gender roles as children begin to associate particular behaviours and characteristics with being male or female.

3–5 years. Strong sense of gender identity has developed in most children. Body and genital exploration continues and can learn that genital touching is normal and pleasurable but they should do it in private. Also learn ownership of their bodies and that they can set limits around touch. Learning about nudity and gender continues.

6–11 years. Peer groups are often the same gender. Friends and media influence sexual attitudes. Interest and natural curiosity about ideas around pregnancy, birth, sex and gender roles. Learning occurs around these issues as well as exploration of attraction towards others.

Puberty. Period of considerable physical, emotional and social development. Sexual interest in others and interest in relationships and physical and sexual intimacy increases. Considerable uncertainty and confusion related to these changes and related to comparison with others and reassurance seeking.

framework to understanding of gender development and these stages of gender identity are outlined above. The theory underlying these stages has been supplemented with ideas drawn from social learning theory (Bandura, 1986) and social-constructionist theory. Cultural factors clearly play a strong role in the development of gender role (Keighley, 2002). There is also growing evidence of the complexity of interactions between physical and biological factors in human gender development. For example, high prenatal androgen levels have been found to affect children's behaviour in ways that are constructed as gender related (e.g. levels of rough and tumble play, toy choice) (Berenbaum & Hines, 1992; Servin *et al.*, 2003).

As children become increasingly aware of and interested in their sexuality, this is enacted in play and peer relationships. Sexual exploration games between young children are very common with an estimated fifty to eighty-five per cent of children playing these games including 'kiss-chase', fantasy sexual play, exposure of genitals or bodies or stimulation of genitals

(Lamb & Coakley, 1993; Okami *et al.*, 1997). This play can occur within and between genders and is unrelated to later sexual orientation. All of these experiences of sexual play may shape adult sexuality in an unhelpful way if experienced as shameful, unpleasant or upsetting. Lamb and Coakley (1993) found a strong relationship between coercive or manipulative experiences that were felt to be abusive and cross-gender play and reflected that power and domination played out in childhood games may mirror wider social inequalities.

LEARNING ABOUT SEX AND SEXUALITY

Childhood is also a time where children begin to learn about sex, reproduction and their bodies. Early messages about sex and sexuality can have significant effects on sexuality later in life (e.g. sex is painful/dangerous, masturbation is a sin), particularly if they are echoed or reinforced by other social or cultural narratives. There is consistent evidence that provision of good sex education before young people become sexually active leads to a delay in the onset of sexual activity and to increased sexual well-being in later life (Baldo *et al.*, 1993; Berman *et al.*, 2001). Sex and relationship education (SRE) that encompasses learning about sex, sexuality, emotions, relationships, sexual health and ourselves, is now accepted as being an essential part of early social and biological education and has recently been made mandatory in the UK (Young London Matters, 2009). There is also a need for provision of information about how gender roles influence men and women's behaviours and sexual expectation as these contexts can exert more influence on sexual expression, desire and arousal than physiological factors themselves (Tolman, 2001).

In older childhood and adolescence, learning should encompass relevant knowledge and information about sex and sexuality and also the necessary skills such as assertiveness and negotiation to be able to engage in safe sexual behaviour (Health Protection Agency (HAP), 2008) and promote sexual well-being. Exercise 5.2 encourages the reader to reflect on their own learning about sex.

Exercise 5.2 How did you learn about sex?

Consider the following questions about how you learned about sex. This exercise can be done in pairs or individually. As always consider how comfortable individuals may be in sharing their responses if working in larger groups. These questions can also be useful clinically in thinking about early formative experiences and developing understandings about a client's sexual identity and beliefs about their own sexuality.

1   When did you first learn about sex? Where were you? How old were you?
2   What information were you told (or not told)? What questions did you ask (or not ask)? What kind of language was used (factual, slang, metaphor)?
3   What were the main sources of information from which you learned about sex e.g. parents, siblings, peers, school, movies? How did your parents talk to you about sex?
4   How did your early sex education affect your experience of sex – as an adolescent/as a young adult/later in life?

As when working clinically, there are no 'right' answers. You may want to reflect on how your responses might affect your work.

- What would enable you to manage your own understandings about sex and sexuality in order to work effectively with clients?
- Do you feel you have good enough information about sex and sexuality to discuss these areas with clients?
- Do you feel you need to be 'expert' in this area to talk about it in your clinical work?

As talking about sex and sexuality often raises anxieties in therapist and clients alike, you may be more aware of concerns about 'getting it right'. However, just as you don't need to be an expert in all areas of religion and culture before you discuss these areas with clients, you don't need to be a 'sexpert' to open these conversations with clients. More ideas about being curious and checking out assumptions in talking about sex are overviewed in Chapter 2.

COERCIVE EARLY SEXUAL EXPERIENCES

Although this is not a clinical manual for therapy and sexual problems, it is important to consider the difficult and distressing area of child sexual abuse (CSA). Abusive sexual experiences have been shown to have wide-ranging and profound effects on individuals' emotional, social and sexual functioning (Di Lillo, 2001; Ussher & Dewberry, 1995) and sexual identity. Female survivors of CSA report less positive sexual self-schemas and view themselves as less romantic and passionate and experience negative affect during sexual arousal (Meston *et al.*, 2006). In male survivors of child sexual abuse, Kia-Keating *et al.* (2005) discussed the importance of raising awareness about masculinity myths as part of developing a healthy sexual identity and balancing conforming and resisting traditional masculine roles as well as making conscious choices not to become perpetrators. Prevalence of child abuse is problematic to ascertain due to issues of silencing, shame around disclosure, ambiguous or absent memories of early experiences as well as the wide range of definitions about what constitutes abuse. Loeb *et al.* (2002), using a broad definition of unwanted sexual experience, report that as many as one in three girls and one in ten boys have reported some experience of sexual abuse.

Two theories outlined in Leonard and Follette (2002) explore the relationship between early sexual abuse and sexual dysfunction. These highlight the importance of emotional experience, including experiential avoidance (Polusny & Follette, 1995) and impaired emotional development (Greenberg & Pavio, 1997) in understanding the problems experienced by CSA survivors. In women with a history of child sexual assault, there is often a development of negative sexual schemas based on these aversive early experiences. Meston *et al.* (2006) suggest that these schemas are mediated by mood-related sequelae of the abuse such as distress, depression and post-trauma symptoms and found an increased experience of negative emotions such as fear, anger and disgust, during sexual arousal in women with a history of abuse.

In *New Feminist Stories of Child Sexual Abuse* (Reavey & Warner, 2003) authors try to untangle some of the complex ways in which stories of abuse and the narrative of harm can shape lived experiences of abuse. Assumptions of damage and harm related to abuse need to be explored gently and carefully with the client, as the degree to which these experiences shape sexuality varies widely. Non-consensual sexual experiences can occur at any age, although children, young people and other vulnerable individuals such as those with learning disability or mental health problems are more at risk. Previous sexual experiences shape the way sexuality is experienced in adulthood. When these experiences go wrong, or when sex becomes problematic in adulthood, more detailed models of pathology or dysfunction are required and a few such resources are listed at the end of the chapter.

ADOLESCENCE

Adolescence is a period of rapid physical and emotional development that was rather aptly labelled by Freud as the 'genital phase'. It is a time of shift in social role, individual responsibility and negotiating significant milestones in education and social relationships. Physically it is a time of significant development and changes such as secondary sexual characteristics and the release of a maelstrom of sex hormones. These complexity of changes make it an important time in the development of sexual and self-identity. The physical changes associated with puberty last about two years however the emotional and social development around sexuality continues well into adulthood. There is a gendered response to the changes in stature and build that occur in adolescence with boys generally feeling positive about increases in height and weight and girls having more negative responses. These responses reflect the societal values around larger physical size that differ across gender in Western culture (O'Dea & Abraham, 1999).

During adolescence and adulthood sexual scripts that guide interactions in potentially sexual relationships are developed. Flirting behaviours enable individuals to display interest and see if this is reciprocated. Sexual negotiation skills that enable individuals to navigate whether and how they will participate in sexual activity also emerge. The negotiation of sexual involvement can become problematic due to difficulties in sexual communication often set in the context of power imbalances or cultural contexts, such as men being positioned as initiators and women as regulators of sexual activity (Metts, 2008).

Adolescents and sex

The influence of cultural effects on sexuality in adolescence has been highlighted in a comparative study looking at changes in young people's sexual attitudes and behaviour over the last half century. Wells and Twenge (2005) reported that attitudes toward premarital intercourse have became more lenient, with approval increasing from twelve to seventy-three per cent among young women and from forty to seventy-nine per cent among young men and this has been accompanied by a decrease in feelings of sexual guilt in sexually active young people. They also found a gender difference with correlations between attitudes and behaviours stronger among females than males.

One of the most common expressions of sexual behaviour in adolescence is the use of fantasising about sexual issues and encounters (Crockett et al., 2003). Fantasy plays a role in the exploration of sexual wishes and desires, and allows for role play of interactions and behaviours in a safe and private personal space. The RIPPLE study (Stephenson et al., 2004) reported that although most teenagers are sexually active, half of those aged 16 to 19 have not had penetrative intercourse. In Western societies there has been a significant decrease in the age at which women first have sexual intercourse. In the 1950s, five per cent of women reported having sex before the age of 16, this figure is currently around twenty-five per cent (Stephenson et al., 2004).

Exercise 5.3 What is 'normal'? – developmental perspectives

As you read the vignettes below, either individually or in pairs, note your response to the following scenarios and reflect on how your formulation is shaped by the lifespan context of the client.

Case A
A client presents to you concerned about their difficulty in reaching orgasm either through penetrative sex or masturbation. The client is concerned that this is 'not normal'. Their regular partner is unconcerned about this and does not see this as problematic.

Case B
A client presents with their partner. They report discrepant sexual desire with your client concerned that they are not having 'enough' sex. They are both satisfied with the kind of sex they have but the tensions arise around frequency of sex. They report that they have sex about once a fortnight.

What is your response to these scenarios and how would your formulation shift if the client was:

1   a 48-year-old man;
2   a 16-year-old girl;
3   a 75-year-old woman.

Having noted your our own expectations about gender, age and sexuality, you may choose to reflect on which narratives inform these assumptions about normality and sex e.g. family, media, religion, academic reading. Definitive statistics on 'what is normal' in terms of sex are problematic as sexual behaviour is so diverse and shaped by a complexity of factors including age, culture, gender, sexuality, relationship issues, reproductive health. There is a general acceptance that frequency of sexual activity diminishes with age, but these behaviours themselves are influenced by powerful social constructions about age and sexuality. Studies are also hampered by methodological issues such as the reliance on self-report.

Due to concerns around high rates of sexually transmitted infections and teen pregnancy rates in young people in the UK (HPA, 2008; the UK Collaborative Group for HIV and STI Surveillance, 2006) many health narratives about adolescent sex are informed by a public health framework and emphasise the need for contraception, safe sex and access to abortion (e.g. National Collaborating Centre for Women's and Children's Health, 2005). Conversations about the need for teenagers to practise 'safe sex' have also highlighted the need for them to be better informed about sex education or sexual well-being. Young people need to learn about having sex for the first time, sexual orientation and homophobia, pressures to have certain kinds of sex (e.g. penetrative vaginal sex) as well as issues around contraception and safer sex choices (Stephenson et al., 2004).

The development of sexuality is played out among strong cultural discourses around sex and sexuality. The objectification of women and denial of female sexual pleasure for its own sake, as played out in pornography and women being viewed as a commodity in advertising, can construct and position women's sexuality as secondary or in service of men's needs (Tolman, 2001). These same contexts also shape the sexual socialisation of men and reciprocally limit the male sexual role by adding to narratives about the male sexual drive, men's role as instigators of sex and penetration as the definitive sexual act.

Uncertainty about what is 'normal' in terms of desire, arousal, orgasm and sexual behaviour is characteristic of adolescent sexuality. Taking a developmental perspective that normalises these uncertainties and anxieties fits with social-constructionist understandings of sexual functioning that emphasise contexts and social constructions around sex. In terms of sexual functioning and diagnostic criteria, adolescent 'sexual problems' are so ubiquitous as to make the term an oxymoron (Tolman, 2001). In female adolescents, absence of orgasm during sex, and lack of certainty as to what an orgasm actually is, is a common experience. As Tolman (2001) observes, it is interesting that this is not constructed as a sexual problem in need of a solution. This can be compared with the vigorous medical and pharmaceutical response to orgasmic difficulties in older males that are seen as problematic and treatable. 'It is still not normal and not acceptable and in some corners considered immoral for girls to believe that they can or should have their own sexual desire and pleasure – and therefore can or should think about querying its absence' (Tolman, 2001: 197).

In male adolescents, the transition from childhood exploration and experimentation to a satisfactory adult sexuality is complicated by social contexts that exaggerate fears of femininity and homophobia. Cultural expectations about male gender roles can also be confusing due to differential parental and peer socialisation of males (Bolton & MacEachron, 1988). As discussed earlier, discourses of sexuality in adolescents are often problem saturated and linked to public health concerns around sexually transmitted infection and unwanted pregnancy and this is reflected in the dominance of conversations about repression and prohibition of sexuality and minimisation of sexual risk and condom use in health and educational settings.

As sexuality develops, individuals begin to learn how to have the kinds of sex they want and enjoy. This involves being able to negotiate between levels of sexual intimacy, awareness of different ways of having sex and a range of sexual behaviours and feeling able to say no to unwanted sex. Young women are at increased risk of unwanted sexual experiences and over a quarter of sexually active students have had unwanted sex at some time in their lives, commonly related to alcohol use or pressure from a sexual partner (Fisher *et al.*, 2000). Women who have experienced sexual assault in childhood or adolescence are more at risk of subsequent sexual victimisation and tend to make riskier behavioural choices around sex (Crawford *et al.*, 2008; Wilson *et al.*, 1999). The miscommunication model of coerced sex (Crawford, 1995) proposes a difference in communication styles between men and women, which makes it difficult for sexual consent to be accurately heard by the opposite sex. However, this theory has been criticised with more recent studies finding that men and women reported feeling confident in being able to discriminate between what constitutes (and does not constitute) consent (O'Byrne *et al.*, 2006).

Exercise 5.4 Sexual assertion

Thinking about the way that sex and sexual behaviour are negotiated can be important in clinical work, such as working with clients who have unwanted sex or risky sex, to develop sexual assertion skills. The questions below encourage reflection on the challenges and dilemmas in sexual communication.

1   What factors may affect an individual's ability to say no to sex in different contexts (e.g. age, familiarity with each other, power differentials)?
2   Name some different ways someone may communicate their consent to sex and how might this be open to misinterpretation?

Negotiation of initial sexual contact involves complex verbal and non-verbal communications such as flirting, and other displays of interest and attraction. Sexual negotiation enables people to determine whether and to what degree they will participate in sexual activity. Power differentials between individuals such as age, gender and degree of sexual experience may powerfully shape how easily individuals can say no to sex or certain sexual acts. Sexual assertion in young people has been found to be shaped by: difficulties in talking about sex, the gender role expectations brought to an encounter, the stage of the relationship and gendered power relations (Wight, 1992). Individuals may also hold established sexual scripts (e.g. 'I'm not able to say no to sex if I have removed my underwear as it would be "leading them on"' or 'I can't say no to sex if I have been taken out to dinner/it's the third date' etc.) that are shaped by broader societal contexts as well as issues such as fear of rejection, being judged, sexually transmitted infections/pregnancy or using sex to meet other needs such as for affection or intimacy. Conversations around sexual risk and condom use can also be difficult because of concerns that discussions will interfere with arousal (if taking place just prior to sex) or by fears that promoting condom use implies you carry a degree of sexual risk.

Sexual behaviour can be negotiated directly during sex either verbally (e.g. 'I like that, keep going') or non-verbally by responsiveness to sensations and touch or by physical guiding or repositioning your partner. Sexual behaviour can also be negotiated before sex takes place (e.g. 'I only do it with a condom so I hope you have one') or afterwards (e.g. 'I really loved it when you . . .')

CONSENTING TO SEX

In clinical practice assessing risks and establishing the nature of consent within formative relationships can be complex. For example, the age of consent varies widely across different cultures and some young people may appear to be willingly engaging in invalidating relationships.

Exercise 5.5 Case study

The following case example asks the reader to consider the contexts of age and culture within a clinical setting.

A 14-year-old Somalian girl attends a sexual health clinic for a sexual health check-up and reveals to staff that she is in a consenting, loving, sexual relationship with a 25-year-old man from her country. She met him via the internet and sees him when she is truanting from school. Her mother does not know about the relationship. The girl has found out from tests carried out in the clinic she is pregnant and has chlamydia. Concerns are raised about her at a team discussion meeting.

- Individually (or in pairs) consider what you would take into account in your possible judgements of consent and the immediate and long-term consequences for this young person?
- What action might you consider if you were involved in this case?

Be aware of what may be a problem for whom, and how your assumptions around this will shape your responses, e.g. how would your responses differ if the girl and her boyfriend are keen to marry and raise the baby? Further clinical and ethical frameworks for reflecting on this case are discussed below.

The Department for Education and Skills has created a common assessment framework for children and young people (2005) that could be used as prompts when considering the issue of consent.

- The development of the young person – health, emotional and social development, behavioural development, identity including self-esteem, self-image and social presentation, family and social relations, self-care skills and independence.
- Parents and carers – whether they are providing basic care, safety and protection, emotional warmth and stability, guidance, boundaries and stimulation.
- Family and environmental – family history, functioning and well-being, wider family, housing, employment and financial considerations, social and community elements.

It is important to assess competence to consent according to relevant national guidelines (e.g. Gillick competence and Fraser guidelines (Wheeler, 2006)) and to ensure that risk assessment and awareness of child protection issues are an important part of any clinical assessment. Ability to give sexual consent and vulnerability to sexual assault is affected by a range of factors including power imbalances in relationships, mental health difficulties, cognitive impairment and the use of alcohol or other substances (Cybulska, 2007). Clinicians are directed to further reading and resources at the end of this chapter.

Non-heterosexual youth

Sexual identity is an important part of the development of self-identity during adolescence. How young people identify their sexuality – both privately and publicly – is influenced, and in turn influences, their sexual behaviour and experience of their sexual orientation. Sexual orientation can also be conceptualised as fluid and different people may relate and identify with different sexualities at different points in their lives (this is further explored in Chapters 1 and 4), with adolescence often being the starting point for this journey.

The range of sexual identities within which individuals identify is shaped by their cultural context. For young Western women new identities such as 'bicurious' and 'mostly straight' are emerging as alternatives to the more categorical constructs of straight or gay/lesbian. In a study on college students, Thompson and Morgan (2008) found that 'mostly straight' women fell between, and were significantly different from, exclusively straight and bisexual/lesbian women. Narratives about sexual identity development for 'mostly straight' women revealed the complexities of sexual identity exploration, uncertainty, and commitment within this population. The emergence of this 'heteroflexibility' illustrates how developmental and cultural ideas about sexuality intersect to produce differing narratives across the lifespan but also across historical context.

As a teenager there is a growing awareness of all aspects of sexuality. For gay, lesbian and bisexual adolescents, two significant development processes may occur at the same time – self-awareness and definition of sexuality and public identification of sexuality or orientation. If same-sex attraction or identification with a lesbian, gay or bisexual (LGB) sexuality is present, there may be a process of aligning self and public identification of sexuality by 'coming out'. This may be seen as a process of developing a positive awareness of sexuality or gender identity, developing social ties with LGB individuals and becoming confident in self-disclosing sexuality to others (Laird & Green, 1996). This is a lifelong process of deciding when and whether to disclose sexuality in new situations and contexts (coming out is also explored in Chapter 4).

Sexual behaviour and sexual identity are not always congruent. Young people who identify as, or feel they may be, LGB may have sexual relationships with the opposite sex and many individuals who identify as heterosexual may have same-sex experiences, crushes or fantasies. These experiences may develop into a fixed and stable part of sexual identity or can remain outside self-defined sexual identity (e.g. bicurious) even if these same sex experiences reoccur in different contexts or over time.

Young people may choose not to label their sexuality until they are comfortable and confident with their identity or because they do not wish to be defined by their sexual orientation. There may also be fear of discrimination and prejudice towards them as being part of a sexual minority. This can also raise concerns of being 'outed' or having other people discuss or disclose one's sexual orientation.

The consequences of being 'out' or publically identifying as LGBT can be traumatic and stressful due to social stigma and discrimination. It can result in rejection or ostracism from friends or family resulting in social isolation or homelessness. Individuals may also be subject to bullying, harassment or violence and are at risk of depression and suicide (Rivers, 1995). LGBT youth may internalise these negative messages and feel negatively about this part of themselves (PACE, 2004). Internalised homophobia and external victimisation associated with being perceived as different can lead to self-harm, absenteeism, delays in 'coming out' and long-term effects such as depression, loneliness, post-traumatic stress disorder, anxiety and distancing from friendships.

SEX AND SEXUALITY IN ADULTHOOD

Sexuality and sexual identity continue to develop and evolve throughout adulthood. These processes continue to be shaped by individual experience, social contexts, cultural norms, beliefs and expectations. Masters and Johnson (1970) referred to the development of a sexual value system whereby individuals invest sensory experiences with erotic meaning. They posit that details of specific and successful sexual events are drawn upon in this process and circumstances and social values make these experiences acceptable or valued as sexual stimuli. This sexual identity is not fixed but evolves and changes. Andersen and Cyranowski (1995: 1079) conceptualise this as a sexual self 'derived from past experience, manifest in current experience, influential in the processing of sexually relevant social information and guides sexual behaviour'.

A comprehensive lifespan theory of sexuality, from childhood to old age, has yet to emerge. Useful theories need to account for the power and plasticity of sexuality, the variability in intensity of sexual desires, the diversity of stimuli that elicit arousal in different people, the mixing of sexual and non-sexual meanings in sexual and non-sexual behaviour and the diverse position sexuality occupies across cultures. Laws' (1980) developmental model of sexual identity meets this in part by listing over the lifespan the many factors conducive to positive sexual expression in men and women, e.g. changes in sexual scripts over time, occurrence of role transitions such as change of partner, developmental increase in capacity to choose and control one's sexual life resulting from accumulated experience.

Exercise 5.6 Adult sexuality

The following exercise is recommended for self-reflection only, given the personal and sensitive nature of the topic.

At this point in your adult life, are there still sexual experiences you are curious about that you have yet to try (e.g. being tied up during sex, watching a particular type of porn, sex with more than one partner)? Do you feel able to bring these ideas into your sexual fantasies? Are there steps you could take to bring them into your real life? If you prefer to keep them only as objects of curiosity or fantasy, why is that? What would it mean about you and your sexuality if you had engaged in these experiences?

In young adulthood, the freedoms of leaving full-time education and earning money are accompanied by opportunities for personal, social and sexual development and exploration. The tasks required to advocate for your sexual and emotional needs are complex and include making decisions about contraceptive use, when to have sex with someone and what type of relationships you are seeking, as well as negotiating about safe sex, initiating the sex you want and declining the sex you don't. Being able to talk about sex and communicate openly with friends, families, partners and health professionals can be important for negotiating this exciting and sometimes confusing or overwhelming stage of life.

In adulthood and middle age the dominant socially constructed significant tasks of heterosexual life such as completing education, engaging in employment, developing stable romantic relationships and establishing a family, might run alongside establishing a positive sexual identity. Women often experience increased confidence in their social roles in adulthood and have developed better awareness of their bodies and familiarity in the sexual role. As a result, many women report an increase in sexual satisfaction and more women than men report increases in sexual activity, frequency of orgasm, interest in sexual activity, sexual urge and subjective pleasure in sexual activities in adulthood (Adams & Turner, 1985).

Adulthood can involve establishing and settling into a long-term relationship that brings concomitant changes in intimacy, desire and sexual expression. This may vary from positive feelings of being more intimate, connected and safe to concerns about reduced desire or sexual attraction and sex becoming too familiar or routine. Developmental tasks may include communicating around sexual needs, negotiating discrepancies in libido or desire and working to maintain a sex life that is mutually fulfilling. Within the context of committed relationships, ideas around monogamy versus polygamy have been more or less acceptable in different historical, social and cultural contexts. For example: in some relationships between gay men, sex outside the main relationship may be negotiated or acceptable; communal living or open marriages in the post-sexual revolution 1970s; in some Islamic Arabic and African countries polygamy for men is legal and acceptable.

Exercise 5.7 Relationship norms

This exercise can be done in pairs or small groups if used in training. It encourages a wider perspective on how relationships could be conducted and questions where messages of 'healthy' relationships come from.

What form of relationships do you see around you (e.g. single mothers, serial monogamists, non-monogamists, decisions not to have children)? In your contexts, is the 'nuclear family' the most typical relationship?

What messages about a 'healthy' relationship have you heard (e.g. they should be long term, monogamous, private, building towards living together and having children)? Where do these ideas come from? What alternate messages to this might be available?

In middle age, as in adolescence, men and women experience a range of physical and social changes. Transitions in work and home life can be profound at this time such as careers ending, relationship changes, divorces, children growing up and illness or death of parents. Such life-disrupting events understandably affect a sense of self and may temporarily erase erotic feelings. Changes in health status may also affect body image and change of role in relationships, which will also affect the ways that sexuality is experienced and expressed and are discussed in Chapter 3.

Sexuality and reproduction

The decisions around parenthood, and/or the event of pregnancy and parenthood itself, can have significant effects on sexuality and sexual identity. Conversations around if or when to have children (and how many) are a key part of adulthood and have significant effects on relationships, sexuality and sexual behaviour.

For LGB adults, decisions to have a family may involve accessing a range of reproductive technologies. This can be a stressful and vulnerable period where discourses of stigma and prejudice can be re-experienced. The law in the UK was amended in 2002 to allow same-sex couples to name both partners on their child's birth certificate when their child's birth is registered and also made provision for joint adoption by same-sex couples. Despite these legislative changes, there remains considerable stigma for LGB parents that is often played out in conversations around the capabilities of LGB parents to raise children. Susan Golombok (Golombok & Tasker, 1996; Golombok, 2002) has done several studies around this and found no difference in the development of children raised by lesbian and gay parents and those raised by heterosexual parents in terms of quality of family relationships, psychological adjustment or quality of peer relationships. With respect to sexual orientation, the large majority of children from lesbian families identified as heterosexual in adulthood although views around homosexuality were different to those of children raised in heterosexual families (LGB issues in parenthood are discussed further in Chapter 4).

Interest in sex after childbirth is affected not only by physical changes such as recovery from labour, temporary changes in vaginal shape and size and body image concerns and fluctuating hormones, but also from the enormous change in role and the effects of exhaustion, fatigue and sleep deprivation that accompany caring for a newborn. Breastfeeding also has different effects on women: for some it is enormously pleasurable, for others it is uncomfortable and anxiety-provoking. It can also directly affect sexual functioning as it can suppress ovulation and the production of oestrogen that may cause lubrication problems.

Partners may find that they feel anxious or insecure and may want to resume having sex before the new mother feels able or willing to do so. Sex with a partner may also be problematic due to the changed role of the female form from a sexual and erotic context to one that is functional and maternal. This may be highlighted by perceptions of breasts as 'belonging to the baby' whereas in other relationships the new size, production of milk and increased sensitivity of the breasts is felt to be highly erotic.

Menopause and sexuality

The menopause, the physiological endpoint of a woman's reproductive capacity, has a range of associated physiological and psychological changes that can directly and indirectly influence sexuality (Hawton *et al.*, 1994; Nusbaum *et al.*, 2005). Often women in this period may be reluctant to raise concerns or complaints about their sexual life and it can therefore be helpful for therapists to initiate conversations around this (Nusbaum *et al.*, 2005).

The menopausal period encompasses the slowing of ovarian activity and the cessation of menstruation. Post-menopause, the ovary no longer produces oestrogen directly but other sex hormones and androgens work together to provide some continuation of oestrogen. The hormone testosterone is important for muscle and bone strength and is well known for its role in libido. Levels of this hormone drop in younger reproductive years but there is almost no change in testosterone at the time of menopause and only a very gradual decline as the woman typically enters her sixties.

Women often experience hot flushes and night sweats during the active menopausal period. Physical changes associated include changes in the shape or elasticity of the vagina due to thinning of the vaginal wall. In some women diminished sensory response may reduce the intensity of orgasm (Goldstein & Alexander, 2005). A decrease in vaginal lubrication can also occur in some women. Simple water-based lubricants such as KY jelly are helpful for this. These changes are normal, but for some they may make penetrative intercourse difficult or painful, although for many, their ability to enjoy sex or penetration is undiminished. Continuing to have sex and remaining sexually active has been found to help keep the vagina healthy (Leiblum, 1983). In a study of 400 women, Dennerstein *et al.* (2002) found that the most important aspect of maintaining sexual function is having good sexual function before entering the menopause. There is evidence that desire in women decreases with age but most research has indicated that this seems to be accounted for by menopausal effects rather than due to ageing itself.

Male ageing and sexuality

As men age, they notice it takes longer to get an erection or that the erection is not as hard as in earlier years. The physiological sensation of 'inevitability to ejaculate', which is part of the male arousal response, may be shorter or may disappear, but this does not affect the ability to orgasm. The refractory period – or time before another erection is possible after orgasm – also becomes longer. Many men find more stimulation of the penis is required to gain an erection than previously (Ramage, 2005). Being aware of these changes, which are a normal part of ageing is important to minimise any performance anxiety that misattribution of these changes may bring.

In addition to the changes in erectile functioning, there is also an increased risk of impotence or the loss of ability to achieve orgasm. Erection difficulties are relatively common in men over 50 and are so highly prevalent that they are often considered a consequence of normal ageing. Mulligan *et al.* (1988) found that, although more common in old age, this is often related to comorbid illness, such as diabetes, heart disease and high blood pressure, rather than ageing alone. Even when related to health conditions or ageing, erectile functioning can be improved by increased stimulation and use of medication such as Viagra. However, satisfying sexual expression can encompass behaviours other than penetrative intercourse. Schiavi (1990) conducted a critical review of the empirical literature on the sexuality of ageing men and found significant age-related declines in sexual desire, sexual arousal and activity and erectile capacity but no difference in sexual and marital satisfaction.

Ideas about emerging narratives in male sexuality are detailed by Zilbergeld (1999) who outlines several common male misconceptions about male sexual roles that can be used as prompts for discussion. These include:

- that men should be liberated and comfortable with sex;
- that men don't have and express feelings;
- that all touch is sexual or should lead to sex;
- that men are always interested and ready for sex;
- that real men are good sexual performers;
- that all sex is centred around large, hard and erect penises;
- that if there are erectile problems then a pill is the solution;
- sex is only penile penetration;

- men are responsible for female orgasm;
- good sex is spontaneous and does not involve communication.

These myths about masculinity can confine and problematise sexuality for both men and women as often these stereotypes involve gender reciprocity e.g. male as active/female as passive, male as instigator/female as gate-keeper. They also limit possible expressions of sexuality and humanity and contribute to prescriptive notions of gender role and expression. Further, the notion that sex is a skill or series of techniques that men need to develop to stimulate women renders sexual pleasures solely as a masculine competence (Hill, 2008).

SEX, SEXUALITY AND OLDER AGE

Sex and sexuality continue to play an important role across the entire lifespan. Despite myths and prejudices about sexuality in older age, desire and expression of sexual impulses are present and many people are sexually active into their seventies and beyond (Myskow, 2002). Physical changes may affect the way that sexual desire is expressed or experienced just as at other points in the lifespan, but enjoyable and fulfilling sexual relationships and other expressions of sexuality continue. An awareness of the physical changes that can occur in older age may be helpful in normalising experience and sustaining the complex balance of emotional and physical factors that affect the way sexuality is experienced. A range of health problems that are more common or severe in older age, such as diabetes, dementia or cancer, can directly affect sexual functioning, as can the side-effects of medications (this is discussed further in Chapter 3). As recovery and adjustment to health changes occur, people may feel reluctant to raise the subject of sex or the possibility of becoming sexual active, perhaps in different but still rewarding ways. Discussion of these concerns and exploration of expectations about what is a 'normal' sex life can help individuals to maintain a positive self-identity and sexual identity throughout later life. Physical changes can and do affect sexual functioning and libido but these effects are often overemphasised relative to psychological factors.

Changes in social roles in later life, such as retirement, financial and family losses or changes, also affect an individual's sense of self and identity. If older people have fewer opportunities to feel valued and useful, this has a profound influence on sense of self, social relationships, mood and sexual expression. For the majority of older persons, marital and relationship satisfaction take on central importance after retirement due to the reduction of other social networks such as friendships and work (Trudel et al., 2008). As Weeks (2002) observes, the most prevalent psychosexual problems of older men and women are mainly the result of social context and relationship factors such as insufficient physical affection, lack of intimacy and loneliness.

Exercise 5.8 Self-reflection on sex throughout the lifespan

The aim of the following exercise is to link your own experiences and current developmental context with ideas about sexuality in older age. It can be done individually or in small groups depending on the setting.

1   What differences have you noticed in your enjoyment/attitude/ preferences/confidence around sex as you have aged? At what stage of your life was it more difficult to negotiate having the kind of sex you like? When has it been easiest?
2   Spend a few minutes thinking about what sort of sexuality you envision for yourself in 20, 30, 40 years time.
3   Recall a story or film that you know well that depicts old age. How was sex and sexuality portrayed in this context? How is this similar or different to your hopes/expectations for your own sexuality in later life? How is this similar or different to your family stories about what happens as you grow old?
4   In discussing or reflecting on your answers, be aware of age-related myths or stereotypes that may be present. What kinds of sexuality are absent from media portrayals that may be part of your hoped for future sexuality? Where are alternative stories possible?

This exercise can be helpful with clients as well as in training settings in exploring and opening up ideas and possibilities for sexuality in older age that go beyond those commonly presented in Western media.

The lessening in sexual activity and deterioration in sexual relationships are ageist assumptions, based largely on misconceptions (Weeks, 2002). Reduction in sex drive may not reflect reductions in other expressions of sexuality and sensuality or in desire for other forms of intimacy. As discussed earlier, sexual identity changes and evolves and is shaped by societal expectation, media and other cultural contexts. Myths and stereotypes about sexuality and old age reflect attitudes to ageing generally. Narrow constructions exist as to what kind of work, activities, appearance and relationships are appropriate for older people (Heath, 2002). These ageist stereotypes have powerful effects on individuals in many areas including sexuality and sexual expression.

Desirability, eroticism and sexuality are often predicated on youth, vitality and physical appearance in Western society (Heath, 2002). Ideals of beauty and attractiveness, particularly for women, are also limited to characteristics associated with youth e.g. unlined smooth skin, pert breasts, hairless bodies (Wolf, 1990; Tiggemann & Hodgson, 2008). Sex is often positioned as belonging solely within the contexts of youth, beauty and reproduction. 'Older women in general, in contrast to the attention and strong sexualised value placed on younger women, are considered to be neither sexual, or sexually attractive, beings' (Weeks, 2002: 232). Older men and women are also disadvantaged by ageist depictions of sexual interest or activity as being perverse or unwanted. Sexuality is often even more invisible or stigmatised in older LGBT adults due to the double stigma of ageing and minority sexuality.

Contrary to these stereotypes, older people often live active and fulfilling sexual lives. Sexual satisfaction has also been found to be a key indicator of quality of life in a study on long-term geriatric residents within a care setting (Spector & Fremeth, 1996). Weeks (2002) explored the gendered experience of people with dementia living in care, whereby male expressions of sexuality were perceived as problematic and discouraged or punished and female expressions of sexuality were seen as signs of vulnerability. Ward *et al.* (2005) reflect how embodied experiences of ageing differ according to gender and highlight the invisibility of the LGBT population in care settings due to heteronormative assumptions in the set-up of accommodation as well as in the beliefs and expectations of care staff.

Exercise 5.9 Case study

The following case study explores ageist and heterosexist ideas and can be used in small groups as a training exercise.

Mary is 73 and living in a residential setting due to deteriorating health. Her long-term female partner, Joan, died 15 years ago. Care staff often joke about trying to 'find her another husband'. She doesn't feel able to correct them when they say this. When asked about the picture of Joan, she refers to her as 'a companion'. She has recently started to develop a close and reciprocated relationship with another female resident in the home, Ann.

How do assumptions of heteronormativity affect the provision of care in this setting? What are the challenges in thinking about Mary's sexual needs? How might care staff respond to the development of a sexual relationship?

> You may want to reflect on factors that affect disclosure of sexu-
> ality in health and social care settings. In the scenario above this may
> be further complicated by Mary's physical dependence on staff
> providing her care, the experience of homophobia in older cohorts
> and staff, the cultural context of staff providing her care and how that
> may be similar or different to her own. In considering Mary and
> Ann's capacity to consent and their mutual relationship, staff need to
> balance the rights of clients and their need for autonomy with their
> professional and ethical responsibility for the well-being of the client.

Sexual functioning in older adults is increasingly relevant to therapists as
the population ages. Older adults are in a difficult position of defining their
sexual identities within a societal context where, for them, a robust libido,
pursuit of sexual activity and interest in others as potential sexual partners
are positioned as non-normative or not acceptable. With increased awareness and critiquing of these narratives in more recent years, Weeks (2002)
invites individuals not only to choose to avoid these stereotypes as they age
but to oppose them constructively instead.

CONCLUSION

Across all stages of life, sexuality and sex shape our experiences of ourselves, our bodies, our relationships and our desire and need for intimacy
and love. Establishing a sexual identity, finding meaningful and satisfying
relationships and integrating sex and love are the tasks of a lifetime.
Sexuality across the lifespan is defined by constantly evolving narratives
around how we think about sex, sexual feelings, sensual touch, sexual risk-
taking and well-being. A detailed understanding of sex and sexuality
encompasses neurobiology, hormonal influences, developmental psychology, attachment, personality and rich social and cultural contexts. Current
theories and knowledge are also powerfully shaped by limits and prohibitions on what areas of sex and sexuality it has been permissible to research.
Remaining curious about our own, and our clients', stories about sex and
sexuality can help us to develop rich and compassionate understandings of
these complex and changing narratives and facilitate ways to talk about sex.

FURTHER RESOURCES

Development of sexuality

Hill, C. (2008). *Human sexuality: Personality and social perspectives.* Sage Publications. http://www.sagepub.com/hillhsstudy/ for online resources.

Women's Aid. National domestic violence charity has free resources for teaching children and young people about healthy relationships, respect and what to do if you are experiencing abuse. http://www.womensaid.org.uk

Pike, L.B. (2009). *Sexuality and Your Child: For Children Ages 3 to 7*. Missouri, US: Department of Human Development & Family Studies, Uni Missouri. http://extension.missouri.edu/explorepdf/hesguide/humanrel/gh6002.pdf

No Outsiders Project – booklet and resources for use in primary schools and early years settings to support teachers and children to address lesbian, gay, bisexual and transgender equality. http://www.nooutsiders.sunderland.ac.uk

Children and young people

Brook. National voluntary sector provider of free and confidential sexual health advice and services specifically for young people under 25. Advice for professionals on sex and the law. http://www.brook.org.uk

London Safeguarding Children Board. Service support for children professionals and local communities in safeguarding children. http://www.londonscb.gov.uk

HM Government (2006). *Working together to safeguard children: A guide to inter-agency working to safeguard and promote the welfare of children*. London: TSO. http://www.everychildmatters.gov.uk/resources-and-practice/ IG00060/

Beautiful Thing (1996) (Director Hettie McDonald). Warm and funny gay coming out movie set in working class area of South East London.

By The Way, I'm Gay (2008). Award winning 3-minute black and white film made by teenagers light-heartedly overviews some of the issues gay teens and their friends face. Available to view at http://www.pinknews.co. uk/news/articles/2005-8877.html

Juno (2007) (Director: Jason Reitman). Oscar winning film with positive depictions of teenage pregnancy.

Sexuality, reproduction and adulthood

PACE. Charity promoting the mental health and emotional well-being of the lesbian, gay, bisexual and transgender community and has useful resources on gay and lesbian parenting. http://www.pacehealth.org.uk/Resources/PACE/Documents/LGBT%20Parenting%20Final%20Report%202007.pdf

Pink Parents. Offers support and guidance in relation to all lesbian and gay parenting issues. http://www.pinkparents.org.uk

Kissing Jessica Stein (2001). (Director: Charles Herman-Wurfeld). Romcom which explores a character's journey across the straight–lesbian–bisexual continuum.

Foxcroft, L. (2009). *Hot flushes, cold science: A history of the modern menopause*. Granta: London. Explores taboos and social construction of menopause as a medical condition.

Sexuality, menopause and ageing

American Psychological Association (APA) *Ageing and Human Sexuality Resource Guide*. References for empirical evidence on ageing and sexuality, summary chapters, case presentations and resources to use for education in teaching settings or with clients. http://www.apa.org/pi/aging/sexuality.html

Athill, D. (2008). *Somewhere towards the end*. London: Granta. Sex affirmative memoir of older age.

Kimmel, D., Rose, T. & David, S. (2006).*Lesbian, gay, bisexual, and transgender aging: Research and clinical perspectives*. New York: Columbia University Press.

Trudel, G., Turgeon, L. & Piche, L. (2000). Marital and sexual aspects of old age. *Sexual and Relationship Therapy*, 15, 381–406.

The Daisy Network. The Daisy Network Premature Menopause Support Group is a registered charity that offers advice and support for women who have experienced a premature menopause. http://www.daisynetwork.org.uk/index.html

The British Menopause Society. The BMS is a charity directed at health professionals specialising in post-reproductive health with a range of useful information and resources. http://www.thebms.org.uk/

Menopause matters. Independent, clinician-led site aiming to provide accurate information about the menopause. http://www.menopausematters.co.uk

Away from Her (2006) (Director Sarah Polley). Based on a short story by Alice Munro. Depicts an older woman with Alzheimer's who loses her memory of her husband and develops a relationship with another nursing home resident.

Sexual dysfunction and sex therapy resources

Finkelhor, D. (1986). *A sourcebook on child sexual abuse*. London: Sage.

Hawton, K. (1985). *Sex therapy: A practical guide*. Oxford: Oxford University Press.

Heiman, J.R. & Lopiccolo, J. (1988). *Becoming orgasmic*. London: Piatkus.

Kashak, E. & Tiefer, L. (2002). *A new view of sexual problems*. New York: Haworth Press.

Leonard, L.M. & Follette, V.M. (2002). Sexual functioning in women reporting a history of child sexual abuse: review of the empirical literature and clinical implications. *Annual Review of Sex Research*, 13, 346–388. http://findarticles.com/p/articles/mi_qa3778/is_200201/ai_n9032343/pg_1

Stewart, E. & Spencer, P. (2000). *The V book*. London: Piatkus.

Zilbergeld, B. (1992). *The new male sexuality*. New York: Bantam Books.

REFERENCES

Adams, C.G. & Turner, B.F. (1985). Reported changes in sexuality from young adulthood to old age. *Journal of Sex Research*, 21, 126–141.

Andersen, B.L. & Cyranowski, J.M. (1994). Women's sexual self-schema. *Journal of Personality and Social Psychology*, 67 (6), 1079–1100.

Baldo, M. Aggleton, P. & Slutkin, G. (1993). Does sex education lead to earlier or increased sexual activity in youth? *International AIDS Conference*, 9, 792. WHO Global Programme on AIDS, Geneva, Switzerland.

Bandura, A. (1986). *Social foundations of thought and action: A social cognitive theory*. Englewood Cliffs, NJ: Prentice-Hall.

Berenbaum, S.A. & Hines, M. (1992). Early androgens are related to childhood sex-typed toy preferences. *Psychological Science*, 3, 203–206.

Berman, J., Berman, L. & Bumiller, E. (2001). *For women only: A revolutionary guide to reclaiming your sex life*. Virago: New York.

Birnbaum, G.E., Reis, H.T., Mikulincer, M., Omri, G. & Orpaz, A. (2006). When sex is more than just sex: Attachment orientations, sexual experience, and relationship quality. *Journal of Personality and Social Psychology*, 91 (5), 929–943.

Bolton, F.G. & MacEachron, A.E. (1988). Adolescent male sexuality: A developmental perspective. *Journal of Adolescent Research*, 3, 259–273.

Crawford, E., O'Doughtery Wright, M. & Birchmeier, Z. (2008). Drug-facilitated sexual assault: College women's risk perception and behavioural choices. *Journal of American College of Health*, 57, 261–272.

Crawford, M. (1995). *Talking difference: On gender and language*. London: Sage.

Crockett, L.J., Raffaelli, M. & Moilanen, K.L. (2003). Adolescent sexuality: Behaviour and meaning. In G.R. Adams and M.D. Berzonsky (eds), *Blackwell Handbook of Adolescence*. Malden: Blackwell.

Cybulska, B. (2007). Sexual assault: Key issues. *Royal Society of Medicine*, 100, 1–4.

Davidson, O. (2000). HIV/GU-Medicine/Sexual Health. In N. Patel, E. Bennett, M. Dennis, N. Dosanjh, A. Mahtani, A. Miller & Z. Nadirshaw (eds), *Clinical psychology, 'race' and culture: A training manual*. Leicester: BPS Books.

Davis, D., Shaver, P. & Vernon, M.L. (2004). Attachment style and subjective motivations for sex. *Personality and Social Psychology Bulletin*, 30, 1076–1090.

Dennerstein, L., Randolph, J., Taffe, J., Dudley, E. & Burger, H. (2002). Hormones, mood, sexuality and the menopausal transition. *Fertility and Sterility*, 77 (suppl. 4), 542–548.

Department for Education and Skills (2005). *Common assessment framework (CAF) for children and young people*. London: DFES.

Di Lillo, D. (2001). Interpersonal functioning among women reporting a history of childhood sexual abuse: empirical findings and methodological issues. *Clinical Psychology Review*, 21, 553–576.

Fisher, B., Cullen, F. & Turner, M. (2000). *The sexual victimisation of college women: Findings from two national-level studies*. Washington, DC: National Institute of Justice and Bureau of Justice Statistics.

Foucault, M. (1978 [French publication: 1976]). *The history of sexuality, Vol. I: An introduction*, translated by Robert Hurley. New York: Vintage Books.

Freud, S. (1962). *Three essays on the theory of sexuality*. New York: Basic Books.

Goldstein, I. & Alexander, J.L. (2005). Practical aspects in the management of vaginal atrophy and sexual dysfunction in perimenopausal and postmenopausal women. *Journal of Sexual Medicine*, 2 (3), 154–165.

Golombok, S. (2002). Adoption in lesbian couples. *British Medical Journal*, 324, 1407–1408.

Golombok, S. & Tasker, F. (1996). Do parents influence the sexual orientation of their children? Findings from a longitudinal study of lesbian families. *Developmental Psychology*, 32, 3–11.

Greenberg, L.S. & Paivio, S. (1997). *Working with emotions in psychotherapy*. New York: Guilford Press.

Hawton, K., Gath, D. & Day, A. (1994). Sexual function in a community sample of middle-aged women with partners: Effects of age, marital, socioeconomic, psychiatric, gynaecological, and menopausal factors. *Archives of Sexual Behavior*, 23, 375–395.

Health Protection Agency (HPA) (2008). Sexually transmitted infections and young people in the United Kingdom: 2008 Report. London: HPA. http://www.hpa. org.uk/web/HPAwebFile/HPAweb_C/1216022461534

Heath, H. (2002). Sexuality and later life. In H. Heath & I. White (eds), *The challenge of sexuality in health care*. London: Blackwell.

Hill, C. (2008). *Human sexuality: Personality and social perspectives*. Sage Publications.

Horne, S.G. & Biss, W.B. (2009). Equality discrepancy between women in same-sex relationships: The mediating role of attachment in relationship satisfaction. *Sex Roles, A Journal of Research*, 60, 721–730.

Kaschak, E. & Tiefer, L. (2001). *A new view of women's sexual problems*. New York: Haworth Press.

Keighley, A. (2002). *Sexuality in childhood and adolescence*. In H. Heath and I. White (eds), *The challenge of sexuality in health care*. London: Blackwell.

Kia-Keating, M., Grossman, F.K., Sorsoli, L. & Epstein, M. (2005). Containing and resisting masculinity: Narratives of renegotiation among resilient male survivors of childhood sexual abuse. *Psychology of Men & Masculinity*, 6 (3), 169–185.

Kohlberg, L. (1966). A cognitive-developmental analysis of children's sex-role concepts and attitudes. In E.E. Maccoby (ed.), *The development of sex differences*. Stanford, CA: Stanford University Press.

Laird, J. & Green, R. (eds) (1996). *Lesbians and gays in couples and families: A handbook for therapists*. San Francisco, CA: Jossey-Bass.

Lamb, S. & Coakley, M. (1993). 'Normal' childhood play and games: Differentiating play from abuse. *Child Abuse and Neglect*, 17, 515–526.

Laws, J.L. (1980). Female sexuality through the lifespan. In P.B. Baltes & O.G. Brim, Jr. (eds), *Life-span development and behaviour*, Vol. 3, 207–252. New York: Academic Press.

Leiblum, S., Bachman, G., Kenmann, E., Colburn, D. & Swatzman, L. (1983). Vaginal atrophy in the post-menopausal woman. The importance of sexual activity and hormones. *Journal of the American Medical Association*, 249, 2195–2198.

Leonard, L.M. & Follette, V.M. (2002). Sexual functioning in women reporting a history of child sexual abuse: review of the empirical literature and clinical implications. *Annual Review Sex Research*, 13, 346–388.

Lewis, R.J. & Janda, L.H. (1988). The relationship between adult sexual adjustment and childhood experiences regarding exposure to nudity, sleeping in the parental bed, and parental attitudes toward sexuality. *Archives of Sexual Behaviour*, 17, 349–362.

Loeb, T.B., Williams, J.K., Carmona, J.V., Rivkin, I., Wyatt, G.E., Chin, D. & Asuan-O'Brien, A. (2002). Child sexual abuse: associations with the sexual functioning of adolescents and adults. *Annual Review Sex Research*, 13, 307–345.

Masters, W.H. & Johnson, V.E. (1970). *Human sexual inadequacy*. Boston: Little Brown.

Meston, C.M., Rellini, A.H. & Heiman, J.R. (2006). Women's history of sexual abuse, their sexuality, and sexual self-schemas. *Journal of Consulting and Clinical Psychology*, 74 (2), 229–236.

Metts, S. (2008). *Sexual communication – Couple relationships.* http://family.jrank.org/pages/1501/Sexual-Communication.html

Mulligan, T., Retchin, S.M., Chinchilli, V.M. & Bettinger, C.B. (1988). The role of aging and chronic disease in sexual dysfunction. *Journal of the American Geriatric Society*, 36 (6), 520–524.

Myskow, L. (2002). Perimenopausal issues in sexuality. *Sexual and Relationship Therapy*, 17 (3), 253–260.

National Collaborating Centre for Women's and Children's Health (2005). *Long-acting reversible contraception.* NICE Clinical Guideline 30. London: NICE. http://www.nice.org.uk/CG030

Nusbaum, M.R., Lenahan, P. & Sadovsky, R. (2005). Sexual health in aging men and women: Addressing the physiological and psychological sexual changes that occur with age. *Geriatrics*, 60 (9), 18–23.

O'Byrne, R., Rapley, M. & Hansen, S. (2006). 'You couldn't say "no", could you?': Young men's understandings of sexual refusal. *Feminism and Psychology*, 16, 133–154.

O'Dea, J.A. & Abraham, S. (1999). Onset of disordered eating attitudes and behaviours in early adolescence: interplay of pubertal status, gender, weight, and age. *Adolescence*, 34, 671–679.

Okami, P., Olmstead, R. & Abramson, P.R. (1997). Sexual experiences in early childhood: 18-year data from the UCLA family life-styles project. *Journal of Sex Research*, 34, 339–347.

Okami, P., Olmstead, R., Abramson, P.R. & Pendleton, L. (1998). Early childhood exposure to parental nudity and scenes of parental sexuality ('Primal scenes'): An 18-year longitudinal study of outcome. *Archives of Sexual Behaviour*, 27, 361–384.

PACE (2004). *Guidelines for best practice in LGBT youth work.* London: PACE.

Polusny, M. & Follette, V. (1995). Long-term correlates of child sexual abuse: Theory and review of the empirical literature. *Applied and Preventive Psychology*, 4, 143–166.

Ramage, M. (2005) Management of sexual problems. In J. Tomlinson (ed.), *ABC of Sexual Health* (2nd edn). Oxford: Blackwell Publishing.

Reavey, P. & Warner, S. (eds) (2003). *New feminist stories of child sexual abuse: Sexual scripts and dangerous dialogues.* New York: Routledge.

Rivers, I. (1995). Mental health issues among young lesbian and gay men at school. *Health and Social Care in the Community*, 3, 380–383.

Schiavi, R.C (1990). Sexuality and ageing in men. *Annual Review of Sex Research*, Vol. 1, 227–249.

Servin, A., Nordenström, A., Larsson, A. & Bohlin, G. (2003). Prenatal androgens and gender-typed behavior: A study of girls with mild and severe forms of congenital adrenal hyperplasia. *Developmental Psychology*, 39, 440–450.

Spector, I.P. & Fremeth, S.M. (1996). Sexual behaviors and attitudes of geriatric residents in long-term care facilities. *Journal of Sex & Marital Therapy*, 22, 235–246.

Stephenson, J.M., Strange, V., Forrest, S., Oakley, A., Copas, A., Allen, E., Babiker, A., Black, S., Ali, M., Monteiro, H. & Johnson, A.M. (2004). Pupil-led sex education in England (RIPPLE study): Cluster-randomised intervention trial. *The Lancet*, 364 (9431), 338–346.

Thompson, E.M. & Morgan, E.M. (2008). 'Mostly straight' young women: Variations in sexual behaviour and identity development. *Developmental Psychology*, 44 (1), 15–21.

Tiggemann, M. & Hodgson, S. (2008). The hairlessness norm extended: Reasons for and predictors of women's body hair removal at different body sites. *Sex Roles: A Journal of Research*, 59 (11–12), 889–897.

Tolman, D. (2001) Female adolescent sexuality: An argument for a developmental perspective on the *New View of Women's Sexual Problems*. In E. Kaschak & L. Tiefer (eds), *A new view of women's sexual problems*. New York: Haworth Press.

Trudel, G., Villeneuve, V., Anderson, A. & Pilen, G. (2008). Sexual and marital aspects of old age: an update. *Sexual and Relationship Therapy*, 23, 161–169.

UK Collaborative Group for HIV and STI Surveillance. (2006). *A complex picture: HIV and other STIs in the UK*. London: Health Protection Agency.

Ussher, J.M. & Dewberry, C. (1995). The nature and long-term effects of childhood sexual abuse: A survey of adult women survivors in Britain. *British Journal of Clinical Psychology*, 34, 177–192.

Ward, R., Vass, A.A., Aggarwal, N., Garfield, C. & Cybyk, B. (2005). A kiss is still a kiss. The construction of sexuality in dementia care. *Dementia*, 4, 49–72.

Weeks, D.J. (2002). Sex for the mature adult: Health, self-esteem and countering ageist stereotypes. *Sexual and Relationship Therapy*, 17, 231–240.

Wells, B.E. & Twenge, J.M. (2005). Changes in young people's sexual behavior and attitudes, 1943–1999: A cross-temporal meta-analysis. *Review of General Psychology*, 9, 249–261.

Wheeler, R. (2006). Gillick or Fraser? A plea for consistency over competence in children. *British Medical Journal*, 332, 807.

Wight, D. (1992). Impediments to safer heterosexual sex: A review of research with young people. *AIDS Care*, 4, 11–23.

Wilson, A.E., Calhoun, K.S. & Bennett, J.A. (1999). Risk, recognition and trauma-related symptoms among sexually revictimized women. *Journal of Consulting and Clinical Psychology*, 67, 705–710.

Wolf, N. (1990). *The beauty myth*. London: Chatto & Windus.

Young London Matters (2009). *SRE core curriculum for London: A practical resource*. London: Government Office for London. http://www.healthyschools. gov.uk/Uploads/Resources/fcc57d09-facf-42de-8640-33442c1c4a10/SRE%20Core %20 Curriculum%20Guidance.pdf%202009.pdf

Zilbergeld, B. (1999). *The new male sexuality*. New York: Bantam Books.

Chapter 6

Culture, sex and sexuality

Catherine Butler and Angela Byrne

> One half of the world cannot understand the pleasures of the other.
>
> Jane Austen

This chapter reflects on sex and sexuality within the context of culture. It does not describe different sexual practices from numerous different cultures as this would take up the whole book. More importantly, such an approach could fall into the trap of assuming that 'culture' refers only to those from minority cultural backgrounds, whereas the dominant culture is seen as 'standard' or 'the norm' and thus the cultural influences in that context become invisible. What this chapter does instead is to argue for the importance of considering culture in relation to sex and sexuality, discuss ethical issues in relation to some sexual practices, but most importantly to allow the reader to reflect on their own position on this topic, as well as provide exercises for training.

WHAT IS CULTURE AND SUB-CULTURE?

Cultures shift and change across time and place. D'Ardenne and Mahtani (1999) define culture as 'the shared history, practices, beliefs and values of a racial, regional and religious group of people'. However, this definition would not cover some uses of the word culture, for example 'gay culture' that is based on a shared sexuality. Sue and Sue (1990) perhaps provide a wider definition of culture as 'consisting of all those things that people have learned to do, believe, value and enjoy in their history. It is the totality of ideas, beliefs, skills, tools, customs, and institutions into which each member of society is born'. Beliefs and practices are not universal within a defined culture, and so sub-cultures represent some of the diversity that can exist within a wider group. So, to take the example of gay culture again, being a 'leather man' would not apply to all gay men, but to a group of men with a sexual interest in wearing leather, who go to specific clubs with their own set of unique rules.

Anthropologist Kate Fox proposes that our culture shapes:

> where we meet our partner, how we flirt, what we eat at dinner and how we eat it, how we talk, the jokes we make, what we drink and the effects of alcohol on our behaviour, the car we drive home in and how we drive it (or our conduct on the bus or in the taxi), the house we take our partner home to and how we feel and talk about it, the dog who greets us, the music we play, the nightcap we offer, how the bedroom is decorated, the curtains we close, the clothes we take off.
>
> (Fox, 2004: 347)

After which point, Fox suggests culture stops and human instinct kicks in.

However, it can be argued that culture continues to shape what happens next. So the response to the following sexual scenarios will be different depending on your and your sexual partner's cultural norms:

- suggesting anal sex;
- suggesting sex during menstruation;
- genital piercing, pubic shaving or anatomical alterations (such as labial stretching);
- using vaginal drying agents or lubrication;
- suggesting sex without penetration;
- suggesting turning the lights out.

Culture, age, sexuality, gender, religion and history will all affect what is thought of as 'normal sex' (see Chapter 1 for further perspectives on this). Culture also influences what sources of information and expertise we draw on in relation to sex, the relative influence of family or friends and issues of gender and power (Davidson, 2000).

Patel *et al.* (2000) capture the importance of reflecting on our own cultural framework. They explain that our culture 'acts as a social standard by which individuals can judge, select and negotiate the respective value systems that each individual brings into an interaction or relationship' (Patel *et al.*, 2000: 44). This applies to the interaction between the therapist and the client, as well as the interaction between the client and their sexual partner.

Exercise 6.1 Identifying your cultural influences

This exercise helps the reader self-reflect on their own cultural influences about sex. If used in training it could be set as a small group or pair exercise.

Based on Sue and Sue's (1990) definition of culture, note down the following as they relate to how you live your own life.

- What values or morals do you hold about the type of sex you have, and with whom and in which circumstances you have sex?
- What 'skills' do you think you have in relation to sex and what 'skills' would you like to develop?
- Do you use any sexual 'tools' (such as the use of fantasy, sex toys, etc.)? If so, how were you first introduced to them? And if not, why not?
- How would you describe your sexual 'customs' to a person from a different culture? Are these different with a new sexual partner to a long-standing partner?
- What institutions do you associate with sex (e.g. family planning) and what messages about sex might these institutions pass on to you that you may or may not agree with?

Put the piece of paper somewhere safe and come back to it a week from today. When you re-read it consider the following.

- How did you feel before you read it?
- What was it like to read it again?
- How might you have felt if someone had found it?
- Would you change anything you wrote a week ago or do you want to expand on anything?
- If you were reading this about someone else, what kind of cultural influences would you notice? What might that person's rules of sex be?

This exercise is designed to promote self-reflexivity in the reader. The first set of questions aims to highlight the multiple influences on sexual beliefs, values and behaviours. For example, readers may identify sources of influence that include personal experience, family, religion, media or other social or cultural influences. Being able to articulate one's own sexual values and norms should help the reader to be aware of assumptions they might make in therapy when working with clients of similar and different cultural backgrounds. The second set of questions invites the reader to take a different (observer) perspective on their own sexual values, norms and practices and to think about what it might be like to share these with another person. This aims to promote empathy with clients when they discuss their sexual concerns in therapy.

CULTURAL DIFFERENCE AND SIMILARITY

This section is about how your cultural attitudes and beliefs about sex might help or hinder a therapy session, through being either different or similar to those of the client.

'Differences' in culture and sub-culture between the therapist and client have both affordances and constraints. Clients may sometimes prefer to work with someone they perceive to be culturally different to themselves. This can be for a variety of reasons, including fears regarding confidentiality within their community, or fear of being judged or criticised especially around sexual behaviour that may be disapproved of within their culture or religion. From a therapist's perspective, obvious cultural or sub-cultural differences may make us more aware of the potential for misunderstandings and assumptions and help us make a more careful assessment of the client's needs, beliefs and values relating to sex.

Cultural difference may also have constraints. For example, a client may fear being misunderstood or stereotyped or feel pressure to 'educate' the therapist about their culture. The therapist may feel deskilled or that their understanding of the issues may not fit with those of the client. Reaching a shared formulation may be challenging in these circumstances.

Working with someone from the same culture or sub-culture may sometimes result in the client and/or therapist feeling more comfortable, but it can also lead to assumptions of shared understandings and values that may be unwarranted. Cultural similarity might also prevent us questioning the cultural influences on the client's sexual experience and our own understandings of their experience. Exercise 6.2 and Table 6.1 further explore issues of working across cultures.

Exercise 6.2 Cross-cultural work

The following exercise provides a framework to consider the potential benefits and challenges of cultural similarities and differences in the work that you and your client might bring into the therapy room. Complete Table 6.1, reflecting on your own cultural messages and hypothesising about those of the client.

How might you discuss these differences and similarities with the client? What might you share or not share? How might you then monitor if 'censored messages' are influencing the therapy?

Exercise 6.2 focuses the reader on the cultural influences that they and their clients bring to the therapy. It can highlight further areas for questioning if the therapist is unaware of some of the issues influencing their client. It

Table 6.1 Cultural messages

Messages about sex you have received from . . .	You	Your client
Politics		
Family		
Peers		
Religion		
School		
The medical profession		
Sexual partners		
The media		

also asks the reader to identify areas of similarity and difference. It should be emphasised that there can be challenges and opportunities in both similarities and differences. For example, similarity can result in greater comfort or shared understandings but it can also lead to unwarranted assumptions of shared understandings and stop therapists being curious or questioning about particular influences. Differences may highlight a potential conflict of values or beliefs but can also be a helpful source of difference, curiosity and new perspectives in therapy. The question about what the therapist might share with the client invites reflection on self-disclosure and the degree to which this is done will inevitably be influenced by the therapeutic orientation of the therapist. However, the exercise invites all therapists to think about the impact of sharing or not sharing this information. It also draws attention to the fact that values and judgements, even if not shared, will still influence therapy and invites the therapist to develop ways of monitoring this influence.

SEX IN WESTERN CULTURAL CONTEXTS

The Diagnostic and Statistical Manual of Mental Disorders (DSM-IV) (American Psychiatric Association, 1994) lists various 'culture bound syndromes' relating to sex, such as Dhat syndrome (a condition reported in the cultures of the Indian subcontinent in which men complain of premature ejaculation or impotence and believe they are passing semen in their urine) and genital retraction syndrome or 'Koro' (a belief that the external genitalia are retracting into the body, shrinking or disappearing. At various times and in different cultures, this has been associated with 'penis panics' seen as a form of 'mass hysteria' in which a number of men in a population suddenly experience genital retraction syndrome). However, it can be argued that all sexual practices and problems are in fact culturally determined. Foucault (1978) analysed the history of sexuality in Western Europe and revealed the powerful discourses that shape our historical and contemporary understandings of sexuality. Of particular importance to current Western conceptualisations of sex was the medicalisation of sexual behaviour in the nineteenth century where sex moved from being primarily understood and regulated within the domain of religion to dominant medical discourses (with the development of categories of disorders such as sexual dysfunctions, Gender Identity Disorder, paraphilias etc.). A number of writers, such as Boyle (1993, 1994) and Ussher (1989) have discussed the assumptions inherent in these new understandings of sexuality, such as the notion of sexual dysfunctions as properties of individuals and the consequences of the classification systems that developed as a result. In particular, these writers have addressed issues of gender and sexuality. For example, Boyle (1994) highlights the assumptions about gender relations inherent in the early sexology writings, such as the equation of sex with heterosexual vaginal intercourse and the idea of male dominance and female submission as the 'natural order'. Despite the more recent emphasis on female sexual pleasure and orgasm, echoes of this persist in current classification systems, e.g. with the lack of a female equivalent of 'premature ejaculation' (cf. Boyle, 1994). Additional discourses that shape understandings of sex and sexuality are discussed in Chapter 1.

The twentieth century also saw the development of a rights-based discourse of sexuality in the West and elsewhere, with movements for women's rights, lesbian and gay rights and the human rights of other sexual minorities to enjoy sexual expression without fear of discrimination, persecution or coercion. The World Health Organization (WHO) also discusses sex in terms of human rights (e.g. WHO, 2006) including the right to high standards of sexual health (e.g. access to sexual and reproductive health care services), sex education, choice of partner and consensual sexual relations and to pursue a satisfying, safe and pleasurable sexual life. Even this is not uncontroversial and wherever these 'sexual rights' are listed they are accompanied by a disclaimer to the effect that they do not necessarily represent the official position of WHO.

Public health discourses around sex have been prevalent in Western cultures since the identification of sexually transmitted infections, such as syphilis. In the nineteenth and early twentieth centuries there were a proliferation of discourses relating to these infections, which constructed notions of risk and responsibility. These were seen as problems of immoral and risky people, especially women who were prostitutes or otherwise 'sexually promiscuous', and men were encouraged to avoid such women for their own protection and that of their (virtuous) wives as, for example, in health promotion literature from the Second World War (Quétel, 1992). A number of writers have noted the similarities between these discourses and those that arose around HIV/AIDS from the 1980s to the present time (Quétel, 1992). These include the notion of risky groups of people who tend to be those in minority power positions within the wider cultural context, such as gay men, injecting drug users or African immigrants. The impact of this stigma and prejudice has been documented elsewhere (e.g. Dodds *et al.*, 2004).

To summarise, in all cultures there are notions of what is 'good' or 'desirable' sexual activity and what is disapproved of or seen as less worthy. The activities in each category change across time and culture, for example, masturbation which was once seen as sinful and potentially harmful is now routinely prescribed as 'homework' by sex therapists and women's magazines.

Sex as skill, orgasm as achievement

One of the most powerful discourses relating to sex in Western culture today is that of the idea of individual skill or personal achievement. The sexologists Masters and Johnson (1970) introduced the idea of sex as a learned skill with a new emphasis on the 'skilled lover'. In both popular and medical discourse one may 'achieve' an orgasm. This is also the view of sex commonly promoted in Western media and popular culture, which is often a major source of information on sex for many men and women. This is typified by representations of sex in lifestyle magazines as skills to be mastered with an implication that relationship satisfaction will follow.

Exercise 6.3 Cultural messages

This exercise explores the messages given in popular culture about sex.

Go to your local newsagents and browse the magazines for men and women (either targeted at heterosexuals or lesbians/gay men) that have articles about sex. Identify some of the discourses underlying the advice given to improve one's sex life.

Exercise 6.3 is designed to draw attention to the discourses about sex that are widely disseminated through popular culture and that may be influencing clients' understanding of their difficulties and what they see as appropriate solutions. The reader should pay attention to the language used as well as the advice given. The following questions are an aid to this reflection, but as there are no 'right' answers it is left to the reader to think about their meaning to them. How does this language relate to that of sex therapy? Is it different for heterosexual women and men, gay men and lesbians? In which publications does sex receive the most or least attention and what might this tell us about who is seen as most or least concerned about sex and as most or least responsible for sex? Which groups of people might be 'absent' or not represented in these publications (e.g. older people or people from Black and minority ethnic communities)? What might this indicate about our cultural values? What impact might this have on people from those groups?

This discourse also underlies most 'sex manuals'. The model is of sexual problems as a deficiency of knowledge or skill and that these may be taught or rectified. A related discourse concerns the assumed optimum amount of sexual activity and interest for both men and women. For example, it can be argued that lack of interest in sex is now seen as pathological. In the case of women, this represents a shift from earlier notions of lack of interest as normal or even desirable among women, and so they could be a restraint on their husband's excessive sexual desire (Zilbergeld, 1999).

Exercise 6.4 Case example

This case example invites you to consider some of the cultural influences that may be operating when a client refers herself for sex therapy. If used in training it can be discussed in small groups.

Emma, a 28-year-old White British woman, refers herself for sex therapy with complaints of low libido, occasional pain on intercourse and difficulty having orgasms. She has had a number of casual partners in the past and two previous long-term relationships. She reports that she is able to have an orgasm when masturbating using a vibrator but has never found it easy to have an orgasm during intercourse. She has been with her partner, Peter, a Black British man aged 26 years, for two years and has begun to worry about the impact of these difficulties on their relationship as they have begun to argue about her lack of interest in sex. Emma fears that she is 'boring' and 'not good in bed'. She tried discussing these difficulties with her female friends but they didn't appear to have the same problems and this left her feeling even more anxious. She has occasionally faked orgasm but this has left her feeling resentful. She tells you she just wants to have a 'normal sex life' like her friends.

- What cultural ideas might be influencing Emma's (and Peter's) understanding of the difficulties described above?
- How might you begin to help her understand the influence of her culture on her experience of sex?
- Are you from a similar or different culture to Emma or Peter?
- How would this influence the way you might work with her/them (e.g. what are the affordances and constraints)? What cultural resources or challenges might there be?

This case example is designed to draw attention to some of the contemporary cultural influences that may be operating for a young heterosexual couple. Culture is likely to influence their expectations about sex, e.g. that it is something to be enjoyed, that women should have orgasms, that being 'good in bed' is important and desirable for a woman and also what it means to be 'good in bed'. Culture is also likely to influence their understanding of their difficulties and what is 'normal', for example, there is an implication that Emma may see not having orgasms through vaginal intercourse as a problem. The different solutions open to Emma and Peter are also likely to be influenced by culture, e.g. talking to friends, faking orgasms, using a vibrator or self-referring for sex therapy.

The reader is invited to consider how they might begin to help Emma understand these influences. This could refer to particular questions a therapist might ask, e.g. how it was decided that Emma would refer herself rather than the couple referring themselves? What are each partner's ideas about 'good sex' and where do these ideas come from? Or the use of exercises such as those provided in this chapter, e.g. 6.1 or 6.2, which can easily be adapted for use with individual clients or couples. Understanding the cultural influences on their sexual beliefs and behaviour may help clients to see their views of the problem not as 'truths' but as ideas that may be more or less helpful and open up the possibility of new perspectives. Readers from a similar cultural background to Emma may find it more difficult to identify cultural influences than those from a different cultural background. If used in training settings, possible reasons for this should be discussed.

CULTURAL DIVERSITY AND MULTIPLE IDENTITIES

In a culturally diverse society, it can be difficult to define exactly what one's culture is. Recent immigrants find themselves having to adjust to a new culture and the second generation often describe themselves as having, or negotiating between, two cultures – that of their parents and the British culture in which they have grown up. Many couples come from different cultures (such as Emma and Peter in the previous example) and their children increasingly will negotiate across all these cultural groups, with those of 'mixed race' or mixed heritage being the fastest growing demographic group in Britain (Scott et al., 2001).

Culture also interacts with all other aspects of identity, such as gender, age, sexuality etc. Roper-Hall (1997) has used the term social GRRAACCES (i.e. gender, race, religion, age, ability, class, culture, ethnicity, sexuality) to describe the range of social difference. Those who are from more than one marginalised or minority culture may have to deal with double discrimination, prejudice and misunderstanding. For example, Black lesbians and gay men may have to deal with racism and discrimination within the gay scene and homophobia and heterosexism in Black communities as well as in the dominant culture. For many Black people, the strong relationships and support of family and community are extremely important in dealing with racism and discrimination in everyday life and this can make the issue of 'coming out' more complicated. The potential risks of 'coming out' may include losing that support and some people also fear bringing 'shame' or 'dishonour' to their families (Brauner, 2000). When this is coupled with racism, discrimination and 'other-ing' within gay communities, it constitutes a significant barrier to 'coming out'.

In addition, the whole concept of 'coming out' has been described as Eurocentric (Smith, 1997; Brauner, 2000) since it depends on a Western notion of sexual identity as an attribute of the individual. According to Smith (1997), 'coming out' is often seen as a necessary step towards psychological health and conversely not coming out is seen as something negative. Smith (1997) describes an alternative Afrocentric strategy in which African–American families may 'take in' a same-sex partner and accept them as part of the family without the overt declaration of sexual identity implied by the term 'coming out'.

Exercise 6.5 Case example

This case example highlights some of the complexities that multiple contexts bring to issues of sex. Work through it yourself using the questions as a guide to thinking, or set it as a small group exercise if used in training.

Abdul is a gay man living with HIV. He is from a South Asian country and a Muslim. He is referred to psychology by his HIV doctor following concerns that he has had a number of sexually transmitted infections. The doctor states that she thinks Abdul is depressed and isolated. Abdul describes feeling 'split' in terms of his identity and that he doesn't feel he really fits in anywhere. His family are not aware that he is gay and he fears they would reject him if they knew. He has Muslim friends who he socialises with and sees at the mosque. They also don't know about his sexuality. He has some gay friends but rarely goes out on the scene. When he does go to a gay bar or club, he is often asked if he knows this is a gay venue and this makes him feel unwelcome. He generally has sex with White men and finds it difficult to negotiate condom use. He struggles with the thought that HIV is a punishment from Allah. He said it doesn't feel possible to have a gay identity while also being a Muslim. When the therapist talked to Abdul about a sexual health project for Black and minority ethnic communities (Naz Project London http://www.naz.org.uk), he was initially quite sceptical and reluctant to make contact. However, after reading their leaflet on HIV/AIDS and Islam and talking to one of the workers on the phone, he began to attend a support group and gain a new sense of 'community'.

- Which social GRRAACCES might be relevant to Abdul?
- How might these influence his sexual health and well-being?
- What are the affordances and constraints in his different contexts?
- What other interventions or resources might you consider for him?

This case example invites the reader to consider multiple levels of context in the experience of one individual. It draws attention to 'double discrimination' in that Abdul faces homophobia from family and friends as well as racism in the gay scene, e.g. being constantly asked if he knows 'this is a gay venue' communicates to him that he doesn't 'fit' in this scene. The impact of these experiences in terms of isolation and depression is highlighted. However, readers are also invited to think about the positive aspects or affordances in Abdul's different contexts. This example also raises the issue of identity and the challenges of feeling that different parts of one's identity are in conflict, e.g. religion and sexuality. If used in a training setting, a useful discussion point can focus on the pros and cons of having services for specific cultural groups as opposed to generic services and the difficulties of 'challenging' beliefs or practices associated with important aspects of a person's culture, e.g. religion. As is the case in the example above, this is often most effective when the challenging voices or different perspectives come from within that person's culture or religion.

WORKING WITH INTERPRETERS

When working with non-English speaking clients, the use of a professional interpreter or advocate is paramount, particularly when discussing sexual matters that might be inappropriate or uncomfortable to discuss in front of friends or family members. However, interpreters themselves may be embarrassed (Raval, 2003) if having to interpret intimate questions about sex. Harvey (1986) reports that omissions, additions and substitutions of words by interpreters are common. This could be to aid the interpretation, or the lack of vocabulary relating to sex, or because of the interpreter's discomfort, or to shelter the client from 'intrusive' or 'inappropriate' questions. Asking how the interpreter feels about the content of the session before and after the therapy is important, as well as factors such as age and gender, which might affect the client or interpreter's comfort in discussing sex.

In the same way that this chapter has focused on highlighting your cultural attitudes and beliefs about sex, the interpreter is also bringing their attitudes and beliefs about sex into the therapy room. This will influence the language they use and how evasive or expansive their questions and descriptions are. If you know the interpreter, or are working on an ongoing piece of work, it might be worth discussing this in detail with the interpreter outside of the session, sharing your own influences, and agreeing how you might be able to work together. Some of the exercises in this chapter might be a starting point to have these conversations. Even if it is a single session, checking the content of the session before and after therapy is important to facilitate a collaborative working relationship. It is also important to check the exact translation and connotation of certain terms, e.g. when using words like 'lesbian', 'gay' or 'homosexuality', check that the term in translation has a neutral or positive connotation, rather than one that may imply 'abnormality' or 'perversion' and be offensive to lesbians or gay men.

If the interpreter is from the same country, culture or religion as the client, they may be able to tell you their understanding of some of the influences about sex that the client might have been exposed to. In this way the interpreter also acts as a cultural consultant. This could even be discussed in front of the client so that the client can agree or disagree with the interpreter's ideas. However, putting the interpreter in this position needs to be with their consent, as it places them outside the strict definition of the role they are employed to do during the session. In addition, it is important that the therapist retains overall responsibility for the session and the information shared and how it is used in therapy.

WORKING WITH RELIGIOUS BELIEFS

Western science has a secular base (Patel *et al.*, 2000) and so religious and spiritual experiences and beliefs tend to be minimised or neglected. How much training have you or your colleagues received on working with clients who present with clear religious beliefs? Research in this area has found that for many people their religious and spiritual cultures influence the structure of their lives and need to be taken into account to make sense of presenting difficulties (e.g. Boyd-Franklin (1989) and Krause (1994) write about African–American and Asian religious cultures and Wieselberg (1992) about Orthodox Jewish culture). It is important to view faith or religion as another potential cultural influence on attitudes and behaviours to do with sex. The client may not raise religious beliefs as they may not consider it appropriate in the session, however, asking about these ideas can provide helpful information. This can include asking what relevant holy texts or a faith leader would say about the sexual matters being discussed. There are often contradictory views held within the same religion so it is also worth exploring alternative ideas or practices. For example, homosexuality is not accepted in most mainstream religious traditions, yet lesbian and gay faith groups exist in all the major religions and find ways to reinterpret the texts and combine religious beliefs and a sexual minority identity.

WORKING WITH SEXUAL PRACTICES THAT THERAPISTS MAY FIND CHALLENGING

In work with clients, therapists may hear about sexual practices that leave them feeling uncomfortable for a variety of reasons. This might be because they know nothing about it and feel deskilled, or because the practice itself is something they disapprove of or might be illegal. At these times the therapist must act within professional and legal frameworks and take appropriate action. Some practices might not be deemed illegal, but the therapist still finds working with them difficult. Exercise 6.6 and Table 6.2 explore these issues.

Table 6.2 Personal and professional responses to potentially challenging client presentations

Scenario	Response
Your client gains sexual gratification by being beaten	Professional response: Personal response:
Your client has several young children and is exhausted. Her religion forbids the use of contraception	Professional response: Personal response:
Your client uses herbs to dry her vagina prior to sex	Professional response: Personal response:
Your client has had no sexual experiences with anyone other than his partner of 45 years	Professional response: Personal response:
Your client regularly uses sex clubs and saunas to have extra-relationship sex with their partner's consent	Professional response: Personal response:

Exercise 6.6 Potentially challenging client presentations

Some examples of potentially challenging client presentations are detailed in Table 6.2; what would be your professional and personal response to each?

If your personal and professional responses are different, how will you be able to work effectively with this client? What could you do to facilitate this? Will you be able to discuss these issues openly with your supervisor?

Therapists may sometimes be working with a woman and learn that she has experienced female genital mutilation. This can raise a range of feelings and questions, as well as ethical and legal concerns. The key issues around this topic are presented in Box 6.1.

Therapists working with individuals or couples may learn that sado-masochistic sex is practised, which may or may not be something the therapist feels familiar with. The key issues that relate to this topic are presented in Box 6.2.

Box 6.1 Female genital mutilation

Female Genital Mutilation (FGM) (also known as 'female circumcision' or 'female genital cutting') refers to a set of practices that can raise numerous political, ethical, legal and practical issues for therapists.
Definition: FGM is defined as 'the partial or complete removal of the external female genitalia or other injury to the female genital organs whether for cultural or any other non-therapeutic reason' (World Health Organization, 1997). Four types of FGM have been described:

- Type I: excision of the prepuce with or without excision of part or the entire clitoris;
- Type II: excision of the prepuce and clitoris together with partial or total excision of the labia minora;
- Type III: excision of part or all of the external genitalia and stitching or narrowing of the vaginal opening (infibulation);
- Type IV: pricking, piercing or incising of the clitoris and/or labia; stretching of the clitoris and/or labia; cauterisation by burning of the clitoris and surrounding tissue; scraping of the vaginal orifice or cutting (Gishiri cuts) of the vagina and the introduction of corrosive substances or herbs.

Legal status: it is illegal to perform FGM or to facilitate FGM in the UK. It is also illegal to take a child out of the country to procure FGM (Female Genital Mutilation Act 2003). Under the Children Act 1989 local authorities can apply for court orders to prevent children being taken out of the country for FGM. The Foundation for Women's Health Research and Development (FORWARD) estimates that there are currently 86,000 women and girls in the UK who have undergone FGM and a further 7000 girls who are at risk. If a therapist or other worker knows or suspects that a child is at risk of FGM, they should contact their organisation's Child Protection Department, or their local Social Services Department or Police Child Protection Unit.

FGM and sex: FGM may have a dramatic impact on sexual and psychological functioning. Sexual dysfunction is a commonly reported consequence for women and their partners. However, this is not inevitable. Sexual enjoyment and even clitoral orgasm may still be possible. This is because the clitoral system is much larger than the external clitoris (Hite, 1981) and also because, even in the most extensive types of FGM such as infibulation, part of the sensitive clitoral or labial tissue may remain and there are also reports of other parts of the body becoming more sensitised (e.g. Lightfoot-Klein, 1989).

Talking about FGM: When working with clients who may be circumcised, use of the term 'mutilation' may be off-putting as it communicates a judgement about the practice. It is preferable to ask 'are you circumcised?'. This is not to pretend that therapists do not or should not make judgements nor be transparent about these. However, in order to discuss different views of FGM, it is important to have established a trusting and respectful relationship. It is also important to understand the meaning of FGM for each individual woman and her partner. Women and men may have a variety of views of FGM, from seeing it as an important part of their cultural identity that they value to something that they experience as oppressive and vehemently oppose.

Resources:
The Foundation for Women's Health Research and Development (FORWARD) provides useful resources and information as well as campaigning on FGM and can be found at http://www.forwarduk.org.uk
See also: Adamson, F. (1992). *Female genital mutilation: A counselling guide for professionals*. London: Forward UK.
British Medical Association (2006). *Female genital mutilation – caring for patients and child protection*. Guidance from the Ethics Department. London: BMA. Available at: http://www.bma.org.uk/ethics/human-rights/FGM.jsp

The National Advisory Group on Female Genital Mutilation has a website: http://www.fgmnationalgroup.org with useful resources such as position statements, references and reviews of the literature on the psychological impact of FGM.

Box 6.2 Sadomasochistic sex

Definitions: SM or sadomasochism in the most literal sense refers to sexual gratification in inflicting pain ('sadism') or having pain inflicted upon the self ('masochism'). However, the term SM has come to be applied to a wide variety of consensual practices or interests that are not necessarily sadistic or masochistic, such as bondage, fetishism, role-playing games, fisting, piercing, etc. (Bridoux, 2000). The term BDSM (bondage and discipline; dominance and submission; sado-masochism) is perhaps more representative of the variety of 'kink' or non-'vanilla' (i.e. conventional) sex.

SM in the DSM: whereas earlier editions of the *DSM* categorised SM fantasies and practices as psychosexual disorders or 'paraphilias', *DSM-III* (American Psychiatric Association, 1994) amended this to include only those fantasies, urges or behaviours that 'cause clinically significant distress or disturbance'. This is similar to the replacement of homosexuality as a disorder with 'ego-dystonic' homosexuality (i.e. causing distress to the individual) as a disorder in *DSM-III* (American Psychiatric Association, 1980). Critics note that the current system still implicates SM as the source of distress rather than the stigma surrounding it (e.g. Barker, 2006).

Legal status: despite its consensual nature, people have been prosecuted in the UK for taking part in SM activity, most notably in the 'Operation Spanner' case of 1987 in which a group of adult gay men were convicted for taking part in consenting SM activities. Their convictions were upheld by the House of Lords and the European Court of Human Rights who ruled that there could be no consent where acts resulting in serious harm (defined as more than 'trifling and transient') are involved. In the UK, it continues to be the case that consent to injury is not a defence. The Criminal Justice & Immigration Bill 2007 criminalised possession of 'extreme pornography', including images of consensual SM acts.

Issues for therapists: the fact that some SM activities may be illegal in the UK may raise concerns for therapists. However, it is important to remember that it is not illegal to discuss such activities for the purposes of providing information to protect people's health (including mental health) and lives (Alcorn, 1995, cited in Bridoux, 2000). It is also important to remember that the majority of BDSM activities would not be seen as illegal in that they do not cause serious and lasting injury. In working with people who practise SM, Bridoux (2000) and Barker (2006) highlight the importance of not assuming that the person's SM lifestyle is relevant to their presenting problem. Bridoux (2000) asks therapists to consider the 'ecology' of the person's SM activity, i.e. to consider the consequences of a behaviour on all facets of their personality and relationships and allow for the possibility of positive consequences instead of focusing on narrowly defined concepts of 'harm'.

Resources:
The Spanner Trust http://www.spanner.org/
Critical sexology http://www.criticalsexology.org.uk
Centre for the Interdisciplinary Study of Sexuality and Gender in Europe http://www.sall.ex.ac.uk/centres/cissge
Langdridge, D. & Barker, M. (eds) (2007). *Safe, sane & consensual.* Basingstoke: Palgrave Macmillan.

CONCLUSIONS FOR TRAINING ON SEX AND CULTURE

Culturally competent training in sexuality should:

- address self-awareness as part of cultural awareness, i.e. participants are encouraged to explore their own cultural understandings of sex and sexuality and think about how these influence their work;
- locate theories and interventions for sexual problems in their historical and cultural context;
- avoid cultural stereotyping and assumptions of heterogeneity within cultures. One way of doing this is to introduce ideas such as the social GRRAACCES;
- address linguistic competence, e.g. finding a shared language for discussing sex and sexuality and skills for working with interpreters;
- challenge and address prejudice, discrimination and inequalities;
- take steps to inform yourself about the culture or sub-culture relevant to a client's presentation if you are unfamiliar with it.

FURTHER SAMPLE TRAINING EXERCISES

The following exercises are slightly less personal than those used so far in this chapter, and are designed for group training sessions.

Exercise 6.7 Contextual influences on sexual expression

List ways in which sexual expression, social approval and disapproval, might change by variation in the following areas of social difference:
Urban/rural environments; race; gender; age; ability; class; culture; ethnicity, sexuality.

This exercise invites participants to identify multiple contextual influences on sexual expression. It can be done by individuals or pairs but works well in groups because of the wealth of ideas generated. The aspects of identity listed draw attention to the impact of access to resources – both material and cultural; power in society and in sexual encounters; issues of visibility and representation. These contexts are likely to influence the presentation of clients and the range of options open to therapists to suggest. For example, a therapist based in a rural setting and working with a young Muslim gay man like Abdul in Exercise 6.5 is likely to have fewer support services to help him connect with compared with a therapist in an urban setting.

Exercise 6.8 Sexual culture

Think of a sexual culture you do not know much about (e.g. kink, transculture). How have you gained the impression/information you have formed? How might you check or challenge these stereotypes? How might these ideas help or hinder you when working with a client from that culture?

This exercise is designed to promote self-reflexivity in the reader or participant. It draws attention to the impact of not knowing (or feeling that one does not know) about a sexual culture that may be central to a client's sexual life or identity. This exercise could be done by individuals or in pairs. It invites the participant(s) to identify assumptions or stereotypes that they may hold; the sources of these and the potential impact on the therapeutic process. It is hoped that completing this exercise may also encourage therapists to attempt to find out more about different sexual cultures.

Exercise 6.9 Sexual expression in UK culture

Some visitors from outer space land in the UK. They want to understand our sexual culture. Prepare a short presentation for them on sex in UK culture(s), e.g. what is sex for?, what is thought of as good/bad sex, who is allowed to have sex, who is discouraged or prevented from having sex, how people learn about sex etc.

The visitors are encouraged to ask questions.

- What does this tell you about the values and assumptions underlying how sex is viewed in UK culture?

This exercise invites participants to take an observer position on their culture and to make explicit the cultural influences on sexual expression. This exercise works best in small groups. As each small group does their presentation, the other participants take the role of the visitors from outer space, asking questions to elucidate the (possibly) strange new concepts they are hearing about. Each group is likely to have a different presentation, allowing a discussion of the idea that there is rarely consensus about what constitutes a particular 'cultural view' and, therefore, always potential for different perspectives.

REFERENCES

American Psychiatric Association (1980). *Diagnostic and statistical manual of mental disorders* (3rd edn) (DSM-III). Washington, DC: APA.

American Psychiatric Association (1994). *Diagnostic and statistical manual of mental disorders* (4th edn) (DSM-IV). Washington, DC: APA.

Barker, M. (2006). Why I study . . . bisexuality and beyond. *The Psychologist*, 19 (1), 33–34.

Boyd-Franklin, N. (1989). *Black families in therapy: A multisystems approach* (2nd edn). New York: Guilford University Press.

Boyle, M. (1993). Sexual dysfunction or heterosexual dysfunction? *Feminism and Psychology*, 3 (1), 73–88.

Boyle, M. (1994). Gender, science and sexual dysfunction. In T.R. Sarbin & J.I. Kituse (eds), *Constructing the social*. London: Sage.

Brauner, R. (2000). Addressing race, culture and sexuality. In C. Neal & D. Davies (eds), *Pink therapy 3: Issues in therapy with lesbian, gay, bisexual and transgender clients*. Buckingham: Open University Press.

Bridoux, D. (2000). Kink therapy: SM and sexual minorities. In C. Neal & D. Davies (eds), *Pink therapy 3: Issues in therapy with lesbian, gay, bisexual and transgender clients*. Buckingham: Open University Press.

D'Ardenne, P. & Mahtani, A. (1999). *Transcultural counselling in action* (2nd edn). London: Sage.

Davidson, O. (2000). HIV/GU-Medicine/Sexual Health. In N. Patel, E. Bennett, M. Dennis, N. Dosanjh, A. Mahtani, A. Miller & Z. Nadirshaw (eds), *Clinical psychology, 'race' and culture: A training manual*. Leicester: BPS Books.

Dodds, C., Keogh, P., Chime, O., Haruperi, T., Nabulya, B., Ssanyu-Sseruma, W. & Wetherburn, P. (2004). *Outsider status: Stigma and discrimination experienced by gay men and African people with HIV*. London: Sigma Research. www.sigmaresearch.org.uk/files/report2004.pdf

Foucault, M. (1978). *The history of sexuality: An introduction, Vol. 1*. New York: Random House.

Fox, K. (2004). *Watching the English: The hidden rules of English behaviour*. London: Hodder & Stoughton.

Harvey, M. (1986). The magnifying mirror: Family therapy for deaf persons. *Family Systems Medicine*, 4, 408–420.

Hite, S. (1981). *The Hite report: A nationwide study of female sexuality*. New York: Dell Books.

Krause, I.B. (1994). Numbers and meaning: A dialogue in cross-cultural psychiatry. *Journal of the Royal Society of Medicine*, 87, 278–282.

Lightfoot-Klein, H. (1989). The sexual experience and marital adjustment of genitally circumcised and infibulated females in the Sudan. *The Journal of Sex Research*, 26, (3), 375–392.

Masters, W.H. & Johnson, V.E. (1970). *Human sexual inadequacy*. London: J and A. Churchill.

Patel, N., Bennett, E., Dennis, M., Dosanjh, A., Mahtani, A., Miller, A. & Nadirshaw, Z. (2000). *Clinical psychology, 'race' and culture: A training manual*. Leicester: BPS Books.

Quétel, C. (1992). *The history of syphilis*. Baltimore: The John Hopkins University Press.

Raval, H. (2003). An overview of the issues in the work with interpreters. In R. Tribe & H. Raval (eds), *Working with interpreters in mental health*. Hove: Bruner-Routledge.

Roper-Hall, A. (1997). Working systemically with older people and their families who 'have come to grief'. In P. Sutcliffe, G. Tufnell & U. Cornish (eds), *Working with the dying and bereaved*. London. Macmillan.

Scott, A., Pearce, D. & Goldblatt, P. (2001). The sizes and characteristics of the minority ethnic populations of Great Britain – latest estimates. *Population Trends*, 105, 6–16. London: Office for National Statistics, UK.

Smith, A. (1997). Cultural diversity and the coming out process: implications for clinical practice. In B. Greene (ed.), *Ethnic and cultural diversity among lesbians and gay men*. California: Sage.

Sue, D.W. and Sue, D. (1990). *Counselling the culturally different: Theory and practice* (2nd edn). New York: Wiley.

Ussher, J. (1989). *The psychology of the female body*. London: Routledge.

Wieselberg, H. (1992). Family therapy and ultra-orthodox Jewish families: A structural approach. *Journal of Family Therapy*, 14 (3), 305–330.

World Health Organization (1997). *Female genital mutilation: A joint WHO/UNICEF/UNFPA statement*. Geneva: World Health Organization.

World Health Organization (2006). *Defining sexual health. Report of a technical consultation on sexual health*. Geneva: World Health Organization.

Zilbergeld, B. (1999). *The new male sexuality*. Bristol: Bantam Doubleday Dell Publishing Group.

Index